D1557110

Literature, Rhetoric and Violence in Northern Ireland, 1968–98

Also by Patrick Grant

A DAZZLING DARKNESS: An Anthology of Western Mysticism

BREAKING ENMITIES: Religion, Literature and Culture in Northern Ireland, 1967–97

IMAGES AND IDEAS IN LITERATURE OF THE ENGLISH RENAISSANCE

LITERATURE AND PERSONAL VALUES

LITERATURE OF MYSTICISM IN WESTERN TRADITION

PERSONALISM AND THE POLITICS OF CULTURE

READING THE NEW TESTAMENT: Literature and the Discovery of Method in the English Renaissance

SIX MODERN AUTHORS AND PROBLEMS OF BELIEF

SPIRITUAL DISCOURSE AND THE MEANING OF PERSONS

THE TRANSFORMATION OF SIN: Studies in Donne, Herbert, Vaughan and Traherne

Literature, Rhetoric and Violence in Northern Ireland, 1968–98

Hardened to Death

Patrick Grant
Professor of English
University of Victoria
British Columbia
Canada

First published 2001 by
PALGRAVE
Houndmills, Basingstoke, Hampshire RG21 6XS and
175 Fifth Avenue, New York, N.Y. 10010
Companies and representatives throughout the world

PALGRAVE is the new global academic imprint of
St. Martin's Press LLC Scholarly and Reference Division and
Palgrave Publishers Ltd (formerly Macmillan Press Ltd).

ISBN 0–333–79412–5

This book is printed on paper suitable for recycling and made from fully managed and sustained forest sources.

A catalogue record for this book is available from the British Library.

Library of Congress Cataloging-in-Publication Data
Grant, Patrick.
    Literature, rhetoric, and violence in Northern Ireland,
    1968–98 : hardened to death / Patrick Grant.
        p. cm.
    Includes bibliographical references and index.
    ISBN 0–333–79412–5 (cloth)
    1. English literature—Irish authors—History and criticism.
2. Politics and literature—Northern Ireland—History—20th
century. 3. Literature and society—Northern Ireland—History–
–20th century. 4. English language—Northern Ireland—Rhetoric.
5. Northern Ireland—Intellectual life. 6. Northern Ireland—In
literature. 7. Political violence in literature. 8. Social conflict in
literature. 9. Violence in literature. I. Title.
    PR8891.N67 G735 2001
    820.9'358—dc21
                                                        2001021625

10   9   8   7   6   5   4   3   2   1
10   09 08 07 06 05 04 03 02 01

Printed in Great Britain by Antony Rowe Ltd, Chippenham, Wiltshire

Such is the nature of force. Its power of converting a man into a thing is a double one, and its application double-edged. To the same degree, though in different fashions, those who use it and those who endure it are turned to stone.

Simone Weil, ''The Iliad, or The Poem of Force''

For Gloria

Contents

Preface

While researching and writing an earlier book, *Breaking Enmities: Religion, Literature and Culture in Northern Ireland, 1967–97*, I found myself noticing two quite simple points more or less independently of my main enquiry. The first is how extraordinary is the documentation pertaining to the Troubles in Northern Ireland during the past thirty years. I had known that John Whyte once described Northern Ireland as, per capita, probably the most intensely researched community on earth, and that Robert Fisk singled out the political collection in the Linen Hall Library as unique because of the unmatched insight it provides into all shades of opinion about the conflict. I was familiar with these views and others like them, but only gradually came to realize how much the remarkable archive of printed materials pertaining to the Troubles has to offer to students of violent conflict not only in Northern Ireland but in general. Within the confines of a society comprising just over 1.5 million people, we can follow the grain lines of a dispute in which the interests of nation states, ethnic minorities, post-colonial economies, globalization, identity politics and urban guerrilla warfare combine and metamorphose in a compelling and bewildering variety of ways. One main legacy of these troubled years in Northern Ireland is therefore likely to be the sheer richness and density of the documentation provided by sociological and political commentary, journalism, biography, memoirs, academic research, political pamphleteering of many kinds, and a literary renaissance that has produced an extensive body of writing, often of high quality.

The second point that I came – again gradually – to notice is how perplexed yet captivating are the relationships between words and the actual conduct of violence, and I found myself increasingly preoccupied by the complex ways in which a war of words has accompanied and interpenetrated with the actual war. In this context I also came to realize how the Troubles are deeply and pervasively represented in literature of the period, though not always directly, and usually not in a straightforward partisan fashion. Indeed, one main contribution of a good deal of the literature is to challenge traditional oppositions, disclosing how these contribute to violence and demonstrating why they need to be deconstructed rather than re-confirmed. In short, literature has a lot to say about the seductions, demonic intoxications and inevitable failures of violence, communicated through an imagined complexity which is a necessary adjunct to the other forms of written discourse by which the Troubles are recorded.

Understandably, one often feels a disturbing incommensurability between printed records of actual, lethal violence and how violent behaviour is represented in literature. Yet the evaluations and re-evaluations enabled and provoked by works produced by the fictive imagination, as well as by an assessment of how these relate to other forms of discourse, have a vital contribution to make not just in Northern Ireland but in any society concerned to understand how precarious is the order maintained by the rule of law and the conventions of civilized behaviour.

Elsewhere, I have written in detail about some basic positions – religious, political and aesthetic – that also underlie the present study, and in the following pages I attempt to avoid undue theorizing and specialized debate. Although I intend to provide arguments sufficient to sustain the case I want to make, the central idea that literature does not occupy a hermetically sealed, specialized realm will, I hope, sufficiently discourage me from writing as if I inhabit one.

I have received help from a great many people to whom I am immensely indebted, though I will not attempt to list their names here. The Social Sciences and Humanities Research Council of Canada has supported the project through a Standard Research Grant, which I gratefully acknowledge. Permission has been granted by the Blackstaff Press to reproduce "The Iron Circle" from *The Collected Poems* by John Hewitt; by Jonathan Cape to reproduce "The Civil Servant" and "Wounds" from *Selected Poems* by Michael Longley; by the Gallery Press to reproduce "Rage for Order" from *Collected Poems* by Derek Mahon; by the Gallery Press and Wake Forest University Press to reproduce "Apostle of Violence" from *Captain Lavender* by Medbh McGuckian.

List of Abbreviations

BBC	British Broadcasting Corporation
CLMC	Combined Loyalist Military Command (emerged in 1991 to represent loyalist paramilitary interests)
DUP	Democratic Unionist Party (strongly conservative; founded in 1971)
INLA	Irish National Liberation Army (an extreme republican paramilitary group, founded in 1975; is associated with the Irish Republican Socialist Party, IRSP)
IRA	Irish Republican Army (a split in 1970 resulted in two organizations, the Officials and the Provisionals, who are sometimes designated PIRA. In the present study, IRA indicates the provisional wing; is associated with Sinn Féin.)
IRB	Irish Republican Brotherhood (a revolutionary organization founded in 1858; a forerunner of the modern IRA)
IRSP	Irish Republican Socialist Party (founded in 1974; associated with the Irish National Liberation Army, INLA)
LVF	Loyalist Volunteer Force (extreme loyalist paramilitary group, founded in 1996)
MRF	Mobile Reconnaissance Force
NICRA	Northern Ireland Civil Rights Association (founded in 1967)
PUP	Progressive Unionist Party (founded in 1979; associated with the Ulster Volunteer Force, UVF).
RTE	Radio Telefis Eireann (Irish broadcasting network)
RUC	Royal Ulster Constabulary (Northern Ireland's police service)
SAS	Special Air Service (an elite British Army undercover unit)
SDLP	Social Democratic and Labour Party (mainline nationalist party, founded in 1970)
SF	Sinn Féin (political party associated with the IRA)
UDA	Ulster Defence Association (loyalist paramilitary group, founded in 1971; has used the cover name Ulster Freedom Fighters, UFF; is associated with the Ulster Democratic Party, UDP)
UDR	Ulster Defence Regiment (formed in 1970 to replace the B Specials (a part-time police force founded in 1920); merged in 1992 with the Royal Irish Rangers to form the Royal Irish Regiment)

UFF   Ulster Freedom Fighters (cover name for Ulster Defence
            Association, UDA)
UUP   Ulster Unionist Party (mainline unionist party, which also
            governed Northern Ireland from 1921 to 1972, when direct
            rule from London was imposed)
UVF   Ulster Volunteer Force (loyalist paramilitary group, formed
            in 1966; traces its origins to resistance to Home Rule in 1912,
            and is associated with the Progressive Unionist Party, PUP)

1
Introduction: at War with Words

On violence, broadly speaking

Complicity in violence is a condition of being civilized. As everyone understands, order is maintained by observance of law; in turn, law is maintained – as it was established – by force. When disagreements occur between states, diplomacy seeks to avoid the use of force and to settle things by words. But when the fence of words and the citadel of law are breached, the edifice of the civilized itself comes under threat. As always, nightmare lurks closer than we know, whetting its instruments of wastage and madness. It is an old story, the first and last story of history.

Outside the halls of diplomacy, non-violent confrontation has sometimes been efficacious. Mahatma Gandhi and Martin Luther King are the best known modern examples of how non-violent protest might throw into confusion the state's confidence in its right to use force. Something comparable occurred in the decisive civil rights marches of 1968 in Northern Ireland, when the RUC battered peaceful demonstrators, including the present Lord Fitt, then West Belfast MP at Westminster. Yet much depended, on that occasion, on television crews and journalists who made the repugnant facts known to an audience sufficiently conscionable to be concerned. As we might safely guess, had Gandhi, say, been a Kurd conducting a protest against Saddam Hussein, or had Martin Luther King been a Cambodian taking to the streets to challenge Pol Pot, both would have vanished without trace. In short, non-violent confrontation works only in special circumstances, within which it may also assume various forms.

For instance, non-violent non-cooperation and non-violent protest are strategically different and will have different effects. Again, a non-violent group might find itself in uncomfortable allegiance with others who do not share the same principles though espousing the same cause. In a situation where supporters of this common cause mingle in large numbers, non-violence can be difficult to maintain, and its proponents are vulnerable to manipulation. Likewise, just as non-violent protest frequently depends on the conscience of those against whom it is directed, so it may also rely on the mobilizing of a wider jurisdictional power against some local form of oppression. Thus, federal troops were deployed in the southern US to implement deseg-regation; and in Northern Ireland in 1972, direct rule replaced the Stormont regime, which had assumed that an old-style local show of force would yet again secure the *status quo*. Even the professedly non-violent are therefore not always free from complicity in the deployment of force that they theoretically oppose. With this in mind, I want to return to the idea that it is better to talk than fight, but to suggest that the opposition between speech and violence is complicated in much the same way as is the opposition between violence and non-violence.

The philosopher Eric Weil[1] argues that discourse – which he describes as the true end of philosophy – is always inherently opposed to violent action. In reply, Emmanuel Levinas suggests that the conceptual coher-ence at which philosophical discourse aims is itself suspect because it imposes a totality upon others and therefore does not escape the taint of violence altogether. Although Levinas might seem here to extend the meaning of violence excessively, the point he makes is hard to ignore once it is raised. Indeed, the maiming and killing of human beings is clearly incommensurate with the effects of threat, verbal abuse, or argument, and it is well not to lose sight of this difference. Yet, everyday uses of the word "violence" commonly reproduce gradations of mean-ing of the kind to which Levinas points. Thus, we might talk about a violent disagreement, a violent rugby tackle, a violent storm, or a vio-lent opinion. Also, the idea of violence is not far removed from the idea of violation, and we can talk of someone's privacy or integrity being violated, thereby invoking a notion of quasi-violence but not necessarily entailing physically violent action in the usual sense. It seems, then, that we readily attribute violence to nature's unconscious processes, human pastimes, opinions, intentions, and speech, as well as to phys-ically abusive behaviour.

I do not want to discuss these various usages in detail, but simply to notice that inter-relationships between violence and language are com-plex. Jacques Derrida[2] even suggests – developing Levinas – that speech produced "without the least violence" would "determine nothing, would say nothing". Consequently, we find ourselves constrained to oppose violence mainly by some lesser violence, and we should understand how deeply we are compromised by history itself, which forces such a constraint upon us.

Even religious experiences of spiritual liberation – freedom in Christ, mystical intuition, transfiguration, and the like – do not free us entirely from this compromise. As the saints tell us, spiritual experience prepares us to re-engage a violent and damaged world as a token of the authenticity of the spiritual experience itself. Thus, the story of Jesus's transfiguration is not complete until the disciples return to the foot of the mountain, to the griefs of the poor and to the fact of the cross that they initially preferred to deny or ignore. "I came not to send peace, but a sword" (Matt. 10:34) does not enjoin Christians to go to war, but it does entail a tragic struggle with the world, wherein a vision of freedom promised for the end time and intermittently piercing the historical present, confronts the realm of necessity governed by an economy of violence with which we find ourselves required to co-operate if only because we must live under the rule of law. Consequently, as Jacques Ellul[3] says, it is natural for us sometimes to condone violence, even though in the name of freedom we should always refuse finally to justify it.

I want now to suggest a broad description of violence, even though – as we see – such a description itself runs the risk of imposing in a quasi-violent way on the reader. Consequently, I want first to introduce a further, central claim of the present study, namely, that among the many modes of discourse through which violence can be described and assessed, literature is distinctive because it challenges and complicates the conceptual descriptions by which we might contrive to define violence in order to keep it at a safe distance, more or less. This does not mean that we should eschew the conceptual; only that the quest for rational clarity ought to remain alert to the gaps and fissures between ideas and experience. With this in mind, let me now attempt to be – at least tolerably – clear and rational.

Broadly, violence occurs whenever another human being is treated as an object or thing, rather than as a person able to give consent or to refuse to enter into a discourse or relationship. Any attempt to deface or absorb another person without regard for that person's willing co-operation is therefore violent. As Simone Weil[4] eloquently says, violence congeals, hardening and turning the other to stone. Its supreme expression is making a corpse of the other – that is, something wholly inert.

But violence also can congeal life before abolishing it, and this is the condition of the enslaved and oppressed.

Clearly, the most explicit violence is physical, producing corpses and effecting the abjection and silencing of its victims. But violence takes many forms, and finds a principal aider and abettor in lies and propaganda. As we shall see, propaganda simplifies the truth about violence in much the same way as violence simplifies the truth about human relationships. By contrast, the fictive dimension of imaginative literature (itself, paradoxically, a kind of lie) can discover in new ways the deceptions on which propaganda depends – the lies, that is, at the heart of violence. But although literature and propaganda are indeed opposites, this does not mean that there is, somehow, a single literary vision of violence. Rather, each writer's achievement remains distinctive, and the singularity of a personal voice – the individual's personal experience taking the form of words – is itself a value that the impersonal mechanisms of violence would destroy. Still, in unmasking the oversimplifications by which violence is perpetrated, the fictive imagination can help us also to discern and describe certain mechanisms characteristically at work in violent behaviour, operating often beneath the threshold of the perpetrators' consciousness, and frequently as seductive and compelling as they are dangerous.

With this in mind we might suggest that the hardening effects of violence and its sheer instrumentality[5] stand especially opposed to the metamorphic energies of imagination, and in his famous poem about civil war, *Easter 1916*, W. B. Yeats contrasts the stone and "the living stream" in this sense. Edna Longley adapts Yeats's figure in her book, also entitled *The Living Stream*, to comment on – among other things – poetry and violence in Northern Ireland, and recently, Jonathan Hufstader has taken up the stone-and-water contrast in *Tongue of Water, Teeth of Stones: Northern Irish Poetry and Social Violence*,[6] drawing for his title on a poem by Paul Muldoon which in turn alludes to and reinterprets Yeats. To some extent, I am joining this conversation, but, as I have indicated, my point of entry is Simone Weil's insightful study of the *Iliad*, with its reminder of how deeply rooted in Western literary tradition is the notion of violence as a petrifying agency. The trope is of course pervasive, extending through myth towards archetype in the complementary opposition, for instance, of Mars and Venus, the principles of iron and water, *furor* and *amor*, each with its dangerous excess, and each required to temper the other in an always perilous equipoise.

Partly as a consequence of taking such bearings, I do not, in the following pages, directly engage the interesting theoretical debate among academics about how violence is represented in modern Northern Irish writing. The theoretical issues are expertly described by Peter McDonald in his book *Mistaken Identities*, where he outlines the controversy about how ideology might permeate supposedly historical facts, and how "the theoretical 'perspective'" then offers to "redeem violence from the narratives in terms of which it is habitually understood". That is, by precluding objective access to historical events, some analysts propose that accounts of violence are always embodied in narratives which attempt to make sense of violence from a certain (often unconsciously concealed) political point of view. The question then is whether or not literary language also inevitably colludes with or exposes the "encoded narratives",[7] and whether or not poetry is inevitably political, or inhabits its own sovereign realm, the aesthetic.

Although I do not enter into this debate directly, I do none the less engage many issues central to it, as a reader will recognize from the examples cited to support my argument throughout, and how these are discussed. But to return now to the broad account of violence which I want to set out in this chapter, I would like briefly to consider Vergil's *Aeneid* and the gospel stories of Jesus's crucifixion. It might seem odd to begin a book on modern Northern Ireland in this way, but I want to argue otherwise, for several reasons. First, the epic tradition and the New Testament are strong sources, central to Western literary and cultural tradition, and they offer a series of insights about the petrifying agency of violence that constitute a highly effective set of criteria for conducting further discussions of the topic. Second, a main concern of the present study as a whole is to re-situate Northern Ireland in a larger cultural history from which it is often too conveniently dislocated. The Northern Ireland Troubles are not just an archaic tribal aberration which the impartial British are attempting to referee. The Troubles are also a product of fraught relationships between imperialism and Christianity which have a broad historical and cultural significance. Third, Northern Irish writers themselves resort explicitly and not infrequently to the paradigm I will propose by way of Vergil and the gospels. Thus, modern Northern Ireland is imagined by an interesting cross-section of writers as a colony of ancient Rome beset by divisions and controversies deriving from Christianity. We find this in John Hewitt, Frank McGuinness, Seamus Heaney, David Rudkin, Medbh McGuckian and Michael Longley (who looks, however, behind Vergil to Homer). In each chapter I will deal in some detail with at least one of these authors, thereby developing a *leitmotif* implicit in the literature, and which confirms my own interest in the foundational texts which I want now to consider.

Refining the criteria: Vergil and the Gospels

On the surface, the *Aeneid* and the gospels are propagandist. The first was written by command of the Emperor to celebrate Roman civiliza- tion, and the second to proclaim the *kerygma*, the saving truth about Jesus. Yet both exceed their propagandist aims, engaging and forcing us to encounter and re-encounter the seductive prejudices, radiant hopes, tragic bitterness and various intimately experienced complexities that impede or unaccountably aid us as we make our human way in a recalcitrant world. In short, through a sheer, captivating excess of nar- rative and symbolism over dogma, both texts achieve a high degree of literary distinction.

Basically, the *Aeneid* interprets Homer's great epics for the Latin West, and Vergil, like Homer, remains deeply preoccupied with the tragic relationship between violence and civilization. In the gospels, which were written close in time to the *Aeneid*, Jesus also promises a new city, a kingdom precluding the violent ways of this world, which are repre- sented especially by his crucifixion. In much the same way as Vergil draws on Homer, the gospels draw on the religious genius of the Hebrew scriptures, and the Christian message was transmitted across the civ- ilized world established by ancient Rome. Still, despite considerable areas of shared insight and concern, the gospels and the *Aeneid* remain opposed and incommensurate, and out of this asymmetry, in turn, have arisen the profoundest explorations of evil and violence in Western literary tradition.

Three episodes from the *Aeneid*[8] can exemplify Vergil's representation of violence in the poem as a whole. The first is the night attack on Troy in Book II, after the wooden horse has been admitted and the Greeks open the city gates. The second is the ambush set for the Trojans by Turnus and his warlike female ally, Camilla, and which results in Camil- la's death, described in Book XI. The third is the death of Turnus, the main anti-hero, at the hands of Aeneas in Book XII, at the very end of the poem. All three episodes deal directly with violence, and are inter- connected in ways that subtend and inform Vergil's overarching vision of the relationship between violence and civilization.

Troy is sacked after the wooden horse is admitted by means of a charade verging on the ridiculous until it unleashes a torrent of blood- lust. The attack occurs at night, and as Troy burns, the flames provide a lurid and frightening half-light. Ambiguous signs, portents and dreams also blur the differences between friend and foe, as a frenzied rush to violence confounds prudence on all sides. "Like a fool I seized my sword" (II, 314), Aeneas recalls, "I was ablaze to round up men for war" (II, 315). Young men in plenty rush to follow him, "Like wolves / hot for a kill at murky midnight" (II, 355–6), and soon the dead litter the streets. At one point, the Greek Androgeos mistakes some Trojans for allies, and the Trojans quickly take advantage of his error and kill a number of Greeks. In their exultation, the Trojans then disguise themselves in Greek armour to deceive more of the enemy. Predictably, other Trojans fail to recognize the disguise, and many are killed, "transfixed by friends" (II, 429), until, at last, "grief heartrending, / terror, and death" reign "over all in countless forms" (II, 368–9).

In the phrase "countless forms" ("plurima mortis imago") Vergil nods in the direction of the philosophical view that violence annihilates identity and produces in the end a formless chaos. Thus, the identities of friend and foe are confused and accidents determine who is struck down and who escapes. Violence operates therefore as an automatism abetted by panic and confusion that robs the combatants of better judgement while filling them with an exultation that they easily mistake for bravery or heroism. One result is the "countless forms" of a destruction that obliterates friend and foe indifferently, leaving grief, terror and death in its wake. Thus Troy is broken, but some Trojans escape and seek to found another city in Italy, breaking, in turn, the rulers who would oppose their design. For Vergil the *pax Augusta* is, at last, less a renunciation than a cessation of violence by a state so powerful that it prevents further challenges to its authority.

The second episode deals with armed resistance to the Trojans in Italy, and especially with the Volscian princess, Camilla, who adds her strength to Turnus, prince of the Rutuli. Camilla is an attractive figure along the lines of Shakespeare's Hotspur, and in Book XI she joins Turnus, leaping from her horse and, full of high spirits, plotting with him to ambush Aeneas. She is engaging and glamorous, but also reckless and does not imagine adequately what she is getting into – as Diana, her protectress, observes ruefully. Consequently, Diana sets Opis to guard Camilla and to strike whomever harms her.

When the fighting starts, Camilla soon becomes incensed, and Vergil lists her victims and their grisly deaths as they fall beneath her incandescent fury. At last, the wily Arruns circles behind her, and as she pauses to deck herself "in golden spoils" (XI, 780) he kills her. Arruns runs off, elated, but Opis quickly tracks him down, and finds him, in turn, "all glittering arms and foolish pride" (XI, 854), whereupon she kills him as Diana had instructed.

This episode duplicates the main motifs evident in the sacking of Troy. An initial sense of preparation for war as a game or sport is quickly replaced by a frenzy of killing as victims fall right and left and the intoxication of battle drives on the combatants. But in the Arruns episode Vergil develops more clearly the implications of those fatal disguises the Trojans assumed in Book II. Here, Arruns stalks Camilla and succeeds in killing her, but he is unwitting that he also stalks himself. By divine edict, whoever kills Camilla will also die, and, ironically, Arruns seals his own fate even as he thinks of himself as victorious. His situation mirrors Camilla's, and he is hunted even as he hunts, proudly dressed in glittering armour to signify a triumph which in fact is a defeat. Victor and victim thus resemble one another, and the circle of violence returns to destroy the perpetrator. The ironies, illusions and bitterness depicted here remain central to Vergil's vision of the Augustan empire that his poem officially celebrates. All of which in turn helps to explain the painful complexity of the episode with which the *Aeneid* ends.

In Book XII, Aeneas has defeated Turnus and holds him at swordpoint. Turnus capitulates, and does not ask for mercy for himself but only for his aged father, Daunus. Aeneas then hesitates, checking the fatal blow he is poised to strike, and in this hesitation the poem suggests that the enemies might recognize how they resemble one another, despite their differences. This glimpse of a possible, higher morality comes to us in Aeneas's momentary pause, but then he sees that Turnus is dressed in the armour of the boy Pallas, Aeneas's favourite whom Turnus slew, and "a flame of fury and dreadful rage" (XII, 946) flares up as Aeneas avenges the boy by striking Turnus dead. Not only anger, but also righteous indignation harden Aeneas at the end, as he makes of the entreating Turnus a speechless corpse.

Again, Turnus is killed because he has killed, and the cycle of violence continues even to the end of this remarkable and poignant poem. Consequently, although Aeneas stands at last triumphant, Vergil leaves us with a resonating, profound sense of bitterness and sadness. This plangency, for which he is justly famous, emerges from the heart of his poem as a quality of language, sensibility and vision, attesting to the disturbing truth that civilization – the grandeur of Rome – rests on a violence that may be contained but is not overcome. Vergil therefore praises civilized order mainly because it is powerful enough to suppress an always latent violence, which, if let loose, would be worse than the repressions required to keep it at bay. His poetry achieves its characteristic, resonant beauty partly from a deep understanding that each person needs to realize, from within the confines of a particular, historically contingent subjectivity, this tragic contradiction between death and civilization, violence and the rule of law.

As I have mentioned, I concentrate on Vergil because of his importance to the Latin West. Medieval exegetes even sought to link him directly to Jesus as a sort of pagan prophet whose epic depiction of Augustan Rome could offer comfort and support to the onward marching Christian soldiers of the converted empire. But there are key differences between Vergil's depiction of violence and the main example of violence in the New Testament, namely the public torture and execution of an innocent man, put to death outside the city.

Basically, the Romans killed Jesus as a scapegoat. As René Girard[9] explains, a scapegoat symbolically bears the sins of a social group, which then experiences an enhanced solidarity – its own internal animosities, competitive bitterness and repressed resentments having been projected onto the sacrificial victim. Whereas the *Aeneid*, therefore, celebrates first of all the earthly city as a guarantor of law and order, the crucifixion protests in the name of the sacrificial scapegoat against violence inherent in the rule of law itself. Yet, in so doing, the crucifixion also returns us imperatively to the challenge inherent in Aeneas's moment of hesitation as he is poised to kill Turnus. The gospels teach that such a moment alone holds the key to the kingdom, as distinct from the parody of peace with which we are mostly familiar, and which is secured by laws underwritten by force and by preparation for war. The resurrection occurs whenever this truth about reconciliation with an enemy is recognized and embodied in our relations with others.

The centrality to Christianity of Jesus's violent death and of the resurrection that overcomes and defeats it, is confirmed by the fact that the earliest strata of the New Testament texts all focus on these events.[10] The passion story is the oldest consecutive narrative about Jesus, as we see, for instance, in the formulas of Acts 2:23, 32; 3:14–15; 4:10, and I Corinthians 15:3–4. The ministry narratives are less clearly ordered, and were developed to preface and explain the events of Jesus's final days in a manner reflecting the christological emphasis of the gospel in question. Certainly, the earliest materials do not emphasize Jesus's birth and family; rather, as Paul and the sermons in Acts show, the resurrection is the key evidence of Jesus's divinity. Consequently, the main aim in the gospel narratives is not biographical; the intent is to proclaim that through the crucifixion and resurrection death itself is defeated and the kingdom made present.

Understandably, as the gospels developed, a more elaborate picture was presented of Jesus's earthly mission and career, suggesting that his divinity was evident at earlier points in his life, though often unrecognized, even by his disciples. Thus, Mark tells us that Jesus was proclaimed Son of God at his baptism; Luke and Matthew add the birth narratives and announce Jesus's divine begetting; John makes Jesus the pre-existent logos, divine even before entering into history through the Incarnation. But the scandal of the cross and significance of the resurrection remain central, and the spare, devastating simplicity and concentration of the passion narratives place the problem of violence at the heart of Jesus's teaching about the kingdom, and at the heart also of the various elements and traditions that subsequently were shaped into the canonical gospels.

As Girard points out, Jesus's death makes conscious the scapegoat mechanism, thereby showing in a singular fashion how readily historical societies conceal from themselves their own violent impulses, which erupt periodically in communal acts of cruelty. Yet, as Moltmann[11] says, by and large Christian institutions have gilded the cross, concealing the hard message about scapegoating and softening, for instance, the sheer horror the disciples must have felt as they fled in fear and confusion away from that dreadful spectacle. And so it is well to remind ourselves of the grotesque cruelty of Jesus's death and of the sadistic, theatrical display accompanying it. Thus, in a ritual parody of coronation, Jesus was dressed up, crowned, paraded and enthroned on the cross, every stage of this royal progress turned into a calculated infliction of agony. His mockers apparently found it hilarious (if also, no doubt, terrifying), and here a further dimension of the economy of violence is touched upon in a way that we do not quite see in Vergil, with the exception perhaps of the remarkable death scene of Dido. For there is something of an absurdist play in the passion narratives, shot through with the sounds of a harsh and horrified laughter. The execution ritual that produces this effect both diminishes and exalts the authorities responsible for it. They are diminished in so far as their cruelty gives rise to spontaneous protest, a recoil, perhaps deflected partly into laughter, against a naked display of state power that mocks at ritual even as it flaunts its own ritualized and absolute control of the instruments of terror and pain. They are exalted because the protest is itself immediately quashed and co-opted by awe and fear of the power so displayed and proclaiming itself legal; the laughter of irreverence then is re-directed to the victim, the mocked and despised scapegoat. In short, like the rest of us, those who witnessed the crucifixion found themselves compromised, and such will continue to be the way of the world until the scroll of history is itself rolled up, as Revelation promises.

As I have said, I begin with Vergil and the gospels because these texts tell a series of truths about violence that I take to be exemplary – strong sources, as Charles Taylor[12] would say. I want to maintain that representations of violence ignoring or eliding the kinds of insight and understanding revealed here are missing something important. This does not mean I want to claim that the *Aeneid* and the gospels have so clearly determined what violence is that we need read only them. Words always fall short of the mystery, and no amount of reading saves us, for instance, from the violence of nature that disposes of us all by and by. Thus, among other things, distinguished literature – and here I include the scriptures of the world's major religions – gives us various, differently angled glimpses, more and less profound, of our vulnerability in a violent world. In each case a personal voice offers witness, shaping in order to make habitable an often glorious, often richly amusing and gratifying, but in the end ungovernable world into which we are thrown and which condemns us to death. No amount of generalization about what great writers say in common can substitute for the centrality of the fact that each of us is born and dies alone; yet, in the meantime, we are able to reach across a shared separateness to shape and forge a variety of civilizations and cultures that might provide us some degree of safety and comfort, even though never quite enough, and never finally. Much literature reminds us of this, while showing us also the same points that I have derived from the texts which I have so far discussed. Homer, Sophocles, the Jahwist compiler, Dante, Shakespeare, Goethe, Dostoevsky, Melville among many others could equally well provide examples. All of which brings me now to my second reason for singling out Vergil and the New Testament, which is historical rather than literary.

Northern Ireland and the historical debate

In his study of modern nation states, *God Land*,[13] Conor Cruise O'Brien correctly looks both to Vergil and to early Christianity as foundational to the story he wants to tell. He points out that in adapting itself to the classical heritage of Greece and Rome, Christianity inserted between the earthly and heavenly kingdoms a "political layer", represented first by the Imperial Court, which "provided Christianity with classical legitimation", making "the Christian Emperor the fulfillment of the classical past". O'Brien argues that the "acceptance of Virgil as a central figure in the culture of medieval Christianity" is crucial to this process, and he points out that the *Aeneid* acquired "quasi-Scriptural status", as indeed it did. But Vergil's promised land remains the earthly city, and in Christianity after Constantine, a new, territorial vision develops, inheriting, as O'Brien says, the "notion of the transcendent importance of the terrestrial patria". The subsequent contention within Christendom between the claims of the heavenly and earthly kingdoms was to remain stubbornly durable, and O'Brien points out how readily new Western nations continued to depict themselves as "true heirs of the Empire". This is the case with medieval Germans, Revolutionary French, Victorian English, and the American founding fathers, who saw themselves at once as a Biblical chosen people and as "transfigured Romans". Though O'Brien does not say so, Ulster's Protestants and the American founding fathers have a good deal in common, seeing themselves alike as a chosen people, a new Israel under siege, and also as the enlightened champions of civil liberties against the Caesaro-Papism of a tyrannical, paganized Christian church, where the balance of values deriving from ancient Rome and the Bible had, apparently, gone very wrong. Thus, the Reverend Ian Paisley preaches regularly on Fridays outside the Belfast City Hall, and the juxtaposition here of reformed evangelical radicalism and Victorian neo-classicism catches exactly the re-combination of traditional elements, as a Christian new Israel and transfigured Roman civic virtue re-enforce a certain ideal of Christian liberty.

Understandably, from the start the "political layer" between heaven and earth described by O'Brien was a source of unease. On the one hand, Rome seemed providentially ordered to enable the spread of Christ's message throughout the empire; on the other, Rome was an earthly tyranny that persecuted Christians and stood opposed to God's kingdom, much as Babylon stood opposed to Jerusalem. It fell especially to Saint Augustine, mainly in his great work *The City of God*, to effect some authoritative compromise between these contending claims. Basically, Augustine envisaged a continuing struggle through history between the forces of Babylon and Jerusalem, but the wheat and tares would not be finally separated until the end time. Consequently, political Augustinianism came to depict the state as legitimate in so far as it acted as an auxiliary of the church, maintaining law and order in a fallen world awaiting the final coming of a kingdom in which the state itself would pass away. Meanwhile, in so far as the state is judged to be legitimate, it acts as the secular arm of ecclesiastical authority, and in medieval philosophy and theology, the state was held to be an instrument of force rather than violence (which in turn was defined as the illegal use of force). This distinction between force and violence was thus held to indicate the key difference between a supra-individual authority and the wilful rebellion of individuals. That is, only individuals can be violent; the state, by contrast, is the agent of legitimate force. Although the casuistry behind this theory is patent, it is remarkable with what persistence human societies still contrive to convince themselves that the violence they do to their enemies is different from the violence done by their enemies.

Theoretical ingenuities notwithstanding, the fact remains that Roman civilization – the earthly *patria* – and the kingdom of heaven proclaimed by the crucified and risen Christ remain fundamentally opposed for the simple reason that, in so far as the state survives by threat of force, it precludes the kingdom, the reign of God. None the less, as is obvious from day-to-day experience, we all need state protection – the lesser violence that is our hedge against the worst violence. Consequently, the question of how the use of force is legitimized by modern nation states inheriting this historical tradition of debate remains highly contentious, as is evident not least in Northern Ireland, where matters of principle deriving from Christianity find themselves variously in collusion with and opposed to the instruments of state power, and where the legal use of force and the individual use of violence once more prove tortuously difficult to adjudicate.

To summarize: as the epic tradition shows, violence radically over-simplifies human relationships, and people in the grip of fear and anger may rush into it spurred to apparent bravery by heroic ideals that blind them easily to the consequences of their actions. Certainly, epic heroism has a value, but one characteristic of the heroic disposition is to approach violence as a game or sport, cultivating a levity and comradeship that simultaneously conceal and protect against a horror that is too stern to contemplate until it is too late to turn back. Once violence is unleashed, its proponents rapidly find themselves locked into its automatism, a blind process that lurches unpredictably, escaping the best laid plans. What follows is a hardening to death in two senses: the perpetrator is hardened to the humanity of an enemy, who consequently becomes merely a representative, but the perpetrator's hardness is also self-destructive. Thus, the violent stalk themselves unwittingly, and violence at last turns upon itself, as the revolutionary cohort turns the instruments of revolutionary war upon dissenters, including its own party members – and as Satan, in Revelation, is exterminated at the end of history by the violence he let loose during it.

The unmaking power of violence and the theatricality of the spectacular productions by which it partly hides itself from itself can produce also a kind of intoxication, a claustrophobic but thrilling, fear-drenched intensity, such as Aeneas and Camilla experience, but which in turn easily spills into sadism, attracting to even the most elevated cause a fringe element of psychopaths and criminals. The gospel passion stories catch something of the feel of such a thing, of violence ritualizing itself as theatrical display, entertaining the mob. If, as Bergson says, laughter occurs when we observe someone behaving under compulsion while believing the action free, then the violent, who submit to and are taken over by the dehumanized mechanisms of blind force, can appear absurd – grotesquely laughable – when they proclaim that they are doing this to uphold the law, or to defend freedom, and the like.

As we see, the unconscious compulsions under which the violent frequently act can partly be explained by the scapegoat mechanism, projecting onto a chosen victim the unacknowledged aggressions and hatreds within one's self or one's group. Because such projections typically remain concealed, justifications of violence depend on disguising its actual causes. As everyone knows, violence thrives on propaganda, which can be difficult to identify, concealed as it often is by ideology and made to appear as self-evident.

And so we return to the notion of a war of words and to the elusive separations and interconnections between language and violent action. Words do not protect us finally against violence, though they might prevent it. Yet words may also incite violence, or contribute to its continuance by perpetrating the lies of propaganda and the illusions of ideology on which violence feeds. In a world where the best we can do is to choose a lesser violence, the war of words by which we might hope to wrest a degree of freedom from the realm of necessity remains difficult and complex. In light of this, the kind of commentary that proposed, for instance, in the early years of the Troubles in Northern Ireland that IRA violence was caused by local boys who resented soldiers going out with local girls[14] is not just trivial; it harbours an attitude of contempt, and there has been a good deal of that kind of commentary over the years. But there has also developed over the past decades a formidable body of analysis, much of which is impressively intelligent. It is produced by a wide range of writers – journalists, academics, artists – and through the patient co-operation of many community-based groups and public agencies. How much this remarkable expenditure of creative, intellectual effort has contributed to saving Northern Ireland from the catastrophe of all-out war cannot be simply assessed or finally proved, but its salutary effects are probably far-reaching.

In this context, I want to argue that literary approaches to the violence of the Troubles are likewise often marked by an indirection that is the best means of finding directions out, as is always the way with imagination. Not surprisingly, relationships between such "literary" and other "non-literary" writing about violence are perplexed and asymmetrical, as the war of words engages the pathologies of violence along many fronts. As we see, where words reach their limit, the violent turn their victims to stone – silent, congealed and abject. Yet new and personal recognitions can also be effected, intimating a peace that surpasses understanding, and in which language also again becomes silent.

Between these poles, the designs that would bring us to Jerusalem still contend with the powers of Babylon, and imagination struggles still with the compromises that always pre-engage us in a world where fact and fiction interpenetrate in bewildering ways. As usual, the violent remain unconscious of their projections upon their scapegoat victims, and how their own punitive rituals conceal and manipulate terror. Propaganda still conflates heroism with actions driven by hatred in a confused half-light, and dismisses real issues by oversimplifying them. The enemy is still routinely depersonalized in order to be killed and the killers reel with intoxication, a temporary elation that might spill easily into remorse, depression, and worse. Still, the violent stalk themselves unbeknownst to themselves, and the automatism when it takes over betrays every ideal as it always does because it is, as it must be, utterly indifferent. The worst violence remains a grotesque, unpredictable absurdity that could evoke a horrified laughter of fearful contempt, perhaps deflected into mockery; and it entails, as ever, a double hardening to death by which enemies are bound together in a vicious circle of revenge and recrimination which is broken only under the direction of a higher morality than that which seeks to justify the necessity of its own violent continuance. In the following chapters I want to consider how language attempts to describe and negotiate such issues, and how compellingly the Northern Ireland conflict shows what such negotiation entails.

2

The Iron Circle: on the Core Mechanisms of Violence

Entrapment: variations on a theme

In the first chapter I suggested that imaginative literature gives us special access to the workings of violence, showing the mechanisms by which it perpetuates itself, and also the means by which the violent conceal from themselves and others the consequences of their actions. Yet there are no clear lines of demarcation between "literary" and "non-literary" texts; people who give interviews about their experiences, journalists reconstructing an event, social workers explaining the problems they encounter – these and others may offer testimony that becomes resonant and moving as some local instance engages us, achieving the compelling power of metaphor or symbol. By contrast, more self-consciously produced imaginative literature might well be banal or tendentious, all-too evidently trivial in comparison with the many harrowing accounts of violent events compiled by writers concerned to avoid the fictitious altogether. Yet the avoidance of imagination is never complete in the construction of narrative, even among writers scrupulously concerned to tell what in fact happened. Just so, no work of fiction can really engage us unless it evokes in some compelling way our experience of the actual world. In short, there is a shifting scale along which imagination comes into play to shape meaning in the form of words, persuading and urging us to re-evaluate, to think again about things we thought we knew well enough already. With this in mind, I want in the present chapter to concentrate on some central mechanisms by which violence is conducted, and to consider how these are represented in a range of printed texts.

As we have seen, violence depends on a *depersonalizing* of the enemy, who thereby is reduced to the status of an object to be acted upon. To enable this depersonalizing, the enemy is usually treated not as an individual but as a *representative* of a despised or feared group which is accused of some prior fault, justifying the violence which then occurs. A representative victim also readily becomes a *scapegoat*, the bearer of repressed or unacknowledged fears and enmities within the culture of the victimizers, who consequently experience an enhanced solidarity among themselves. In turn, members of the social group to which the victim belongs will see themselves attacked in and through the victim, and will be strongly tempted to reply in kind. Reprisal then opens the floodgates of a *mutual recrimination*, whereby the difference between accuser and accused all but disappears as the opposites come to mirror one another, locked into an *anonymous mechanism* of reciprocal exchange. I will refer to this combination of effects as the "iron circle", a phrase suggested by a poem of the same name by John Hewitt.[1] Here it is:

The Iron Circle

> Here, often, a man provoked has said his say,
> stung by opinion or unjust event,
> and found his angry words, to his dismay,
> prop up his adversary's argument,
> for bitterness is not allowed to die,
> is fanned and fuelled, in this crazy land:
> the brandished gun demands a gun's reply;
> hate answers hate, our crest the Bloody Hand.
>
> My friend, who followed coursing on this ground,
> and sought its lore and logic everywhere,
> suggested once, the Hare must need the Hound
> as surely as the Hound must need the Hare.
> In my mood now I fear that he was right:
> the chase continues, with no end in sight.

Initially, when the angry man has "said his say", protesting against an "unjust event", the suggestion is that the grounds for protest seem to him self-evident. But to his "dismay" he then finds that his well-intentioned indignation is construed by his adversaries as a mark of prejudice, rather than as a cause for complaint that a reasonable person would acknowledge. We are left to imagine how the unsympathetic listeners seize on the speaker's latent assumptions as evidence of prejudice, and it is a pity that Hewitt does not develop this element of the poem further. Instead, in the second stanza he offers an analogy featuring hares and hounds, but this weakens the poem because the analogy surrenders the central idea of reciprocation suggested by the iron circle – after all, the hare does not turn and attack the hounds, and "the chase" of the last line is a one-way affair and not a circle at all. Still, Hewitt is insightful in noticing how "angry words" might lead – even inadvertently – to mutual accusation, reciprocal bitterness, and violence. Thus, when "the brandished gun demands a gun's reply", it is as if the gun takes over the argument independently of any actual person wielding it, just as the man's complaint is also taken impersonally, in a manner he did not intend.

In a later poem, "The Anglo-Irish Accord", Hewitt describes the "mirror hate" through which both sides in the Northern Ireland conflict become victims even as they victimize, and in "A Little People"[2] he harks back to "The Iron Circle" while also using the image of a mirror to describe how "baffled wits ignite to violence / as frightened face its mirror image meets". Hewitt's "little people" are the Protestant descendants of the seventeenth-century planters, and they continue to fear "that other tribe" which they displaced. Now, that "empire-Commonwealth runs down", the once prosperous Ulster Protestants find themselves under special duress, but Hewitt hopes that toleration and friendship will prevail.

"A Little People" is also strikingly close in theme and sentiment to "The Colony",[3] a poem described by Hewitt as "the definitive statement of my realisation that I am an Ulsterman".[4] Both deal with the Planters' modern descendants and the conflicts that have ensued through a perpetual enmity with the native, Catholic Irish. But "The Colony" develops this theme also through an extended analogy between modern British Northern Ireland and an ancient Roman settlement, and implicit throughout is the idea that Northern Ireland is not just a British colony by analogy with ancient Rome in the early years of Christianity, but is also a product of the history that developed from those foundations. The speaker is one of the Romans, and he makes all the same points as would a liberal modern Ulster Unionist, so that the Roman experience is developed as a sort of parable, summarizing various elements of Irish history since the seventeenth century. Thus, the speaker admits that the first appropriation of land was unjust, but argues that the settlers now have rights too. He is concerned that the rebellious natives have caused a "terror" that still "dogs us", and that "Caesar" (the British government) might well withdraw as the empire dwindles. He worries as well about the superstitions and strange religious beliefs that fuel resentment and rebellion among the natives as they plot and wait for "a bitter revenge".

A good deal of violent behaviour in modern Northern Ireland confirms all too clearly the cogency of Hewitt's iron circle, as victims typically are treated as representatives of the despised other group, and the violent themselves remain anonymous. As Allen Feldman[5] points out, in Belfast street culture preceding the Troubles, the "hard man" was often an admired local figure, willing to brawl in match fights with all-comers. This quasi-heroic pugilism all but disappeared with the introduction of the techniques and attitudes of urban guerrilla warfare. Now the hard men wear masks and shoot or bomb civilians, often chosen at random or on some unconvincing pretext. A double anonymity thus turns both assailant and victim into faceless people – one a masked assassin, the other a randomly chosen representative of the opposed group.

The callous directness of loyalist graffiti depicting the letters ATD ("any Taig will do")[6] catches something of this grim process as it makes any member at all of the Catholic community a target. As the loyalist Billy Giles explained in an interview with Peter Taylor, "Catholics, nationalists, republicans. Put whatever slant you want upon it. They were all the same", and "The only way to stop them was to terrorise them."[7] The daunting clarity of such declarations is countered by typically more discursive Republican warnings against assisting the security forces and thereby aiding and abetting the British. For instance, an IRA active volunteer offered the following explanation to the journalist Tony Parker:[8] "A hairdresser who cuts a soldier's hair, a barman who serves a policeman with a drink in a pub: to us every one of them is a collaborator"; moreover, "We'll define whether someone's helping the security forces or not: it's not for you to make the definition and criticise us for not agreeing with it" (326). This kind of reasoning led, for instance, to the deaths of eight Protestant workmen who had been servicing a security base in Co. Tyrone in 1992, but it is a line of thought that can also turn unpredictably in the other direction through a Kafka-esque chain of guilt by association, rapidly inducing terror and paranoia among nationalists also, especially those living in enclaves controlled by the IRA. Significantly, the main cause of death among Republican paramilitaries is other Republican paramilitaries,[9] and it is easy to see how IRA definitions of the enemy as anyone deemed to be helping the security forces could extend by association in a manner just as frightening and arbitrary as the blunter loyalist "ATD". Parker's interviewee – whose pseudonym is Eddie Boyle – confirms this intimidating arbitrariness when he goes on to proclaim that "the IRA has its own logic and oh no it's not yours" (324). He then says that he can't add much detail because secrecy is power, and "If you don't know our aims or how we justify them in our thinking, then it's that much more difficult for you to combat us"; in short, "some of our best weapons" are the "capacity to confuse and cause frustration" (325). Here Eddie Boyle acknowledges that sheer instrumental force is effective precisely because it is detached from any justification by which the victim might understand and assess it.

Malachi O'Doherty is singular among commentators in teasing out the implications of this kind of Republican rationale. O'Doherty suggests that releasing violence for its own sake sends a powerful message. The Canary Wharf bomb (1996) is a case in point, and so is the killing of two policemen in Lurgan (Roland Graham and David Johnston) in 1997, just at the moment when the British government was negotiating a ceasefire. O'Doherty suggests that in these instances violence "was being presented by Sinn Féin as a virtual force of nature, which they could show others how to assuage, not as a concerted political campaign that was amenable to reason".[10] That is, the Sinn Féin politicians would be willing to talk, but words alone (including Sinn Féin's words) could not really control the violent (and spontaneous) forces of destruction let loose by the IRA, putatively as a natural and virtually uncontrollable reaction to injustice. The fact that the violent episodes in question made no sense would therefore help to show British politicians what they are up against. In so far as violence and reason are incommensurate, violence is all the more terrifying; it therefore suits the IRA well to act in ways that confirm this disjuncture. Because people usually seek a reason when violence occurs, politicians might attribute some complex strategy to the IRA, and indeed such a strategy might exist. But a lack of strategy can itself be a strategy, showing that force is an automatism that, once released, takes directions impervious to reason. According to the IRA, violence will cease when the British leave Ireland; until then, it will continue as a law unto itself, impersonal as the law of falling bodies, and as indifferent to human concern as a storm at sea.

As the political process increasingly lays hold on the IRA, especially through the inclusion of Sinn Féin in the Northern Ireland Executive – established according to the Good Friday Agreement of 1998 – it is (at the time of writing) a moot point whether or not the ceasefire will break because of a failure to agree on the decommissioning of IRA weapons. The violence that many republican hardliners claim has got them this far might well get them no further if it renders the Good Friday Agreement unworkable, as many nationalists and republicans believe, reflecting a broad public consensus. Yet it is also an illusion to think that those who unleash violence – "legitimate" or otherwise – can simply decide when to stop it, and the strategists who wanted violence to be seen as a blind force of nature may discover that violence is indeed just that. In such circumstances, the politically empowered can expect to prevail uncertainly, and by the exercise of much forbearance,[11] over those who habitually resort to the intoxicating simplifications of a violence on which they ride perilously, thinking themselves in control.

As I have suggested, those caught up in the iron circle typically depend on oversimplifications to sustain and justify themselves. Thus, an IRA volunteer, using the pseudonym "Donnelly", explains that "I don't see the man, only the uniform", then adding that it is necessary to think in this way, "otherwise you would become psychopathic". Another volunteer, "McShane", concurs: "most volunteers got it into their minds that it was the uniform and not the individual that was being shot. This was pointed out to you at every opportunity at lectures to try and prevent you from getting emotionally involved".[12] Interestingly, ex-para and SAS soldier Michael Asher, recalling his experiences in Northern Ireland, reports that he knew very well that the IRA "thought of British soldiers as 'uniforms', not as people with mothers, wives and children". Candidly, he then adds that the same applied in reverse, and the paras' own "worship of violence" likewise "prevented us from remembering that the IRA were human beings like us".[13] And in his confessional book *Killing Rage*,[14] ex-IRA member Eamon Collins also explains how he set out "to kill a UDR uniform", realizing only later that "you can never kill a uniform, you can only kill a person" (2). He goes on to describe the high cost of his attempts to "suppress my instinct for compassion", and how he "fought to curb what I saw as my 'weakness', namely, my readiness to see my victims as ordinary human beings and their deaths as deserving of sympathy" (119). Eventually, the strain was too much for Collins, who became mentally unstable, feeling increasingly "as if I were some sort of automaton" (221) on "the verge of mental and physical collapse" (222).

The best parts of *Killing Rage* are those which come closest to exploring Collins's inner turmoil as he tries to reconcile his commitment to violence with his growing distaste for it, as in the episode when an IRA operative, Robert Carr, is burned alive by an incendiary bomb which he was planting in Newry customs station. Collins was responsible for setting up the operation, and is disturbed by the melted rubber soles of Carr's shoes and by blood on the walls. But Collins's "commitment to the organisation" (71) remains firm even as he tries to comfort Carr's wife Maureen, an old girlfriend with whom he now attempts a new relationship, which soon peters out amidst grief, pain and regret, though not without genuine solicitude and affection.

Such complexities notwithstanding, a main problem throughout *Killing Rage* is that the author's personal troubles and attempts at sympathy tend to be proclaimed rather than evoked ("She was upset at what was happening and felt that her world was collapsing" [196]; "at some human level I regarded Hanna's killing as a foul act" [119]). In short, we do not often experience the gripping power of the contradictions Collins claims eventually almost destroyed him, but which also forced him to revise the oversimplifying strategies by which he sought to kill a uniform rather than a person. One result is that the book itself reproduces the same flatness of affect that it claims is a main characteristic of those indoctrinated to commit violence.

Admittedly, difficult questions lurk, here. On the one hand, the assistance Collins received from journalist Mick McGovern in writing the book indicates that Collins was not equal to the task of bridging the gap between his actual experience and its narrative reconstruction. On the other hand, why should we expect Collins to be an imaginatively sensitive writer, or indeed any kind of writer? Are not the disturbing facts he discloses worth recording, and don't they make some further imaginative dimension seem beside the point? After all, the kinds of data collected about human rights abuses by Amnesty International are not poetic, and the facts about famine and child labour are upsetting merely because we know such things are happening. None the less, I hesitate to relinquish my point about the shortcomings of *Killing Rage*, partly because the meaning of Collins's story is inseparable from its narrative structure, and because Collins himself realizes that imagination is indispensable in the making of moral decisions that would prevent substituting "a uniform" for a person. Consequently, although there is no good sense in making unrealistic demands of Collins's book, neither should we fail to notice how wide is the gap between its theory and practice. After all, the imaginative discernment Collins recommends is not to be applied selectively, and therefore should not preclude an assessment of *Killing Rage* itself.

Among loyalists, a depersonalizing comparable to that described by Collins was acted out especially in a spate of sectarian murders during the 1970s in which innocent Catholics, straying from the safety of enclave areas – usually in finding their way home along bordering streets late at night – were abducted and killed, often after being horrendously tortured. As we see, one reason offered for such behaviour is that it would strike terror into the Catholic community, thereby showing that the IRA were not its able defenders. Also, unlike the security forces, the IRA do not dress distinctively, and the depersonalization represented by "killing a uniform" (which, by the Kafkaesque logic described by Eddie Boyle, includes anyone who *once wore* a uniform) is paralleled by a loyalist willingness simply to kill any Catholic at all. Kenny McClinton (now a fundamentalist preacher, who in earlier days advocated impaling the heads of assassinated Catholics on the railings of Woodvale Park and the Shankill) admits that "the most macabre means"[15] were used to terrorize the Catholic community. Many details of what happened to abducted Catholics have not been published, and the sample that has – for instance, in Martin Dillon's chilling account, *The Shankill Butchers*[16] – produces feelings of horror, revulsion and shame, uncomfortably mixed with a sense that such evidence also needs to be heard. Certainly, the means by which victims were ritually carved while alive stands as an extreme example of making the enemy "a sectarian artifact", as Feldman says, the body having been abstracted "through torture and mutilation into a political token".[17] Thus, in a frenzy of hatred, Lennie Murphy attacked the abducted and badly beaten Joseph Donegan with a pair of pliers, tearing out many of his teeth before ordering the still conscious Donegan to be finished off with a spade. The silencing of Donegan by attacking his mouth with the pliers and then rendering him faceless by destroying his head with a spade graphically materializes an extreme objectification whereby the person is made both speechless and faceless.

Apparently, the killing of Donegan was too much even for the UVF, with whom Murphy was associated (though as leader of a breakaway group), and it was agreed that he would have to be stopped. In the upshot, the UDA, who also had trouble with Murphy, seem to have set him up as a target for the IRA because he had become "a typical psychopath",[18] as one UDA spokesman is quoted as saying. At any rate, Murphy was shot dead on 16 November 1982, and although the circumstances of his death remain murky, he provides a shocking example of how violence attracts psychopathic personalities, and how it spirals rapidly into nightmare. As English-born loyalist Dave Fogel explains, when he was a paramilitary chief he had "the power of life and death over people", and "I must at times have been drunk with it."[19] In Fogel's case, the consequences were less sinister than with the Shankill Butchers, but he acknowledges how dangerous is the allure of violence and how it temporarily inflates the ego, allowing to the violent a fatal illusion (as Simone Weil says) that they are in control, whereas in fact the violence they let loose is less predictable than they think.

The IRA also has tortured people, especially those suspected of being British agents or informers, and the IRA also has its complement of sadists intoxicated by power. Even a less extreme figure, such as Eamon Collins, can (like Dave Fogel) acknowledge a dangerously addictive excitement, and Collins describes being taken over by a "weird intensity"[20] and elation. This kind of emotional heightening stands in dismal contrast, however, to the effects of violence actually committed by paramilitaries who think that they are merely "killing a uniform". Thus, RUC Sergeant Noel McConkey describes how he was injured by a car bomb that exploded while he was clearing an area.[21] "A guy standing at the door of the Landrover up the street saw my arm fly past him", McConkey tells us, going on to describe how relieved he was to notice that both his feet were still where they should be; only later did he discover that his "leg had been blown away", leaving the foot apparently in place. When someone then started beating him with a heavy coat, he wondered, "What the hell are you hitting me over the head for?" not realizing that he was on fire. Although McConkey recovered, he had indeed been blown to bits, and his disabilities are permanent. "If I was put face to face with the people who did it I would shoot them," he says, and then adds, "I'm not religious and can't forgive."

I will return to the question of forgiveness in Chapter 6; for now, I want to note the remarkable objectivity with which McConkey describes his injuries, as if his body were somehow separate from himself, an assemblage of parts, broken asunder. As he tells us, shock prevented him from feeling pain, and he perceives violence as an unleashing of mere force. The pain comes when the person returns, as it were, to the broken body, and the shattered man's suffering and distress then rise in protest against the faceless attackers and their pitiless machinery. The sergeant's assurance that if he were "face to face" with whomever was responsible "I would shoot them" is understandable, a wholly natural sentiment. Yet, in shooting those responsible the sergeant would return bullets for shrapnel, making a corpse of the face he would identify only in order to kill. It is hard to blame him for feeling as he does, for who of us might not feel the same. But the fact remains, as the sergeant also acknowledges, that another possibility beckons, requiring that the entail of the iron circle be broken by forgiveness, however difficult and unpredictable the response required to bring about such a result.

Not surprisingly, one main effect of the iron circle has been to harden the tribal oppositions between Northern Ireland's so-called "two communities'', which, as scholars and commentators increasingly agree, are best understood in terms of ethnicity. Despite the fact that the lives and experience of individual Catholics and Protestants are richly varied, it is impossible, in describing their political and cultural situation, to relinquish the religious labels depicting them as belonging to opposite camps. Even the Opsahl Report (1992), which presents highly convincing evidence of cultural diversity in Northern Ireland, retains the ''two communities'' nomenclature, reflecting the fact that there are two broadly shared kinds of ethnic identity, shaped by distinctive versions of history, different mythologies and acculturization, and a different sense of destiny. These differences are confirmed and sustained by a high degree of segregation in housing and in an all-but universal endogamy and segregated education. In short, the Northern Ireland Troubles can best be understood as an ethnic conflict in which religion is a principal marker of identity (religion, that is, as an indicator of one's lineage, regardless of whether or not one is a believer). Violence, then, especially confirms ethnic differences, creating force-fields of hatred and loathing of the ''other community'' in general, that no political process will easily dispel.[22]

From the beginning of the conflict, the security forces, and especially the police, were seen generally by nationalists as sectarian and aligned with the interests of unionists – that is, the Protestant majority. Certainly, this opinion was confirmed at Burntollet in 1969, when civil rights marchers were attacked, with the collusion of the police, by a mob, many of whom were un-uniformed B-Specials, and also when RUC members baton-charged a peaceful (if illegal) demonstration in Derry. These events led to a serious, official discrediting of the force by the Hunt Report (1969) and Scarman Tribunal (1972). Today, restructuring (or abolishing) the RUC remains a top priority of Sinn Féin, and, in accord with the Good Friday Agreement, the Patten Commission has made sweeping (and controversial) recommendations for reform. Yet, as Chris Ryder's detailed history makes clear, the RUC is far from being merely an instrument of unionist politicians, and has developed into a high-calibre, internationally respected police service. Especially in the wake of the Anglo-Irish Agreement in 1985, loyalists turned violently against the RUC, and many police families were fire-bombed. Ryder reports that by the end of the year ''there had been 564 incidents and 120 police families had had to abandon their homes''.[23] None the less, the fact remains that the RUC has maintained a recruitment rate for Catholics of approximately 7 per cent, and its image as a sectarian force has been difficult to overcome, especially among nationalists who, for their part, by and large refuse to join, thereby confirming the *a priori* assumption that the RUC is overwhelmingly Protestant. Also, some RUC members have indeed engaged in blatant sectarianism and criminal activity.[24] Subsequent to the Anglo-Irish Agreement, some members even appeared masked on TV to warn against the consequences of Britain's collusion with Dublin.[25] The paramilitaries, it seems, are not the only masked men around, and, once again, the tendency of those who deploy violence to mimic the deplored tactics of their enemies remains menacing, whether or not the violence is directed by the state and described as legitimate.

The other main instrument of state force in Northern Ireland is the British Army. As is well known, the army initially was welcomed by the Catholic population in Belfast (to the chagrin of an uncertainly re-emerging IRA), but the honeymoon ended when the army was perceived as an enforcer of Stormont's policies. This became especially clear in the Falls curfew of July 1970, and in the raids of August 1971 when the army conducted a sweep aimed at corralling and interning IRA members, who had been tipped off sufficiently in advance to make good their escape.[26] The soldiers' brutality and the damage they caused to property radical-ized many people in the nationalist community and gave the IRA – and especially the newly emerged Provisional wing – exactly the boost it needed to declare itself a defender of the Catholic population. More-over, the army made no parallel attempt to pick up loyalist paramili-taries or to raid Protestant districts. In short, the Falls curfew and the internment raids were old-fashioned, Stormont-directed acts of sectar-ian oppression (justified under the Special Powers Act), and army spokespersons now admit that they went along with a one-sided policy, which was, as Brigadier (later General Sir Frank) Kitson acknowledges, disastrous.

Another reason sometimes offered for the army's failure to arrest leading IRA members is that the RUC's list of suspects was badly out of date, and so the army managed to pick up mostly old-timers, trade union leaders, and an assortment of civil rights activists and nationalist sympathizers who were not part of the new wave (soon nicknamed the "sixty-niners") of violent republicans at all. Another interpretation of the same event suggests that the RUC deliberately withheld informa-tion from the army as part of a rivalry driven by professional jealousy and mutual distrust which took years to circumvent and was never entirely resolved. Also, it seems that on first going into Northern Ireland the army received briefings which were flatly sectarian. A retired army officer told Martin Dillon that "Our intelligence confirmed that priests were aiding and abetting the paramilitaries on the Catholic side.... We had to treat them all as a potential enemy". Father Raymond Murray confirms that soldiers sent from Germany had received briefings which "were very anti-Catholic Church",[27] as was explained to him by some of those involved. Yet, as Mark Urban reports, it was "important for the self-esteem of many Army officers to feel that the RUC was in some sense tainted by sectarianism, because this view helps to justify their own presence",[28] and clearly the army frequently regarded the RUC as incompetent, or worse, all of which made for a protracted bitterness between the two bodies.

More disturbingly, soldiers who have served in Northern Ireland, and who are willing to recount their experiences,[29] attest to a series of reactions and responses to violence not dissimilar to those exhibited by the paramilitaries and confirming yet again the compulsive, levelling efficacy of the iron circle. Thus, Jimmy Johnson (formerly of the Royal Tank Regiment) confides his indifference about having brutalized a rioter: "To me he was only a Paddy" (51). Soon after, he confirms the point: "They were just two Paddies to me," and "A Paddy is a Paddy to a squaddie" (73). Johnson also describes the alacrity with which soldiers anticipated "payback time" (56), arming themselves with "home made personal weapons" (41), such as hammers, baseball bats, lead pipes, and the like. Another ex-soldier tells of a training routine that involved being "beasted" (that is, brutalized in order to "build your character" [91], though the destruction of character is in fact what he describes), a point confirmed by Michael Asher, who also discusses "beasting" and concludes that the paras with whom he served were reduced, partly as a result of such behaviour, to "a bunch of lunatics" and "savages". As always, the depersonalization entailed by violence turns people into automatons, and Asher reminds us that the paras are known as the "Maroon Machine"; he also describes how soldiers were conditioned "like clockwork toys" to be "wound up and pointed in the right direction", spurred on by the assurance that they were "the iron claw of the British Army".[30] Many soldiers whose experiences are recorded in John Lindsay's collection tell how they continued to behave like clockwork toys even when they had left the army, resorting uncontrollably to violence. One explains that "I call my hands 'bastards' because I hit people without warning" (95).

The combination in these examples of a coarse stereotyping of the "Paddies", unseemly elation at the prospect of exacting revenge, the deployment of illegal weapons such as thugs might use, together with the symptoms of compulsive automatism, indicate that the degenerative effects of violence are not confined to those whose deployment of it is deemed illegal.

Further covert aspects of army operations, in so far as these have been documented, open upon an even more disturbing, shadowy world of undercover operatives, shoot-to-kill ambushes, murders which were covered up (as in the so-called "pitchfork killings"), disinformation and black propaganda (via the "Lisburn lie machine"), the treatment of prisoners in a manner condemned by the European Court of Human Rights as "inhumane and degrading", and the out-of-control killings of unarmed civilians by the paras in the events of Bloody Sunday (1972).[31] In short, even under the fairly close scrutiny permitted by the accessibility of Northern Ireland to journalists and news media, violence conducted by the state all too readily spirals out of control and is consequently masked by undercover operations, concealed by disinformation, confused by internal rivalries, all the while exhibiting the same kinds of vindictiveness and circularity characteristic of violent behaviour everywhere. This is not to deny that there is a real difference in degree between the worst violence – exemplified, say, by the Shankill Butchers and the Omagh bombers – and the violence of the army and police routinely attempting to secure civil order while observing legal guidelines. By and large, this difference in degree is significant and has done much to prevent Northern Ireland from descending into the chaos of civil war, but I am keen to stress that difference in degree is not difference in kind, and the lesser and the greater violence are violence just the same, binding its practitioners into the same frightening oversimplifications and blind hatreds. What, then, might literature add to this already compelling body of information?

One answer is that literature has played a part in establishing the criteria for this analysis in the first place – after all, the metaphor of the iron circle comes from a poem, and its explanatory power is central to this analysis as a whole. Also, the materials I have just been discussing sometimes achieve a degree of literary complexity and resonance, the implications of which are significant for the truth claims being made. For instance, despite its shortcomings, *Killing Rage* can touch us with pathos that enables us to see in Collins's experience a potentiality of our own. Likewise, Tony Parker's skilled editing of extended taped conversations shapes his raw material so that the printed interviews frequently have the compactness and suggestiveness of short stories, as people's personal experiences open up in striking and often moving ways to matters of broad human concern, reaching through the immediate circumstances to engage us imaginatively. Thus, the introduction to Eddie Boyle's monologue reads like a work of fiction: "Tall and well-built, he came out of the darkened sitting-room into the brightly-lit kitchen, closing the door firmly behind him to shut out the sound of the television." Boyle then speaks, in a tone that blends apparent friendliness with a sinister underlay of aggression calculated to make the interviewer uncomfortable: "Sure now and didn't I read a book once of yours Tony, *Soldier Soldier* was it, about the British Army?"[32] Here Boyle reproduces within the conversation something of the deliberately disconcerting effect that he describes as basic to IRA strategy in the field. His ensuing explanations of the IRA's offensive are precise, and a ruthlessness emerges from his combined clarity and conviction. His cajoling but menacing tone and deliberate vagueness about how the IRA identifies collaborators add a further, sinister dimension, so that although he complains about how unfair the propaganda war is, he also contributes to it, as he well knows. In short, Parker offers us in brief compass a portrait of a dangerous man whose intelligence, ruthlessness and self-ironizing combine with a disturbing acknowledgement of the blind instrumentality of violence that might strike anywhere the IRA wishes or happens to decide. There is something of Shakespeare's Iago in this capable, elusive but sinister character, and Parker's skilled handling and editing of the interview enable us to feel a menacing presence that plays upon our pulses, and which we recognize as at once familiar and threatening.

There is therefore some significant if elusive interpenetration between "literary" and "non-literary" in these documents, and, as I have argued in Chapter 1, a key to understanding this intermittent heightening is to consider how imagination engages us as participants in a process rather than merely as observers or analysts. With this in mind, I want now to consider some poems by Michael Longley and a play by Brian Friel.

Michael Longley: violence and the fragility of the civilized

Here, to begin, is "The Civil Servant", the first poem in a group of three by Michael Longley[33] entitled *Wreaths*, all of which deal with the assassination of civilians by paramilitaries.

The Civil Servant

He was preparing an Ulster fry for breakfast
When someone walked into the kitchen and shot him:
A bullet entered his mouth and pierced his skull,
The books he had read, the music he could play.

He lay in his dressing gown and pyjamas
While they dusted the dresser for fingerprints
And then shuffled backwards across the garden
With notebooks, cameras and measuring tapes.

They rolled him up like a red carpet and left
Only a bullet hole in the cutlery drawer:
Later his widow took a hammer and chisel
And removed the black keys from his piano.

One of Longley's main strategies in this poem is ruthlessly to exclude the personal from his account of the murder and its aftermath in the police investigation and the distracted widow's reaction. Thus, the civil servant[34] is un-named; his killer is anonymous; the police are mechanically efficient but nothing more; in her anguish, the widow is almost catatonic, miming the violent intrusion that has destroyed her life. By contrast, the poem also quietly registers the sense of a comfortable domestic space. There are books and music, a garden, a piano, and, *déshabillé*, the man is cooking his Ulster fry. But then "someone" walks in and shoots him. The trajectory of the bullet is carefully described, and the police ("they") are, in their fashion, as without affect as the killer. With the business-like despatch of sub-contractors, they roll up the dead man like a carpet ("red", presumably because of the blood, perhaps also hinting that the importance of the man himself is now a matter of indifference). And when the widow takes a hammer and chisel to the piano, removing the black keys, she is distracted by grief, but she also re-enacts the senseless destruction that has already smashed her domestic interior. These last two lines are the most telling in the poem, suggesting how the impersonal mechanisms of violence catch up even the victims into its process, while also implying a stultifying depth of grief that the language of the poem cannot directly reach.

A main achievement of "The Civil Servant" is to suggest how disturbingly close violence is to the everyday, and how fragile are the amenities of civilized life. There is no question here of heroism or a clash of ideologies; we are presented instead with a monstrous banality, the mechanical and brutalizing simplicity of the act itself, and the helplessness of the man in his pyjamas. This counterpoint between a calm but fragile domestic interior and the pitiless machinery of violence may reflect something of Longley's training in the Classics, and, especially, his responsiveness to this same juxtaposition in the epic tradition. His verse renditions of several episodes in Homer suggest how this might be so, as I will indicate more fully by and by.

The other two poems in the *Wreaths* group ("The Greengrocer" and "The Linen Workers") deal with violent actions in much the same way as "The Civil Servant", presenting a quiet and unassuming good order suddenly interrupted and shattered by an anonymous, implacable force. "The Linen Workers" opens with a surreal stanza announcing that "Christ's teeth ascended with him into heaven" and the wind whistles through a decaying molar as he remains "fastened for ever" by his "exposed canines". There is something bizarre and ferocious in these lines, suggesting that Christ's ascension is imperfect, and that the bleakness of his suffering is not ended. Longley then is reminded of his father's false teeth inside the tumbler of water wherein, presumably, they were placed at night. When the ten linen workers of the title were massacred (a reference to a tit-for-tat killing that resulted in the deaths of ten Protestant workers at Kingsmills in South Armagh in 1976), a set of dentures was found among the detritus of "spectacles, / Wallets, small change". Once again, these bits and pieces suggest the shattering of people's lives, while implying also that violence reduces the people themselves to mere bric-a-brac. In this context, Longley concludes that before he can bury his father "once again" he must place the spectacles on his nose, put money in his pockets, and the set of false teeth in his mouth. These are puzzling lines, but it seems that whatever grief the poet experienced at his father's death was assuaged by remembering him not just as an emptied-out corpse, but as a human face, a physiognomy re-combining the familiar instruments of the everyday (loose change, spectacles, false teeth). A restored sense of personal dignity becomes a means to remembrance that carries solace, and so it should be with the violently dispersed remains of the linen workers. But the poem does not say how we are to effect such a restoration; rather, Longley turns to his father as a partial means of registering a sense of loss that, once more, words cannot directly reach. The poem thus ends by suggesting an imperfect resurrection matching the imperfect ascension at the start, as Christ's agony is perpetuated through history.

For readers of Longley's poetry, the reference to his father in "The Linen Workers" will strike a familiar note. Longley's father had fought in the Great War and was wounded, eventually dying of cancer when his son was twenty years old. Longley elegizes him in several poems, and in so doing also connects the Great War to the Troubles in Northern Ireland. "Before I can bury my father once again" therefore opens out upon

Longley's preoccupation with the First World War, and the massacred linen workers re-awaken for him the violence of the broader European conflict, and especially warfare in the trenches.

"In Memoriam"[35] is the earliest of Longley's elegies on his father, and already a characteristic preoccupation with the limitations of language is evident, as words fail sufficiently to grasp their subject, mirroring instead the liminal "No Man's Land" where the poet's father was left for dead, an innocent involved in war but without quite knowing why: "Your nineteen years uncertain if and why / Belgium put the kibosh on the Kaiser". This idea of innocent complicity, at once dangerous and naive, is central to the poem, and is taken up and explored further in "Wounds",[36] one of Longley's best reflections on this topic:

Wounds

Here are two pictures from my father's head –
I have kept them like secrets until now:
First, the Ulster Division at the Somme
Going over the top with "Fuck the Pope!"
"No Surrender!": a boy about to die,
Screaming "Give 'em one for the Shankill!"
"Wilder than Gurkhas" were my father's words
Of admiration and bewilderment.
Next comes the London-Scottish padre
Resettling kilts with his swagger-stick,
With a stylish backhand and a prayer.
Over a landscape of dead buttocks
My father followed him for fifty years.
At last, a belated casualty,
He said – lead traces flaring till they hurt –
"I am dying for King and Country, slowly."
I touched his hand, his thin head I touched.

Now, with military honours of a kind,
With his badges, his medals like rainbows,
His spinning compass, I bury beside him
Three teenage soldiers, bellies full of
Bullets and Irish beer, their flies undone.
A packet of Woodbines I throw in,
A lucifer, the Sacred Heart of Jesus
Paralysed as heavy guns put out
The night-light in a nursery for ever;

Also a bus-conductor's uniform –
He collapsed beside his carpet-slippers
Without a murmur, shot through the head
By a shivering boy who wandered in
Before they could turn the television down
Or tidy away the supper dishes.
To the children, to a bewildered wife,
I think "Sorry Missus" was what he said.

Again, in this poem Longley recalls his father's experiences in the trenches and his death years later, but now the memories are juxtaposed to recent violent events in Northern Ireland. Innocent complicity is the key idea joining the poem's two main sections, and the cross-currents that run between them constitute a disturbing reflection on the pity and waste of violence that wreaks havoc impersonally and is callously justified by people who do not count its costs.

In the first section, the Ulster Protestant boys going over the top exhibit a wild bravery and zany sense of the absurd as they yell out the shibboleths of Ulster loyalism to inspire them against the Germans – "Fuck the Pope!"; "No Surrender!" His father's reaction (he served in a different regiment, the London-Scottish) remains a mixture of "admiration and bewilderment", acknowledging the young Northern Irish soldiers' brave abandon and also registering confusion, perhaps, at how these boys found themselves dying in such circumstances, and also at what the relevance might be of their battle cries, evoking a familiar tribal solidarity but serving also to suggest fear and displacement. The best they can do facing death is to repeat the sectarian mantras on which they were raised, and we feel here something of the dangerous narrowness of the shibboleths which induce (indeed demand) blind loyalties, even though we might also feel that the boys indulge a reckless humour with which it is easy to sympathize, and which helps to give them courage.

By contrast, the "London-Scottish padre" is not accorded any such admiring response as he is caustically imagined surveying the dead bodies of soldiers in Longley's own regiment, now reduced to the coarse anonymity of "dead buttocks". The indecency of wholesale slaughter seems secondary to the padre's concern in "Resettling kilts" to cover the lesser indecency of exposed limbs. The "stylish backhand" (suggesting that he is practising his tennis stroke), and the trace of arrogance in the name itself of the military symbol of authority, "swagger-stick", indicate a high-handed indifference to the deaths of these young men who will

remain unknown to him. Belatedly – his sacrifice likewise unacknowledged in any official way – the poet's father also dies of wounds received
at the front, but the solace offered by the poet to the dying man is
poignant, and again non-verbal: "I touched his hand, his thin head I
touched."

As with "In Memoriam", the second half of "Wounds" considers a
second burial for Longley's father, again linking the violence of the
Troubles in modern Northern Ireland to the Great War. The "Three
teenage soldiers" were members of the Royal Highland Fusiliers (Joseph
McCaig, 18; his brother John, 17; and Dougald McCaughey, 23), lured
from Mooney's Bar in Belfast in 1971 by IRA members who invited them
to a party. The soldiers were shot on a deserted road while they stopped
to urinate, and died still holding their beer glasses. The incident caused
public outrage, and the IRA initially denied responsibility, though the
murders – still unsolved – are now generally attributed to them.[37]

In the poem, the dead boys' *naïveté* parallels but reverses the situation
of the young Ulster soldiers in a foreign field. Now Ireland is the foreign
field, and the young men again did not understand what they were
getting into. Their disarray, "flies undone", parallels the unsettled
kilts, and in both cases suggests indignity, a far cry from the heroic
language in which warfare is often eulogized. Woodbines were a favourite smoke of Longley's father's generation; the lucifer is a match, but the
trace of theological meaning counterpoints the paralysed Sacred Heart
of Jesus, overlooking but unable to protect the sleeping child in the
nursery (a reference to Patrick Rooney, aged 9, killed while he slept, in
1969, by a stray bullet fired by the RUC). The Catholic icon in turn
parallels the anti-Catholic sentiments of the soldiers at the Somme, as
the cigarettes and the Sacred Heart in turn juxtapose the memory of the
Great War and the contemporary Troubles, suggesting a terrible, impersonal uniformity in the killing itself, which then passes over to the
murder of the bus conductor by another boy, this time sent by his
paramilitary superiors to assassinate the man in his home. The bus
conductor collapsing beside his carpet slippers recalls similar effects in
"The Civil Servant", as the domestic interior, with its protective warmth
and comfort, is rudely violated. Again, the killing is marked by impersonality, as the bus-conductor falls, inert as his slippers, and the "shivering boy" sent to kill him is pathetically, dangerously confused. The
diminuendo of "Sorry Missus" mirrors his incapacity to understand
well enough what he has done, and there is a sense that he, like the
other young men in the poem, is a pawn in the hands of those who give
the orders and who, in turn, are removed from the results of the violence

they cause, condone and justify. This is not to say that the young assassin is not responsible; only that the poem points to a dangerous innocence, a simplification of issues and events which it is always necessary to induce for violence to occur. Although, again, there are important differences between soldiers ordered to the front in the First World War and a boy ordered to shoot a civilian in his home, the poem remains effective because it shows a uniformity in the conduct of violence, and in the pathos and waste in both cases, despite their differences.

Other poems by Longley deal with the Great War in similar ways, constituting an impressive set of meditations on the fragility of the civilized, the anonymity of violence, the simplifications that enable it and the pathos that attends it, beyond words.[38] But in his later work Longley also returns directly to the epic tradition, producing verse paraphrases and reconstructions of episodes in Homer dealing especially with violence and with relationships between fathers and sons. Examples are "Laertes", "The Helmet", "Ceasefire", "Phemios and Medon", "Anticleia", "The Butchers" and "The Camp-fires".

The introduction of Ulster Scots dialect into some of these poems establishes a connection between today's Northern Ireland and Homer's ancient world, at once deploying Homer to redescribe Northern Ireland, and Northern Ireland to "recover and renew Homer", as John Lyon says.[39] Like Homer, Longley is preoccupied by the close proximity of peace and war, and how uncertainly established are the civilized interiors, the domestic spaces that provide a comforting sense of order and privacy. Thus, "The Butchers"[40] retells an episode in Book 22 of the *Odyssey*, when Odysseus returns and slaughters the suitors who have taken over his house in his absence, squandered his goods and pressed themselves upon his wife Penelope. After the suitors are killed, a group of faithless maidservants are forced to clean up and are then hanged. The treacherous Melanthios is also mutilated, and finally Odysseus fumigates his palace, having rid it of his enemies.

Longley's version compresses the original and also expands on it, especially by adding a section on Hermes gathering in the dead souls and escorting them through a landscape with distinctive Irish touches ("clammy sheughs" and "a bog-meadow full of bog-asphodels") to their place of residence among other ghosts and "images of the dead". The poem's concentration on the sheer materiality of violence (the women hanged in a row on a hawser, the dead suitors heaped like fish) is reenforced by the contrary dematerialization that death also effects, taking the slaughtered people out of the world of flesh and blood where they are most fully alive. But the most telling effect of the poem lies in

the casualness with which the violence takes place, and in the comparison of violence to domestic tasks, as a kind of house-cleaning. Thus, the
maids are ordered "to sponge down the armchairs / And tables" before
being hanged like doves, their "heads bobbing in a row" and their "feet
twitching but not for long". There is something almost delicate in the
description, as well as a typically Homeric leisureliness that dwells on
individual pictorial details, unruffled by the fact that a mass execution is
being described. The "need for whitewash and disinfectant" is not given
any different register to distinguish it from the mutilation of Melanthios, whose severed parts make up "a dog's dinner". The horrendous
is made to seem ordinary, and the conflation of monstrously violent acts
with domestic tasks (including the catching of fish and the killing of
doves and thrushes for food – "butchery" in both its domestic and
criminal senses) makes the poem quietly shocking. The people killed
are hardly people at all, so efficient and heartless is their despatch.

Longley has no meditations on Biblical materials comparable to his
poetry engaging the epic tradition. But I would like to end this section
by looking at a poem that deals with the scapegoat mechanism, and
which fills out the depiction of violence in the examples we have so far
discussed. The poem is "Self-heal",[41] from the group entitled *Mayo
Monologues*. It is spoken by a woman looking back on an event that
occurred when she was a girl. The accuracy and self-consciousness of
her language ("his back was hunched, / Which gave him an almost
scholarly air") suggest a grown-up narrator, but when she runs off to
tell "them" how the retardate touched her thighs as she was teaching
him the names of flowers, we are to imagine her as a young girl. In
response to her telling, the grown-ups flogged the retarded man daily for
a week with a blackthorn, and tethered him in a hayfield. In the closing
lines, the speaker reflects:

> I might have been the cow
> Whose tail he would later dock with shears,
> And the ram tangled in barbed wire
> That he stoned to death when they set him free.

Throughout, a restrained leisureliness reproduces something of the
effect we have noticed in "The Butchers", as Longley again provides
the sense of an unnerving closeness of violence to the orderliness of day-
to-day life. Again, the poem makes us think about the girl's innocence,
and causes us to wonder, following her own question in retrospect, to
what degree she might – as she says – have been "leading him on?" As

we see, dangerous innocence is one of Longley's favourite themes. But this poem is also remarkable in the concluding lines, describing how the anonymous "they" wreak a cruelly punitive violence on the retarded man, beating and confining him like an animal. In response, he lashes out, mutilating animals, including the "ram tangled in barbed wire", the scapegoat which he stones to death. There is a Biblical resonance here, offsetting the ironic use of the word "free": the man of course is not free at all, caught up in the mechanism of violence, which he reproduces by a blind, scarcely conscious process – not much different from the soldier who called his hands bastards.

Longley's poetry, then, lets us see some familiar aspects of violence in new ways, cultivating a personal vision that enables us to feel the betrayal of humanity implicit in the fabrications and circumstances which permit violence to thrive. The main criteria for describing the iron circle are evident in his treatment of depersonalization, mechanization, and scapegoating, but the poems awaken us also to how people can be unselfconsciously complicitous with or vulnerable to unanticipated destructions, blind griefs, rage, or cruelties caused even by their own innocence, which in turn destroys the innocence of others. The casualness with which domestic order might all at once be overwhelmed, the pathos that may attend even our strong moral disapproval, and a sense of the grief that lies beyond language – all this combines in a lyrical voice offering a distinctive vision, itself an antidote to the depersonalizing agencies to which it stands implicitly opposed, and opening also upon broader cultural dimensions that extend through the Great War poets to Homer.

In his interesting study of how violence is depicted in recent Northern Irish lyric poetry, Jonathan Hufstader stresses a crucial "breaking of style"[42] which he detects in the mid-careers of the poets he discusses. This leads him to draw a sharper distinction between Longley's Homeric poems and his earlier work than I have done in the previous pages, where I have stressed the continuities enabling us to recognize a characteristic voice in Longley's work as a whole. Consequently, I have suggested that when Longley depicts violence, he does so, typically, by restraint, and the voice we respond to most fully is his own – the lyrical voice of a persona whose tact, clarity and compassion stand as an antidote to the thing he deplores. By contrast, in Brian Friel's play *The Freedom of the City*,[43] a different strategy is at work as the author takes special pains to dramatize other voices, personalizing his victims and allowing us to know them intimately, so that we can deplore the mechanisms and hypocrisies of the violence done against them.

Brian Friel's Bloody Sunday: art containing outrage

The Freedom of the City was first performed at the Abbey Theatre in Dublin on 20 February 1973. It is based on the events of Bloody Sunday, 30 January 1972, in which thirteen unarmed people were killed by British soldiers of the First Parachute Regiment (a fourteenth died later as a result of his wounds). The occasion of these events was a banned civil rights demonstration which proceeded peacefully until a group of some two hundred broke from the main march, which was by this time moving to avoid a confrontation with soldiers blocking the route. The break-away group began throwing stones at the soldiers, who were then ordered to conduct a scoop-up operation. Firing began, and within half an hour thirteen people had been killed. No soldier was wounded, nor was any army vehicle damaged.

The outraged reaction to Bloody Sunday led to a tribunal of enquiry, headed by Lord Widgery, Lord Chief Justice of England. The report was submitted in April 1972, and has been a source of controversy ever since. Widgery confirmed the soldiers' testimony that they were fired on first, but he granted also that none of those killed was proved to have been handling a firearm or bomb. In January 1993, Prime Minister John Major admitted that those killed were innocent, but refused to re-open the investigation. When the Labour government came to power in 1997, Tony Blair reversed Major's decision, and at the time of writing, a new Tribunal headed by Lord Saville of Newdigate has officially opened (March 2000) and may continue with its work for some two years. There seems little doubt today that the Widgery Report was over-hasty, as the interesting book edited by Don Mullan, *Eyewitness Bloody Sunday*,[44] makes clear. Certainly, as Flackes and Elliott point out, "the convulsion caused by the affair was regarded as the decisive factor in the decision to impose direct rule from Westminster",[45] and as Mullan says, "Bloody Sunday changed everything. A new and frightening era dawned, as the innocence of our generation died".[46] One main consequence of this loss of innocence was that young men hastened to join the IRA, thereby fastening themselves into the circle of violent reprisal which was rapidly to confirm its hold, making of the 1970s the most violent decade in the thirty-year history of the Troubles.

On the fateful day itself the paras seem to have broken out of control, and it remains a moot point what accident or provocation caused or enabled them to do so. Asher describes himself and his fellow soldiers in Northern Ireland as continually gnawing at themselves "like leopards in a gin-trap",[47] frantic to unleash the violence that Vergil's sad wisdom assures us is at once the strength and the liability of the *civitas* dependent on its armed forces. Ironically to an almost ludicrous degree, Lt.-Col. Derek Wilford, who commanded One Para in Northern Ireland in 1972, was, according to journalist Peter Taylor, "a lover of the Classics who bemused his men by reading the Roman poet Virgil's epic war story, *The Aeneid*, in Latin".[48] What this might have meant to 18-year-old working-class boys "beasted" into an insensate savagery is difficult to say (among many unsavoury off-duty para pastimes described by Asher is that of a soldier who chewed off the heads of live rats and chickens).[49] Still, for Wilford himself, the aftermath of Bloody Sunday has not been without Vergilian overtones. Weary and disillusioned, he retired from the army in 1981 and now describes himself as a scapegoat, a role he accepted to protect his soldiers. He says that the events of Bloody Sunday eventually "made me anti-war", and he feels that it would be better if British troops withdrew from Northern Ireland.[50] A poignancy that Wilford might recognize also in his favourite *Aeneid*, combined here with his reflections on the scapegoat mechanism, can indicate how readily the local again becomes transparent to those paradigms by which we might attempt to understand how violence continues to blunder its way through history. Certainly, the Bloody Sunday killings released hatreds of such intensity as to ensure the perpetuation and triumph of the iron circle, as a consequence of which, especially during the ensuing decade, the nightmare of Derry in 1972 became for many a condition of ordinary life.

Clearly, Bloody Sunday was a watershed event and was experienced as such at the time. A quarter of a century later, the initial sense of its significance has not diminished, but when Friel wrote *The Freedom of the City* he had not acquired much distance from the shock and horror that gripped Derry (where he grew up), extending then across the globe. Friel himself says about *The Freedom of the City* that "the experience of Bloody Sunday wasn't adequately distilled in me. I wrote it out of some kind of heat and some kind of immediate passion that I would want to have quieted a bit before I did it."[51] Here Friel intimates that "heat" and "immediate passion" somehow curtailed his better judgement, and, his remarkable talents notwithstanding, *The Freedom of the City* does register anger leaning towards the propagandistic, even as the play also denounces the dangers of propaganda.

The Freedom of the City is set in 1970, and focuses on three people who have been on a civil rights march and who take refuge in the Guildhall in Derry when the march is attacked by soldiers. Michael, a young idealist, is blinded by CS gas and is hauled to safety by Skinner, an unemployed and cynical but clever young man whose views are different from Michael's, as we discover as the action unfolds. Lily, a forty-three-year-old mother of eleven children, is also choked by gas, and stumbles into the Guildhall with the other two. Initially, none of them knows where they are, and when they discover themselves in the Mayor's parlour – headquarters of the local authority – they react in different but characteristic ways. Michael is impressed by the furnishings and is guiltily conscious of trespassing. Skinner is resentful, and among other things, he breaks open the liquor cabinet, stubs out a purloined cigar on a leather desk-top and sticks a ceremonial sword into an official portrait on the wall. Lily is at first bewildered, and then makes herself at home, suggesting how to improve the decor with pink gloss paint and a flight of brass ducks. She drinks with Skinner, and a bond develops between them, excluding Michael, though he and Lily get on well enough.

Friel thus gives us three unarmed civilians, each of whom is marching for a different reason. Michael believes that the system can be changed and that reason will prevail. He wants to promote fair play, and is studying at the technical college to improve his prospects. Skinner has been expelled from grammar school (suggesting that he is clever but rebellious), and his quick intelligence provides a realistic assessment of the state of affairs which his two companions are reluctant (or unable) to see or accept. Skinner is marching because he sympathizes with the poor, whom he sees as oppressed by a conscienceless system. As he points out, Lily is a good example of the oppression he deplores, living as she does with her ill husband and eleven children in a two-room flat in a converted warehouse without running water or a toilet. But Skinner is also alienated by his cynicism, and has cultivated a glib irreverence that prevents him from acting effectively in support of his own analysis.

Lily at first conceals the fact (which she eventually admits to Skinner) that she is marching because one of her children, Declan, is "a mongol" (155), and because her distress finds an outlet in the organized protest. Lily has little understanding of the political dimensions of the civil rights campaign, and the incongruities following upon her inability to assess her present situation are often comic. Certainly, she is the play's most engaging character.

As the action unfolds, conversation among the three refugees allows us to know them with some intimacy, and to appreciate their differences. But Friel juxtaposes this knowledge of the insiders to a series of official, public figures who assess the situation from outside. These include a judge who conducts an enquiry after the event, a priest who sermonizes about it, and a sociologist who analyses the underclass. There are also a brigadier, a forensic expert, a pathologist and a TV commentator. Throughout, the judgements of these outside voices are interleaved with the inside conversations by a series of time shifts, locating us at different points before and after the three insiders are shot dead, on leaving the Guildhall. The soldiers claim that the insiders were armed and fired first, and the judge assesses the evidence and gives a verdict that flatly contradicts what we know to be the case.

Although the play takes place two years before Bloody Sunday it clearly alludes to the events of that day, and to the aftermath. For instance, the judge, like Lord Widgery, has a military background (134), and when he insists on conducting ''a fact-finding exercise'' to establish ''an objective view'' (109) confined to the time of the shooting, he echoes Widgery, who likewise said that the tribunal would be ''essentially a fact-finding exercise'', observing a ''narrowness'' in the ''confines of the Inquiry'' for reasons of efficiency.[52] The initial assault with water cannon and CS gas also mirrors the events of Bloody Sunday, as does a speech by an un-named woman who exhorts the crowd, ''Stand your ground!'' (111). These words were in fact spoken to the crowd by Bernadette Devlin at Free Derry Corner as events at nearby Rossville Street got out of hand. The priest crouching and holding a white handkerchief as he attends to the wounded recalls the now famous photograph of Fr. Edward Daly in a scene which, as Mullan says, ''was to become the icon of Bloody Sunday''. An Italian photographer, Mr Montini (142) in the play, had a real-life counterpart in Mr Fulvio Grimaldi, and arguments about paraffin tests and contamination are important both in the play (142) and in the real-life events.[53] The judge's summary at the end (168) also reproduces some of Widgery's main conclusions: for instance, that the ban on the parade should have been respected, and that the soldiers were fired upon first.[54] The additional account of how the three deceased were armed when they came out of the Guildhall, and that two of them opened fire, are determined by the requirements of the play, but in the fifteen seconds of automatic gunfire with which the play ends, while the three stand with ''their hands above their heads'' (169), Friel registers an anger that spills over the borders of his imagined world to comment directly on the political events that inspired it.

Independently of these analogies, the play is powerful and moving, and Friel's contrast between the inside, personal voices and the outside, impersonal ones is by turns engaging, disturbing, and comically infuriating. Thus, a balladeer annexes the insiders to the heroes of 1916 – ''Tone, Pearse and Connolly'' (118) – while providing a good measure of maudlin claptrap. An RTE announcer, Liam O'Kelly, indulges a comparable but condescending sentimentality as he covers the funeral ("surely the most impressive gathering of church and state dignitaries that this humble parish of the Long Tower has ever seen" [167]). The American sociologist Dr Dodds offers a commentry on the subculture of poverty "common to ghetto or slum communities all over the Western world" (110). His explanations help to universalize the events at the Guildhall, even as his analysis remains at an ineffectual distance from the people involved. The priest addressing a congregation shares something of the sociologist's perspective, adapted towards the language of liberation theology, and with echoes of Martin Luther King: "they could endure no longer the injuries and injustices and indignities that have been their lot for too many years", and we are "even more determined to see that the dream they dreamed is realized" (125).

By far the most disturbing outside voices are those which seek to justify the violence, as in the judge's "fact-finding exercise" (109). Thus, the security forces assume that the Guildhall is occupied by "terrorists" (109), and initial rumours (confirmed by the RTE announcer) claim that there are some forty people involved. An Army press release then describes a "band of terrorists" comprising "up to forty persons" and claims also that "they have access to arms" (126). The brigadier tells the judge that the three deceased "emerged firing from the Guildhall" (134), and in response to the judge's observation that the force used was overwhelming, the brigadier responds that these three were considered "the advance group of a much larger force" (134). The judge in turn assumes that the choice of the Guildhall was not fortuitous, but "a carefully contrived act of defiance" against the "legitimate forces of law and order" (149). Why else, he asks, were the building defaced and the furnishings despoiled? Again, the insiders are homogenized so that they become representatives, and are thereby primed for destruction. But, as we see, the insiders are far from being like-minded, and, as individuals, they do not have much in common. To Michael, Skinner is a hooligan and a vandal (138), just the type who is contaminating the "responsible and respectable" (128) civil rights movement and bringing it into disrepute. Although the IRA is not mentioned, when Michael worries about a "hooligan element", and about "a lot of strange characters" who have "knuckled in" (127) on the civil rights initiative, he is voicing a concern that applies to early IRA interest in the Northern Ireland Civil Rights Association (NICRA), and which reflects a fear that escalating violence would draw disaffected young people towards the IRA. The same concern is repeated by the priest, who deplores the fact that the "peaceful and dignified" civil rights campaign has drawn "certain evil elements" to itself which have "contaminated" it, partly by inculcating a "Godless communism" (156). The fear of communism was especially associated with the IRA before the split in 1970 that resulted in the emergence of the Provisionals, as distinct from the increasingly Marxist Officials.

Skinner indeed has a good deal of the "hooligan" in him, but he is also the most intelligent of the three insiders. He is first to identify where they have taken refuge, and he is quick to assess the implications and danger of their situation. He also offers an account of the protest marches that is close to the academic analysis proposed by Dr Dodds. Indeed, Skinner is more convincing than the sociologist because Skinner knows what it is like to live on the margins; yet he is also ineffective because he has neither discipline nor patience, and squanders his talent in cynical and petty rebelliousness fuelled by anger and resentment. Michael points out that people like Skinner would be dangerous if they ever were radicalized, and Friel again has his finger on the pulse, because many young men like Skinner did join the Provos as a result of Bloody Sunday and the Falls curfew in Belfast in 1970.

Towards the end of the play, as the insiders prepare to leave, Michael takes pains to remind the other two of the law, and advises that if you "Give them no cheek" they'll "give you no trouble" (158). But Skinner has a clearer view, and asks why then is the place surrounded by tanks and armoured cars, and the walls lined with soldiers and police. Lily responds, incoherently, by maintaining that "them windows'd be nicer in plain glass", and reassures the others that things will be all right because it looks like she'll get home "in time to make the tea" (158). These different estimates of the situation are entirely characteristic of the people involved. Michael's well-intentioned trust in the system is offset in one direction by Skinner's smarter, less illusioned appraisal, and in the other by Lily's total incomprehension. Still, Lily remains the play's most vital character because of her spontaneity, generosity, and preposterous recommendations on all manner of topics, as well as her unselfconscious good sense, which mixes easily but sometimes surprisingly with her utter *naïveté*. She makes us laugh, even as the situation becomes increasingly threatening and grim. Thus, she scolds Skinner – "Mother of God, will you watch my good coat!" (112) – as he hauls her, half-blinded with CS gas, off the street and into the Guildhall. Soon after, she advises the more seriously gassed Michael, "It's a help if you cross your legs and breathe shalla" (114), and then confides that "CS gas is a sure cure for stuttering", which is why "Celia Cunningham across from us drags her wee Colm Damien into the thick of every riot from here to Strabane and him not seven till next May" (115). Yet such wild notions remain compatible with a vigorous common sense, and when Michael explains how a CS canister burst at his feet, she tells him, "You should have threw your jacket over it" (114). When Skinner edgily asks her, "Did no one tell you the march was banned?" she comes back directly: "I didn't expect them to drive their tanks through us and shoot gas and rubber bullets into us, young fella" (114).

Towards the end, as Skinner and Lily become tipsy, he confers on her the freedom of the city, but this amusing charade is also poignant because Skinner knows how unfree Lily really is, in thrall to poverty and cheerfully unaware of the social mechanisms confining her. By thus introducing something of the carnivalesque, Friel forces us to notice the unsettling proximity of levity and violence, and how people might turn to play and distraction as a means of deflecting or concealing a harsh reality. Clearly, Skinner gets drunk and dresses up in the mayor's clothes to blunt his growing awareness that a heavy price will be exacted for this trespass. Lily's fantastic gossip might partly be the result of a lifetime's habit of putting a cheerful face on difficult circumstances, and there is an element of farce in how she operates on one level as if she hadn't a care in the world, even as, on another, we see her increasingly in the grip of forces that are determining things otherwise.

In various ways, the more closely we come to know the insiders, the more we appreciate their individual imperfections, appealing characteristics and fragility. Certainly, Friel's art allows us to know these people in ways that are incommensurate with what the various public voices say about them, and especially the public voices seeking to justify violence by homogenizing the insiders as "terrorists" – as representatives of a dangerous enemy who must be put down by force. By contrast, the outside voices lack complexity, and here the play is at odds with itself: the judge and the brigadier are mere ciphers, and in objectifying them so thoroughly, Friel reproduces the reductive depictions of others that his play as a whole is at pains to denounce. One main difference between this and the analogous failure I have noticed in *Killing Rage* is that Friel is a talented writer whose art wavers, whereas Collins has no comparable talent to begin with and makes no pretensions to artistic merit or effect.

Although Friel did not know it when he wrote *The Freedom of the City*, at a meeting on 1 February 1972, the British Prime Minister Edward Heath told Lord Chief Justice Widgery that "It had to be remembered that we were in Northern Ireland fighting not only a military war but a propaganda war.''[55] The confidential document recording this conversation was discovered in the Public Record Office in London on 4 August 1995. It may well be that, faced with the Widgery Report, Friel in turn decided to fight fire with fire. But, as I want to argue throughout, it is more salutary to fight propaganda with art, and there is some indication in Friel's own admission of over-hastiness that he recognizes the slippage in question. By the token of the best achievements of the play itself – which are considerable – fighting with the enemy's weapons creates more of the same, confirming the iron circle rather than breaking it. Thus, we return to Hewitt's poem, where, to the speaker's dismay, his own righteous anger inadvertently feeds the conflict against which the anger is directed in the first place.

In this chapter I have been concerned with some central mechanisms of violence. As we see, these depend on an oversimplification that targets others as representatives, thereby depersonalizing them and turning them into scapegoat victims. A double anonymity of victim and victimizer is then confirmed by the use of violence for reprisal, and, in Northern Ireland, this ''iron circle'' has continued to confirm the binary opposition between ''two communities'' locked into an ethnic conflict in which religion is a chief marker of identity – the telling sign, that is, of which tribe one belongs to, whether or not one is in fact a religious believer. The depersonalizing process that enables the iron circle can rapidly become pathological, and one criterion of psychopathic behaviour is that those exhibiting it have no conscience about the violence they commit, and no empathy for the victim, who is regarded not as a person but as a despised object. Even violence conducted by the state and sanctioned by law displays the same instrumentality and easily spirals out of control, soon reproducing the ''mirror hate'' and terrifying methods of the enemy, despite legal constraints.

A variety of sources allows us to see these mechanisms at work in Northern Ireland, and it is not always easy to distinguish between ''literary'' and ''non-literary'' elements in the materials on which I have drawn for examples. Rather, criticism attempts to discern how words inform us about the stratagems and subterfuges of violence that would destroy the civilized amenities allowing criticism itself to flourish. In this context, the kind of writing that enables us to participate imaginatively in the experience of other people, bringing them to life in complex ways as individuals, is what I mean by literature. It follows that, by virtue of its exigent personalizing of experience, literature stands opposed to the means by which we have seen the iron circle perpetuated. With this in mind, I have focused on some poems by Michael Longley and a play by Brian Friel. In Longley, a reserved, dignified and sensitive lyrical voice depicts and protests against the anonymity of violence, allowing us to feel its lethal closeness to the everyday, and the fragility and vulnerability of the civilized. In causing us to think in fresh ways about the dangers of innocence, Longley develops an elegaic compassion, completed in the silence of a contemplative identification with those who suffer. His poems offer a vision simultaneously rooted in particular experience and transparent to concerns that engage the larger cultural history of which they are a part.

Brian Friel is also preoccupied with the impersonality of violence and the schematized rhetoric deployed to justify it. Consequently, the main achievement of *The Freedom of the City* lies in a richly imagined depiction of the three people whom we come to know as individuals, in contrast to the official voices attempting to account for their deaths. Unlike Longley, Friel lets us know these victims intimately, thereby fuelling our indignation when they are killed. Yet, in so far as Friel precludes imaginative identificaiton with the perpetrators of violence, he risks oversimplifying them in a way that runs counter to the play's best insights.

Throughout this chapter, I have wanted to comment on the kinds of rhetoric that most effectively reveal the dangerous coherence and compelling power of the iron circle. In this context, I have suggested that the writers who do most to understand and counteract the core mechanisms of violence have in common, at the very least, a patient insistence on reinvesting the personal with the value and dignity that violence inevitably destroys.

3
Equivocations of the Fiend: Self-Deception and Poetic Diction

Confused and complex diction: Seamus Heaney and others

In this chapter I want to claim that in addition to the mechanisms of the iron circle, violence also breeds dangerous confusions confirmed by double-talk, equivocation and contradiction. Initially, it might seem that I am making two mutually exclusive claims: on the one hand, violence oversimplifies human relationships; on the other, it breeds monstrous and opaque complexities. Yet these opposites are interdependent, and it is not difficult to understand why.

As we have seen, depicting a member of the "other community" as a representative or scapegoat entails a distortion of that person's particular humanity. Violence therefore depends on complicity in the lies that enable such a distortion, and this helps to explain why violence and propaganda are closely allied. When the violent then are called upon to explain themselves, their initial, specious clarity soon encounters the refractory complexities it has been at pains to ignore, and contradictions spring up, to be either glossed over or suppressed. Often, apologists of violence merely repeat a party line, offered as self-authenticating so that critical reflection is curtailed. But, as Fionnuala O'Connor notices, when her interviewees try to justify violence they also typically "airbrush" the main issues and then "contradictions come tumbling out".[1] Sometimes these contradictions are acknowledged and experienced as painful or uncomfortable, but even the most liberal and well-meaning of apologists can remain unaware of being embroiled in a deeply-riven, equivocal discourse. Initial clarity and consequent confused justification are therefore symbiotic. Far from being incompatible, these opposites feed off one another in what is, in the end, a mutually confounding interdependence.

There is a crucial difference between such confusion and the kinds of complexity offered by literature. Poets (let us for the moment have them stand for literature in general) seek to know intimately each ripple in the force-fields of thinking and feeling by which we are inserted into the world in relation to one another. In so doing, they introduce a disturbing, luminous disorder into the familiar patterns of thought and behaviour on which we habitually rely. Yet simultaneously they also invent new forms of order, discovering and reshaping the uncharted, often unacknowledged chaos subtending our everyday lives and experience. The equipoise here is precarious, but it is exact and resonant, revealing the familiar in new and enriching ways, unlike the labyrinthine double-talk deployed by those who attempt to excuse violence by appeals to a party line or to shibboleths of the tribe that all too soon breed nightmarish delusions.

The luminous complexity of poetic diction is a special preoccupation of Seamus Heaney, who is acutely aware of his own need to avoid the oversimplified, stereotypical religious and political allegiances underlying the Troubles. To some critics, this avoidance is a defect and Heaney seems too much an expedient fence-sitter whose poems confirm the *status quo* by refusing to disturb it. But others admire him for respecting the proper boundaries of his art and for insisting that poetry should not be used as a mouthpiece for some political platform. Rather, poets are concerned to bring to the surface complex feeling structures that force us to reshape or reassess conventional categories of naming and labelling, and this is what Heaney means when he says that poetry always "implies a politics"[2] even when it is not explicitly political. As Edna Longley points out, Heaney is best when dealing with "the hovering suggestiveness of thresholds"; by contrast, his work suffers when it comes "to or from political conclusions".[3]

Yet Heaney also lets himself worry aloud about what might appear to be a lack of political commitment on his part. In "An Afterwards", he acknowledges how he is accused of an "Indifferent, faults-on-both-sides tact", and again, in "Station Island", of a "timid circumspect involvement" that confuses "evasion and artistic tact". In "An Ulster Twilight"[4] he discusses a typical avoidance in Northern Irish civil society of embarrassing or inflammatory topics, in this case the fact that the toymaker Eric Dawson's father was a member of the security forces. The poet suggests how, on meeting Dawson again, it would be "A doorstep courtesy to shun / Your father's uniform and gun". Then, as if catching himself in mid-sentence, he adds, "But – now that I have said it out – / Maybe none the worse for that". The poem ends here, with an ambiguity: are things "none the worse" because the uniform and gun are at last plainly named as a source of discomfort, or were things "none the worse" when such naming was avoided? Heaney remains poised between saying and not saying, between registering the need for political clarification and the need to preserve a human relationship that is more valuable than the plain speech that might cause bad feelings. The poem thus makes a statement and draws back from it, and this presumably is what Edna Longley means by the "hovering suggestiveness of thresholds" that poetry can best explore, and on which Heaney bases his own defence of poetic diction.

To clarify the special province of poetic diction, Heaney has translated part of the *Aeneid* as an introduction to his collection *Seeing Things*.[5] He chooses the lines in Book VI where Aeneas receives instructions from the Sibyl about plucking the golden bough, and how difficult it is to return from Avernus even though the descent is easy. Heaney ends his translation at the point where the Sybil explains that "The bough will come away easily" if "fate has called you"; otherwise, even the toughest blade will not be able to cut it. In this prefatory poem, Aeneas's search intimates the underworld journey that Heaney's poetry itself will undertake, and the golden bough becomes a metaphor for poetic inspiration: if "fate has called you", you can have it; if not, there is no way you can make the poetry come to you. In thus recasting the poet as epic hero, Heaney joins forces with the Sibyl, who makes the cave echo "With sayings where clear truths and mysteries / Were inextricably twined". For those who have ears to hear, this combination of "clear truths" and complexity is the voice of poetry itself, the fruit of a heroic labour even though, to those who read the epic more superficially, Aeneas's martial prowess might seem to be the thing that counts.

By contrast with this praise of "clear truths and mysteries", Heaney's most explicit poem about the dangerous relationship between equivocal speech and false clarity is "Whatever You Say Say Nothing", from *North*.[6] The title repeats a well known bit of Northern Irish folk wisdom, and the poem comprises 22 quatrains, the alternate rhymes providing a satiric edge, offset by the looser and more conversational intervening verses. The poem is bluntly contemptuous of journalists' pat questions and jargon ("'escalate' / 'Backlash' and 'crack down,' 'the provisional wing'"), and of the social requirement to be "Expertly civil tongued with civil neighbours". Heaney is caustic also about religious hypocrisies on both sides of the community divide. Although "'Religion's never mentioned here,' of course," Catholics none the less in their "deepest heart of hearts" feel gratified that the Protestant heretics are at last being led "to the stake". Likewise, behind "the great dykes" made by "the Dutchman" (William of Orange), the Protestant community hunkers down, preserving the notion that "to be saved you only must save face / And whatever you say, you say nothing". Being "saved" evangelically and saving face are conflated here, and the political imperative to maintain the *status quo* through a stony defensiveness rests on a barely suppressed sectarianism masquerading as self-righteousness. Religion is therefore the source of an equivalent hypocrisy on both sides, danger-ously annexed to political violence in which each side mirrors the other in a mutual and mutually scapegoating antagonism.

As the poem explores this unfortunate situation further, Heaney looks again to the epic tradition, and specifically to the story of the Trojan horse. Northern Ireland, he suggests, is a land

> Where tongues lie coiled, as under flames lie wicks,
> Where half of us, as in a wooden horse
> Were cabin'd and confined like wily Greeks,
> Besieged within the siege, whispering morse.

Here, Catholic nationalists are the wily Greeks trapped inside Northern Ireland, which is like Troy, defended by Protestant unionists. The ana-logy is not quite accurate if only because Northern Ireland's Protestants know all too well that the nationalist community is by and large ready to bring them into a united Ireland; by contrast, the Trojans (except for the ill-fated Laocoon) think that the horse is a peace offering, and is just as it appears. Still, the stanza is less concerned with this precise corres-pondence than with the turn at the end, bringing Heaney back to language. The coded and whispered words of subversion are a result of the double siege (by analogy, the "double minority" problem), and these coiled tongues are incendiary, provoking violence by refusing to communicate across the divide, just as does the tight reticence of "what-ever you say, you say nothing".

Once more, then, for Heaney the epic returns us to the *agon* of language, and to a heroism represented by the poet's own labour, unveil-ing the hypocrisies concealed by conventional jargon. But although Heaney appeals in this poem to the epic to discover the "fork-tongued" duplicities of Northern Ireland's sectarian factions, he does not (except by the widest indirection) engage the protest against sectarianism and religious hypocrisy registered from the heart of Christianity itself. If anything, poetic diction is offered here as a means of grace unmasking and bringing to consciousness the dangerous evasions and equivocations on which violence feeds.

For all its engaging edginess and interesting concern for linguistic confusion, "Whatever You Say Say Nothing" is not among Heaney's best poems, not least because the satire too often descends into mere reproof. However, the next poem in the collection almost seems to address the shortcomings of its predecessor, not just by developing the conversation about poetic diction in the context of an ancient Roman theme, but also by dealing more thoughtfully with the religious question and by producing a more nuanced and more telling satire. "Freedman"[7] has an epigraph from R. H. Barrow, *The Romans*:

> Indeed, slavery comes nearest to its justification in the early Roman Empire: for a man from a "backward" race might be brought within the pale of civilization, educated and trained in a craft or a profession, and turned into a useful member of society.

Here, Barrow almost says that slavery is justifiable because it helps to civilize "backward" people, and when he talks about "the pale of civilization", the word "pale" – especially in this context – evokes the Irish situation and the problems encountered by the English attempting to civilize yet another "backward" race. As an English writer, Barrow therefore is analogous to the Romans whose techniques of enslavement he all but condones, just as the slaves of ancient Rome are analogous to the Irish under English rule. As we discover later in the poem, "Roman" also indicates for Heaney the Roman Catholic Church, which is depicted as another authoritative and enslaving institution – a capable inheritor of the policies and practices of the Roman Empire that enabled Christianity to spread through the civilized world.

In the second of the poem's four stanzas, Heaney describes the Ash Wednesday ritual during which Catholics are marked on their foreheads. An initial, evocative description of the physical sensation of receiving the ashes is offset by a resentment against ecclesiastical authority that comes with the poet's later reflection on being "under that thumb". Heaney then describes how subsequently during the day he took notice of those whose foreheads were also marked, and how, in turn, the "groomed optimi" took notice of him. That is, the ashes are a visible sign, a public declaration of one's "caste" or religion, and the "groomed optimi" are the Protestant ruling class, on whom no such mark is visible, but who are quick to notice who the Catholics are. The ashes ceremony is thus ambivalently passive–aggressive. It signifies both a submission to the Catholic Church, and also a defiance, an act of tribal solidarity of which the "groomed optimi" had better take heed. The poem registers this defiance in its contemptuous attitude to the "estimating, census-taking eyes", even as it also expresses resentment at being under the thumb of the Church. Both the Church and the ruling class thus figuratively resemble the ancient Roman enslavers, and again, Heaney's means of deliverance from this double servitude is poetry, as a result of which he abjures "all cant and self-pity". "Cant", presumably, is Catholic doctrine and ritual; "self-pity" is the inferiority Catholics feel under the census-taking gaze of the "groomed" ruling Protestants. The poem's last line registers again Heaney's sensitivity about how his faith in poetry might make him seem disloyal: "Now they will say I bite the hand that fed me." But there is a touch of rebuke here too, suggesting that those who would say such a thing have failed to understand, and therefore remain unfree. Consequently, if the poet is now victimized it is because his accusers trust to old allegiances and antipathies which continue to enslave them. In reply, Heaney offers the poem itself, a complex assessment of the patterns of mutual dependence, self-pity, resentment and hard-won understanding that constitute his own liberation, shaped into a discourse that breaks with the stereotypes on which oppression and discrimination thrive. The poet therefore proclaims a means of redemption, operating at once as the conscience and critic of the community, rebuking the propagandists by means of a telling compexity, and the unselfconsciously confused, by means of a luminous precision and the achieved form of the poem.

This brief précis of some aspects of how poetry communicates does not imply that the linguistic confusions on which violence thrives are not effectively treated also in other kinds of writing. For instance, Frank Wright's extraordinary book *Northern Ireland: A Comparative Analysis*[8] shows how similar are the linguistic structures of propaganda and scapegoating in various "ethnic frontier zones" globally. In a comparable study, Clare O'Halloran[9] analyses the "deep contradictions inherent in Irish nationalist ideology", whereby official rhetoric in the Republic keeps masking the fact that partition is accepted in practice but resisted in theory. Consequently, a particular kind of explanatory language has emerged, disguised "to hide the contradictions of the irredentism-in-theory and partitionism-in-practice". Not surprisingly, this language thrives on stereotypes, especially of Northern Protestants, and is marked by a "dishonest thinking" that also produces a flattering self-image. Again, in a ground-breaking study, Duncan Morrow[10] and co-authors show how pervasive in Northern Ireland is the influence of the churches, and how clergy are often constrained by their congregations, who might be willing to listen to rhetorical exhortations about loving one's enemy, but who prevent this happening in practice. Morrow's conclusions confirm John Whyte's[11] observation that a comparison of voting patterns with opinion polls suggests that many Northern Irish people hold less liberal convictions than they openly profess. The culture of politeness that emerges from this typical suppression of hardline opinions enables civil life to continue relatively smoothly, even though it also prevents difficult issues from being openly confronted. As Brian Lambkin[12] shows, people learn how and when to shift their ground in various social situations by a process of "paradigm modulation" that often remains unconscious, so deeply is it enculturated. Once people become aware of this process, it appears as " 'doublethink' or hypocrisy", but it frequently remains hidden to those who go on reproducing it.

Here, now, are two brief examples of the kind of unconsciousness to which Lambkin directs us. The first is spoken by a woman named Irene Marshall, though that is likely to be a pseudonym because she is a policeman's wife who agreed (against her husband's wishes) to be interviewed by Tony Parker.[13] She describes her husband as an honest, unprejudiced and well-intentioned man, serving bravely in the RUC:

> He doesn't do it for honour or glory, but simply out of his sense of duty. He doesn't want to sweep all the Catholics into the sea or make them give up their homes or their jobs or their way of life: he just wants us, the majority, to be allowed to get on with our own lives in peace.

The second example is spoken by the late Cardinal Tomas O'Fiaich,[14] and occurs in a New Year's message delivered in 1989, in which the Cardinal calls for the paramilitaries to stop killing. He warns that "Violence can never solve the problem of Northern Ireland," and that "bombs and bullets only divide" and "never unite". He recommends instead a "union of hearts", acknowledging that Protestants are a minority in Ireland as a whole, but reminding us of Catholic teachings about the "inalienable dignity of every human person". He goes on to suggest that "respect for minorities" is "an index of a country's maturity", and concludes that "Forced unions would only produce coercion in reverse. It would only transfer the violence from a six county into a 32 county framework with Unionists replacing Nationalists as the group feeling coerced."

The ecumenical tone and intent of these two statements at first suggests a liberal convergence whereby each speaker is willing to acknowledge the claims and anxieties of the other community. Irene Marshall assures us that if Catholics could come to see that no designs are being made on their identity or "way of life" by people like her husband, then surely the mutual hostilities between the "two communities" would be lessened. Likewise, the Cardinal argues that Protestants have a place in Ireland that Catholics should respect and accept, the anxieties occasioned by the "double minority" problem notwithstanding. Both speakers concede that the other side feels insecure, and both offer reassurances. Yet both statements are also disturbing in ways almost certainly unrecognized by the speakers themselves.

It is worrisome, for instance, that Irene Marshall tells us her husband "doesn't want to sweep all the Catholics into the sea", if only because the word "all" allows that he might want to sweep away some (even most) of them. But a Catholic would probably be more upset by what Irene Marshall says next: "he just wants us, the majority, to be allowed to get on with our own lives in peace". This appeal to majority rule might initially appear democratic, but to a person from the minority community, "us, the majority" means the Protestant unionists, who want to get on with their lives "in peace", but without taking minority grievances into consideration. Irene Marshall's reassurance thus turns into an example of exactly what is wrong about unionist majoritarianism.

Cardinal O'Fiaich also intended to be reassuring, but when he explains that a "32 county framework" would shift the balance of power, "with Unionists replacing Nationalists as the group feeling coerced", he assumes that the unionists within Northern Ireland today are coercive but without themselves experiencing coercion. Again, this is exactly the opposite of what many unionists do experience (including Irene Marshall), and the Cardinal's nationalist prejudices show through in a way that contradicts the very reassurance he intends to offer. In short, instead of convincing the other party, the Cardinal and Mrs Marshall alike end up widening the gap between them, and their liberal intentions unselfconsciously convey a dismaying counter-message which would be picked up immediately by an interlocutor on the other side of the community divide.

Lies, delusions and propaganda

The closer we move to the actual conduct of violence, the more dangerous such confusions become. As we have seen, exposure to violence rapidly produces an unstable, adrenalin-charged and disorienting intensity. Thus, an IRA volunteer describes himself as "so excited after a job that we shot the wee birds in the wires as we drove back from it".[15] Cusack and McDonald describe the atmosphere during interviews with the UDA Inner Council as "a mixture of menace and bizarre hilarity",[16] at once highly charged and unpredictable. Eamon Collins[17] describes how the killing of two policemen followed by his finding out that he had passed some university exams provided a "double delight", and a "real high", even though he soon found himself in a "contradictory and unstable state", and felt increasingly that he was living in a "fantasy world". Something analogous is suggested by the Shankill Butcher Billy Moore, who broke down and cried on admitting his part in a number of cut-throat murders, complaining, in distraction, "My head's away with it."[18] In short, reason is easily volatilized or stultified by the intensity and unpredictability of repeated violent behaviour, which becomes all the more confused and confusing when it is perpetrated in a world inhabited plentifully by informers and spies, turncoats and double agents. In such a world, the line between legal and illegal is also easily blurred. For instance, the IRA has especially demonized Brigadier Frank Kitson[19] as a prime example of how immoral means can be used to pursue legal ends.

In his book *Gangs and Counter-Gangs* (1960), Kitson describes how his anti-Mau Mau strategies in Kenya depended on undermining the enemy by infiltration and by creating a crisis of confidence focused on doubts about who exactly the enemy was. Thus, counter-gangs were deployed both to win the confidence of and to terrorize the real gangs. In 1971, a year after Kiston was appointed to command the 39 Brigade in Belfast, he published another book, *Low Intensity Operations*.[20] Basically, he argues that the limitations imposed on modern warfare by nuclear weapons will result in a global increase in low-intensity conflict. The army must learn to deal with this new face of modern warfare, and Kitson stresses that effective intelligence networks are the key to doing so successfully (71). To this end, he recommends (among other things) the use of the same kinds of "pseudo gangs" as in Kenya, as well as "psychological operations", propaganda, informers, and captured insurgents who can be persuaded to switch sides. In this context, he takes to task conventional commanders who insist on making "rousing speeches" while indulging in "activities designed to create the illusion of battle". By such behaviour, these old-fashioned soldiers merely lead their men "away from the real battlefield onto a fictitious one of their own imagining" (201). By contrast, for Kitson the real war against insurgency is a battle of minds, and he presents the world of "psy ops", disinformation, and organized treachery as less "fictitious" than the old-fashioned rhetoric of martial heroism indulged in by those who have not yet caught up with the new reality. In a sense, Kitson is right – the rhetoric of martial heroism is indeed frequently self-deluding, naive and dangerous. But the "reality" to which he directs us is hardly reassuring, if only because lies, deceit and manipulation are basic to it, so that the "fictitious" now itself becomes the "real" thing.

When Kitson went to Belfast, he put some of his theories into practice by means of a special unit called the Mobile Reconnaissance Force (MRF), which used agents who could pass for locals, as well as "turned" IRA members who were paid to pass on information and to identify former colleagues. Some MRF operations were alarmingly amateurish – such as the bogus Four Square Laundry which was soon identified by the IRA, who shot the driver of the fake van as it made its rounds of the Twinbrook estate. None the less, the effort Kitson put into cultivating informers and deploying undercover operatives contributed greatly to a culture of paranoia which, among other things, caused all the main paramilitary organizations to turn on their own members, torturing and executing suspected informers and inflicting often ferocious punishment beatings on others held to have stepped out of line. In an atmosphere of high anxiety, filled with intoxicated bravado and pervasive confusion, it is not surprising that such paranoia should run like wildfire. One consequence is that paramilitaries are considerably more likely to suffer extreme violence at the hands of their colleagues than at the hands of the main branches of the security forces.[21] Clearly, this internal predation is closely bound up with the culture of lies and double-speak that helps to create the "fantasy world" described by Collins, as well as Billy Moore's craziness. All of which is even more readily understandable and upsetting in light of the fact that the paramilitary organizations so easily gather to themselves society's free-floating complement of psychopaths, sadists and criminals. It is now no secret that the main paramilitary groups run extensive protection and extortion rackets, engaging in a wide range of criminal activities, some of which have been legitimated and pass as regular businesses.[22]

The combination of this kind of corruption and parasitism with high-minded political language produces a sub-culture of dizzying unpredictability. Thus, when Desmond Boal, QC, cross-examined the INLA informer John Patrick Grimley, discovering in the process Grimley's history of violence, petty crime, and generally feckless behaviour, Lord Justice Gibson abruptly halted the trial, pronouncing that Grimley "lived in a sort of half-world between reality and charade"[23] and that his testimony was worthless. In a report on the unsavoury William McGrath, Judge William Hughes and his committee of enquiry likewise concluded that the personalities under investigation were "a tableau vivant of people wandering lost in a maze of their own creating",[24] and the report was unable to substantiate charges against McGrath and his rumoured involvement in vice and undercover work involving top politicians. As an IRA operative explains, "in this type of war nothing is as it seems", going on then to describe the uncertainties involved in tracking and interrogating informers, and in trying to assess the designs of the other side. In such a process, thinking easily becomes distorted, so that "you begin to wonder what is going on and where the reality lies. This aspect of the war is like a room of mirrors, not just for us but also for the Army."[25] A senior army officer balefully concurs: "If you go into undercover warfare, you know that you will never be able fully to explain that side of life."[26]

Indeed, in 1990, Tom King (who was Secretary of State for Northern Ireland from 1985 to 1989), addressing the House of Commons as Defence Secretary (a post he occupied from 1989 to 1992), admitted that the authorities gave out false information for "honourable" reasons. According to Mark Urban – whose research discovered frequent disparities between official versions of events and what senior army and police officers told him in private – the "Lisburn lie machine" deceived not only the press, but also the courts, a fact which "none of those involved in covert operations whom I interviewed ever denied".[27] Although the dissemination of black propaganda is not entirely surprising, King's use of the word "honourable" is disingenuous, if only because the business of covert warfare, fought with weapons of deception, "official" lies, agent-running, collusion, cover-ups and "honourable" circumventions of the law is soon corruptive, as the supposed guardians of law and order come increasingly to resemble the despised enemy, even while this fact is covered up in a labyrinth of disinformation, black propaganda, and denial. A policeman candidly admits, "There are times you'll say black is white, or you heard something that you didn't, or you didn't hear something that you did."[28]

The interesting and often alarming collection of essays, *War and Words*,[29] edited by Bill Rolston and David Miller, provides abundant evidence of how the propaganda machine has operated in Northern Ireland by means ranging from censorship to outlandish fabrication, forgery, smear campaigns, cover-ups and intricate deceptions of many varieties. Even the judicious and well-trusted Senator George Mitchell, who served as independent Chair of the talks leading to the Good Friday Agreement and whose book *Making Peace*[30] describes his experiences, found himself involved in a smear campaign aimed at discrediting his staff member Martha Pope, who was eventually awarded substantial damages. Mitchell was puzzled and frustrated by the British government's lack of support, and by way of possible explanation he mentions a "widely discussed conjecture" that some people within the British security service who were "opposed to the entire peace process and especially to American involvement" (94), had attempted sabotage. Whatever the truth of the matter, Mitchell concludes: "In all of my years in politics, I have never been involved in anything so despicable" (95), and elsewhere he explains how the pervasiveness of leaks, disinformation, and rumour during the talks led to such confusion that at one point "I could no longer tell fact from fiction, reality from rumor" (4).

Not surprisingly, rumours and fantastic stories have been pervasive throughout the Troubles as a means both of expressing common anxieties and of suppressing uncomfortable truths. For instance, according to Malachi O'Doherty, the initial welcoming of British soldiers by the Catholic community, who plied them with tea and sandwiches, is rationalized in some quarters by the fantastic notion that the women were putting "ground glass in the sandwiches and caustic soda in the tea".[31] Interestingly, this story is mirrored elsewhere by a soldier who explains, "We were told never to accept a cup of tea from a Catholic because it might have powdered glass in it".[32] Here, on a small scale, one fabrication begets another, and the weave of distrust proliferates. Thus, a loyalist woman, anxious to deny that Protestant mobs burned Catholics out of their homes, explains: "This is a fact I'm telling you, a well-known fact. They set fire to their own house and go off to the authorities and say the Protestants have burnt them out. It's disgusting it is, isn't it now? And it's the IRA that sets fire to their houses for them, that's well-known as well".[33] The repeated insistence that the fact is well known arouses more than a slight suspicion that it might be as hard to substantiate as the local rumours about ground glass in the sandwiches and caustic soda in the tea.

One result of these kinds of confusion, fantastic stories and "official" lies, is that many difficult questions about the Troubles remain disturbingly unanswered. For instance, the Stalker and Sampson reports[34] are still sealed (though the Patten Commission has access to them), and the reasons remain unclear why Chief Constable John Stalker – seconded from the Manchester police force – was removed from investigating alleged shoot-to-kill incidents which occurred in 1982, involving the

RUC. Stalker was relieved of his duties in 1986, putatively for disciplinary reasons, though charges against him were later dropped. The enquiry in Northern Ireland was then taken over by West Yorkshire Chief Constable Colin Sampson, and in 1988 Attorney-General Sir Patrick Mayhew acknowledged that the unpublished reports contained evidence of criminal wrongdoing, but for security reasons he decided not to press charges against the guilty police officers. By and by, the truth will probably come out, but once again the ''honourable'' reasons for covering it up conceal an embarrassment at the fact that the forces of law and order behaved in ways neither lawful nor orderly.

Worrisome questions of this kind soon open out upon the further problematic issue of collusion between loyalist paramilitaries and the security forces. One of the best known examples occurred in 1975, when the Miami Showband[35] was halted at a checkpoint set up by men dressed in UDR uniforms. The band was driving on the Dublin Road between Banbridge and Newry. Their van was searched, supposedly for security reasons, but the uniformed men in fact planted a bomb timed to explode as the band entered the Republic, thereby to demonstrate that the band was carrying explosives for the IRA. But the bomb detonated as it was being planted, and the men who were holding the band members at the roadside opened fire, killing three, including the popular lead singer Fran O'Toole. Two others survived, one of whom was seriously injured. (A sixth band member had driven, on his own, to his home in Antrim.) The UDR checkpoint was of course bogus, set up by UVF paramilitaries, some of whom were also members of the UDR.

Another well publicized example involves Brian Nelson, an ex-soldier who became a member of the UDA in 1972, and eventually was promoted to Senior Intelligence Officer. But Nelson was also working for the British Army, to whom he passed information about UDA activities. He was arrested in January 1990, as a result of the Stevens enquiry,[36] which was investigating the disturbing fact that loyalist paramilitaries had flaunted security forces' documents profiling suspected IRA members. As a result of the Stevens enquiry, 94 people were arrested and 59 were charged. No RUC members were indicted, but the UDR was discovered to be so heavily implicated in the transferral of classified information to loyalists, that the ensuing scandal prompted the merging of the UDR with the Royal Irish Rangers to form the Royal Irish Regiment. Conjectures that the Stevens enquiry itself was deliberately sabotaged by a mysterious fire in January 1990, just as Nelson was about to be arrested, remain unresolved. In a compelling summary of the incident in The *Guardian* (20 April 2000), Jack Ware expresses dismay that Labour

Defence Secretary Geoff Hoon threatened former intelligence officer Martin Ingram (a pseudonym) with Official Secrets Act charges instead of pursuing Ingram's allegations that the army broke into the Northern Ireland police authority building and committed arson to cover up its involvement in the assassination of suspected IRA members.

Eventually, Brian Nelson was sentenced to 10 years' imprisonment for conspiracy to murder five Catholics, and for 15 other offences. In the course of his trial, it transpired that he had passed information to the security forces about planned attacks on individuals, but in certain instances this information had not been acted on, as seems to have been the case, for example, with the lawyer Pat Finucane, who was murdered in 1989 and whose death is now subject to further investigation. Although Nelson's defenders pointed out that he had saved many lives (he warned about threats to 217 people), the judge concluded that he had "crossed the dividing line between criminal activity and intelligence gathering".[37] As we see, in the murky world of undercover operations, collusion, and paramilitary gangsterism, this line is frequently blurred beyond recognition, despite the double-talk typically deployed to deny this.

As I have suggested, by making conscious the workings and consequences of these kinds of delusions and self-delusions, poetry implicitly challenges the equivocations in which the violent frequently take refuge. Thus, Heaney's *Freedman* allows us to know how a conventional tribal allegiance can be shot through and complicated by resentments, both against the agencies confirming such an allegiance, as well as by those opposing it. The freedom that the poem declares – exemplified by what goes on in the poem itself – is paradoxically dependent on the very acculturation from which that freedom is also won. The poem therefore holds in perilous equilibrium several contradictory elements, their entanglements brought to order so that they can be felt and understood, their complexities made clear, yet resistant to the reductions of easy partisanship. Whereas Cardinal O'Fiaich and Irene Marshall remain unaware of the prejudices that fissure their intended liberalism, the poem thematizes the tacit interplay itself between secret resentment and outward deportment so that we may recognize such an interplay as a potential of our own behaviour or experience. In short, the ecumenism of poetry is based on accuracy and discernment that the Cardinal and Mrs Marshall fail to achieve. With this in mind, I want to turn in conclusion to some poems by Derek Mahon, who does not often write directly about the Troubles but whose work frequently deals with problems of self-perspective such as I have now briefly described.

Getting a perspective: Derek Mahon's "semantic scruples"

Derek Mahon grew up in Belfast, and although he left Ireland to seek inspiration, as Elmer Andrews says, in the "marginalised figures of the wider, European world" (one might add, also, the transatlantic world), still "there is a centripetal, homing force, implicating him, guilty and responsible, in what rejects him and what a part of him wants to reject".[38] In brief, Mahon's eclectic internationalism and typical ironic detachment have enabled him to assess his native Northern Ireland in interesting ways. The tension created by a caustic intelligence and knowledge of how he has been shaped by a particular cultural inheritance gives his work a distinctive, combined equipoise and exigency by which he explores, especially, the fragile constitution of the self. To this end, he is much preoccupied with the idea of perspective. At one point he asks, for instance, "Why am I always staring out / of windows?"[39] and, as readers familiar with his work will recognize, his poems deal often with windows. Thus, he wonders about the "fitful glare of his high window";[40] he draws the curtains to look out of the window at the city;[41] he contemplates clouds "clearing beyond the dormer window";[42] branches whack against the window[43] and he peers through a window's "cracked panes".[44] There is even a shape poem in the form of a window, made up entirely of the two words "wood" and "window", with the word "wind" in the centre.[45] Also, in his best-known poem, "A Disused Shed in Co. Wexford",[46] the "thousand mushrooms" growing in the shed "crowd to a keyhole", the "one star in their firmament", which is also a tiny window, a frame through which things outside are seen, as the world beckons.

The motif of windows is accompanied in Mahon's work by a further interest in paintings and the idea of framing, or of selecting and holding things to be viewed in a certain perspective. In "Preface to a Love Poem"[47] he is concerned with how lovers handle "thoughts they cannot frame", and in "Van Gogh in the Borinage"[48] the artist paints light "Refracted in a glass of beer / As if through a church window". "Courtyards in Delft"[49] describes a seventeenth-century Dutch painting, as Mahon assesses what it contains and omits, coming thereby to see again aspects of his own Belfast childhood. In "The Hunt by Night"[50] we learn how Uccello's decorative and pageant-like painting of the same name has "Tamed and framed to courtly uses" the primitive and violent quest for food. The poem suggests that the human adventure itself is a sort of hunt by night, and the painting reminds us of this and of the means by which we ritually conceal it from ourselves.

Windows and paintings have in common that they deploy frames, detaching the observer, who, as a result, comes to see certain aspects of experience more clearly, even as other aspects are occluded. But in providing perspective, frames also shape a point of view which is arbitrary. Just so, our sense of self is, in a way, the product of our habitual perspectives – our familiar ways of framing experience – arbitrarily amalgamated and interiorized. In turn, Mahon's frequent reflections on such matters help to explain his acute sense of the incapacity of language (itself a framing device) either to penetrate to the secrets of the human heart or to encompass a harsh and forbidding natural world. The word "silence" occurs often in his work, frequently to indicate the inherent limitations of language, as in the "sullen silence", "unnatural silence", or quietly desperate "patience and silence"[51] in which the mushrooms – all of us in our unconscious longing – listen and wait.

Briefly, then, Mahon has much to say about the instability of the self, framing its perspectives upon an always un-encompassed reality. He is scrupulous about the reach of language even as he deploys language in interesting ways to explore the mutual interdependence of detachment and engagement through a cool and ironic play of intelligence measured against the pull of old allegiances. In all this, his work stands opposed especially to the narrow certainties and false clarities upon which the violent especially depend, as a final example will show.[52]

Rage for Order

Somewhere beyond the scorched gable end and the
                                   burnt-out buses
      there is a poet indulging
         his wretched rage for order –
   or not as the case may be; for his
         is a dying art,
      an eddy of semantic scruples
         in an unstructurable sea.

      He is far from his people,
   and the fitful glare of his high window is as
         nothing to our scattered glass.
   His posture is grandiloquent and deprecating, like this,
         his diet ashes,
      his talk of justice and his mother

> the rhetorical device
> of an etiolated emperor –
> Nero if you prefer, no mother there.
>
> '...and this in the face of love,
> death, and the wages of the poor...'
>
> If he is silent, it is the silence of enforced humility;
> if anxious to be heard, it is the anxiety
> of a last word
> when the drums start; for his is a dying art.
>
> Now watch me as I make history. Watch as I tear down
> to build up with a desperate love,
> knowing it cannot be
> long now till I have need of his
> desperate ironies.

Mahon reminds us here of the gap between actual events ("the scorched gable end and the burnt-out buses") and the poet's detachment and ineffectuality, positioned somewhere "beyond", observing from "his high window" and seeking to frame events as he watches from a distance, "far from his people". Also, the speaker in this poem is not entirely appealing – he is self-indulgent, "wretched", "deprecating", "anxious", and when we are told that his is a dying art, we are hardly invited to lament the fact, but rather to feel that if this is what poets do, we might be better served without them. Clearly, Mahon is vexed as he considers within the poem how off-putting is the acerbic detachment that characterizes much of his own writing (the note of "loneliness and cold distance" well analysed by Peter McDonald[53]) and how words fail to deal effectively with events, all of which can make him disconsolate, bitter, and elegiac. The poem then notices the impotence of the vexed rumination itself, and the "poet indulging / his wretched rage for order" is both the writer whom Mahon describes, and Mahon the writer. This simultaneous split and identification between Mahon and the poet depicted within the poem causes us to engage and then re-engage the question of how poems communicate, and by lamenting the inefficacy of language in such a self-reflexive way, Mahon draws us further into the problem, despite the disavowal of his capacity to do so.

In the final stanza, the "I" who explains the failure of poetry imagines himself instead making actual history – thus, in a sense, returning us to the scorched gable ends and burnt-out buses at the start. The lines "Watch as I tear down / to build up with a desperate love" suggest the intoxicating, unreflective energy that fuels violence, but the "I" that would make history remains Mahon the poet, "knowing" even as he speaks the folly and tragedy of the history-makers who would build only by destroying. And so he checks himself, acknowledging instead a need for poetry's "desperate ironies", exemplified not least in the reversals and refractions that have occurred throughout the poem itself, and especially in the conclusion.

Why exactly the "desperate ironies" are needed is not made clear, except (it is implied) by the poem as a whole. Broadly, it tells us that order requires detachment, a point of view from which to frame events, and that we have a need for order because of our propensity to make chaos, to destroy things in misguided attempts to make things better. Yet the pursuit of order must itself be impassioned to some degree, expressive of desire and not just coldly manipulated. Because the poet needs to be proof against the dangers of oversimplification that are one consequence of a "rage" for order, he watches himself at every turn, aware of his limitations, wary of the exorbitant. The fine assessment of poetry as "an eddy of semantic scruples / in an unstructurable sea" might almost be a counsel of despair, but not quite. The sea remains uncontained, but the scruples, patiently examined, may give us pause, and in that hesitation a life might be spared, a wrong decision avoided, a dangerous lie discovered.

Clearly, it will not do to make too grandiose a claim for the power of poetic diction to change the likes of Billy Moore or John Patrick Grimley or countless others like them, and a "silence of enforced humility" indeed restrains us. But the poet's scruples and resonant ironies, whether obviously efficacious or not, stand opposed none the less, as anodyne and solvent, working to loosen and unravel the knots of equivocation and self-delusion in which the violent are entangled, often unconsciously. As I have argued, the poets unsettle habitual assumptions and also provide new kinds of order – fresh perspectives – enabling us to deal in new ways with the untidiness and refractoriness of experience. In so doing, they embody the combination of "clear truths and mysteries . . . inextricably twined" which Heaney (via Vergil) describes. In this chapter, I have assessed also what some other voices tell us about the un-making of violence and the confusions and contradictions by which it disguises its own destructiveness. In addressing the same issues, poetry especially educates the imagination, and in so doing, its genius and particular "semantic scruples" are the best earnest of a political tact based on discernment and self-perspective. Without such tact, and the education that enables us to acquire it, the propagandists of violence will go on justifying themselves through the many-headed hydra of equivocation and double-talk, serving until the bitter end the lies on which violence thrives.

4
The God of Battles: Violence and Sectarianism

How important is religion, really?

In June 1970, leaders of the four main churches in Northern Ireland issued a statement declaring that whatever else fuelled the fast-spreading conflagration of violence in recent years, religion was not to blame. Oliver Rafferty points out that this view has been widely shared also among liberal academics who want "to characterise the problem as social and political rather than religious".[1] A further suggestion is offered by Simon Lee, as part of a complaint about the lack of serious attention to religion in the current affairs journal *Fortnight*. Lee wonders whether or not the political pundits have found themselves so insecure[2] on the topic of religion that they contrive to ignore or dismiss it by pretending that it is unimportant.

These concerns about how religion is neglected stand all too obviously in contrast to the best known, widespread media descriptions of the Northern Ireland Troubles as a clash between Protestants and Catholics. Here, left-liberal commentators such as Rafferty describes are likely to point out that the mainstream media are merely using religion as a cover for Britain's colonial depredations. That is, descriptions of the conflict as sectarian make it seem an archaic, local squabble with the British attempting to mediate between tribal factions incensed by religious hatreds of a kind that were by and large put to rest in Europe several hundred years ago. British policy in dividing Ireland in 1920 and 1921 by playing "the Orange card" (in the well-known words of Randolph Churchill), thereby securing military bases facing the North Atlantic while also annexing one of the world's finest ship-building industries and preserving the loyalty of Unionist Ulster – all this is circumvented by describing the conflict as a sectarian squabble, at once opaque and repugnant to those who observe it with varying degrees of exasperation and condescension.

This kind of left-liberal analysis typically goes on to point out that sectarianism ensures the hegemony of the ruling classes by dividing workers against one another, leading them to believe that their religious heritage needs protecting above all else. Along these lines, socialist elements even in the fiercely opposed Sinn Féin and Progressive Unionist Party likewise insist that workers have been duped into sectarian killing at the expense of their class interests. Yet this point of view, shared though it is across the loyalist–republican divide, has made a limited impression on hardline opinion bent on preserving the old loyalties and allegiances. Consequently, the political leadership of the PUP is held in contempt by many UVF members, as well as by others in the UDA and in break-away groups such as the LVF. PUP leader David Ervine has even received death threats from dissident loyalists who see his socialism as a sell-out.[3]

The contradiction within the UVF between atrocious sectarian killing on the one hand, and anti-sectarian, leftist political analysis on the other, is well documented by Cusack and McDonald, while Dillon argues that hardliners in both the UVF and UDA purged leftist elements within their organizations in an effort to curb an encroaching Marxism.[4] As is well known, an analogous split divided the IRA in 1970,[5] when the Provos hived off from the parent body led by Cahal Goulding. The split occurred partly because Goulding wanted to avoid sectarian conflict in the North, and advised that Northern Catholics would be better protected by the army and police. Goulding hoped to take the IRA in a Marxist direction, but, as with the UVF, traditionalists resisted the prospect of a godless communism and insisted on re-locating the IRA within the Patrick Pearse-inspired sacred cause, whereby Irish nationalism and Catholicism remained integrally bound together. As a result, the Provisional IRA was formed, and emerged in 1969–70, putatively to defend the Northern Catholic community. The Goulding faction subsequenty became known as the Official IRA, and eventually formed the Workers Party.

Not surprisingly, the split between Provisionals and Officials is far from clearcut, and from its inception as an umbrella organization for various elements that fed into the 1916 rising, the IRA has combined assorted and sometimes ill-matched ideological strands. These include the Marxist socialism of James Connolly, the physical-force republicanism of the old IRB (represented by the revenant dynamiter Tom Clark), the sacrificial martyrdom combining nationalist sentiment and Catholicism as represented by Patrick Pearse, and the political independence movement of the Sinn Féiners, inherited from Arthur Griffith and allied with republicanism especially under de Valera. It is an unstable amalgam, and within the Provisional IRA, the socialist and traditional religious strands continue to cohabit uneasily. One explanation of Gerry Adams's success is that he continually finds ways to strike a balance between traditional Catholic pieties and the secularizing socialist ones, even though he cannot do this entirely coherently. Thus, he proclaims an anti-sectarian socialism (not loudly when he visits the USA), and he is also a devout Catholic who understands very well that his appeal to traditionalists depends on his remaining so, and on valuing a brand of Irish culture that is not fully comprehensible unless the marriage of nationalism and Catholicism is acknowledged.

Understandably, left-liberal critics will continue to argue – à la Goulding – that sectarianism is a mode of false consciousness and a distraction from the real issues. Such arguments are easily made impregnable because only a little ingenuity is required to contain objections within the preferred discourse. This is a problem shared, for instance, by some kinds of psychoanalysis, wherein a patient's strenuous objection to a diagnosis is construed as "resistance", confirming that the analyst is correct after all. Likewise, the remarkable staying power of sectarian animosity in Northern Ireland can be construed to show how powerful the prevailing ideology really is; those who "resist" by suggesting that the religious dimension is insufficiently accounted for by a materialist critique are held, in turn, merely to be victims of that same ideology. One consequence of this hermeneutic impregnability has been, as Rafferty and Lee point out, that the religious question is frequently sidelined rather than addressed on its own terms, with a view, for instance, to persuading religious believers to consider the contradictions between sectarianism and what the New Testament teaches.

Still, it is not quite correct to suggest that religion in Northern Ireland has been ignored to the extent that Rafferty and Lee suggest, and, especially in recent years, several important studies have taken the question seriously. Thus, the declaraction by the joint churches in 1970 was followed in 1976 by a much praised document, again commissioned by the churches, entitled *Violence in Ireland*.[6] The contributors acknowledge that religion does play an important role in the conflict, even though they admit that they are unable to describe this role precisely. Again, John Whyte's landmark study, *Interpreting Northern Ireland*,[7] also insists on the centrality of the religious question, and

Whyte's opinion is developed in studies by Hickey, Gallagher and Worrall, Lambkin, and others.[8] A trilogy of books published by Presbyterian, Church of Ireland and Catholic religious leaders[9] in the early 1990s has also done much to illuminate the place of sectarianism in the conflict, and to provide some understanding of how church leaders are aware of their responsibility to counteract the all too frequent betrayals of Christianity into bigotry and violence within their own congregations. Sociological studies, such as those by Morrow and co-authors, by Radford and by McMaster,[10] provide detailed information about how religious values are mediated to civil life in Northern Ireland, and how pervasive and engrained such values remain, even though experienced in a wide variety of ways. Studies such as *Sectarianism: A Discussion Document*, and Frank Wright's impressive *Northern Ireland: A Comparative Analysis*,[11] also do much to show how religious stereotypes are generated and perpetuated, and how they are locked into the iron circle of violent reciprocation.

In short, a body of work has developed in recent years that provides fascinating new insight into the religious dimension of the Troubles. None the less, the main churches by and large continue to share with left-liberal commentators a resistance to and suspicion of the popular media use of religious labels. Understandably, the churches are embarrassed that the Troubles are made to seem, somehow, a religious war, even though, as the growing body of work on religion suggests ever more clearly, the religious labels cannot easily be dispensed with, and it is important to understand why this is so.

As Doherty and Poole[12] point out, the word "religion" in Northern Ireland is often used equivocally. Thus, for some respondents to the 1991 census, "religion" meant faith, church attendance and the like; for others it pertained to allegiance by birth and upbringing to one of the "two communities". Lambkin[13] goes on to notice a further set of equivocal usages, whereby "religion" might indicate denominational differences within Christianity (Catholics and Protestants are said to belong to different religions), and also differences between Christianity and other world religions. He cites examples where it is impossible to tell which of the various senses of "religion" is intended, and his main point is that equivocation is carefully, and often unconsciously, preserved in much Northern Irish discourse to conceal the starkness of the sectarian divide, thereby enabling people to cope. Thus, "the ambiguity of religion has remained hidden" (51), and, given this largely unexamined state of affairs, it is not surprising that the "role of religion in the conflict has proved so controversial" (51).

Similar differences might well attach to the word "religion" in other cultures, but Lambkin's main point is that the topic is so sensitive in Northern Ireland that an unusually elaborate set of evasive practices is deployed to prevent violent disagreements from surfacing. One result is the "culture of politeness" noticed frequently by observers and commentators on Northern Ireland, but Lambkin insists that such apparently accommodating politeness is in fact the result of an enculturation through which basic group identities and loyalites are formed.

Lambkin also points out that for some people, as we might expect, growing up involves the acquisition of mature religious and political understandings that call into question the unthinking group loyalties imparted by early upbringing and education. For others, however, "the development of their identity will remain arrested at the proto-religious stage", in which case "at least they will know what they are not and hence what they are, either Protestant or Catholic" (54). Although Lambkin does not stress the point, early enculturation typically establishes strong feeling-structures that, once aroused, can play havoc even with the mature opinions acquired at a later stage of development. Consequently, one further manifestation of the "culture of politeness" is that people are likely to reserve judgement about liberal or ecumenical opinions expressed by apparently mature adults, preferring to wait for more telling signs of what "really" lies under the surface. A main appeal of the notorious Reverend Ian Paisley is that he dares to say openly what many people feel secretly, and more people are relieved by this than are willing to say so. His dedicated followers aside, Paisley is generally regarded in the public view with a mixture of embarrassment, repugnance, fascinated horror, and some amusement, and he is widely denounced as dangerously bigoted. But he survives, not only as an MP at Westminster but as one of Northern Ireland's three MEPs. Such a figure would be incomprehensible outside the cultural formations described by Lambkin and others, where the effects of early enculturation are typically managed by stratagems of evasion, themselves so complex as to be often unconscious, yet ensuring that sectarian animosities remain alive and well.

As we see, Doherty and Poole point out that respondents to the 1991 census interpreted religion either as a system of belief or as allegiance to one of the "two communities". These alternatives in turn can correspond loosely to the difference Lambkin notices between adult religious convictions and the "proto-religious" identity acquired by virtually all children growing up in Northern Ireland. Consequently, when the churches in 1970 declared that the fighting was not about religion, they should be taken to mean religion in the first sense: nobody is much concerned to shed blood over theological disagreements or arguments about church organization, and so on. But the way in which allegiance to a community is marked by religion in the second sense is an altogether less rational process, conditioned partly by a sense that one's identity is established by what one is not – that is, one is not a member of the contaminating and threatening "other community". All of which has led commentators in recent years increasingly to describe Northern Ireland as an ethnic conflict zone wherein religion is the chief marker of ethnic identity. Steve Bruce was among the first to offer this interpretation, and he has since been followed by a wide range of commentators, including myself in an earlier study. Bruce takes as normative A. D. Smith's description of an ethnic group as "a type of cultural collectivity, one that emphasises the role of myths of descent and historical memories, and this is recognised by one or more cultural differences like religion, customs, language or institutions".[14] These criteria apply readily to Northern Ireland, where religion is the chief marker of the two main "collectivities" or tribal groupings, which determine loyalty less by religious observance and orthodoxy than by origins and kin groupings. This helps to explain why many unbelievers remain identified with their "Catholic" or "Protestant" communities: the important fact is the group into which one is born, and the enculturation received there. As a member of such a group, one therefore has a representative identity, and in Chapter 2 we have seen how representative violence is a core mechanism of the iron circle. Paradoxically, Christianity would have us break with just such tribal identities in the name of a more fully personal freedom, as is entailed by Jesus's instruction to love our enemies, and by his extending of salvation to the gentiles. Many Christians in Northern Ireland know this, even as they remain loyal to the ethnic group in which they belong by birth and upbringing, and which is labelled "Catholic" or "Protestant".

One result of this state of affairs is that ecumenical clergy are likely to be reined in by their congregations, whose ethnic loyalty prevails over the higher spiritual principles of which the clergy might want to remind them. Consequently, ecumenical activity among the main churches often tends to stop short of encountering the real issues that determine community identity and ethnic difference. As is often pointed out, endogamy is fiercely preserved in Northern Ireland, and this is still the case despite some loosening of taboos against "mixed marriages". Also, education (especially during a child's early years) is highly segregated, despite the recent, heartening successes of the integrated schools and of programmes such as Education for Mutual Understanding and Cultural Heritage. In short, endogamy and education remain the chief mechanisms for preserving community division, and the main arguments presented by both sides for the maintenance of this kind of apartheid are religious.[15]

Still, there are many shades of opinion throughout Northern Ireland on all the main issues I have discussed, and these differences are influenced in various ways by age, gender, denominational allegiance, class, education, geography, and other personal circumstances. Reducing such diversity to the old and tired "Protestant" and "Catholic" binary prevents the assessment of individual experiences which, were they duly recognized, would help to loosen and unravel the familiar and all too convenient stereotypes. For instance, in their study of Belfast churchgoers, Boal, Keane and Livingstone[16] point out that "the complexity of religious commitment and experience" is "largely unexplored" (3), and they offer to counteract the prevailing "tendency towards monolithising ethnic 'others'" (1) typically depicted as two opposed blocs. A great deal of fascinating information then serves to show how the opposed traditions in fact "constitute a diverse array of sites and social spaces within which culture is differentially produced" (172). None the less, at the end of this fascinating study the authors do not fudge the depressing fact that "overwhelming differences between the two communities" remain "crystal clear" (166). That is, on certain core issues, people revert to type, and – as with the Opsahl Report – Boal and colleagues find that they cannot dispense with the "two community" nomenclature, even as they provide information challenging to its cogency. For instance, only 2 per cent of Protestant churchgoers identify themselves as Irish, and only 2 per cent of Catholics identify themselves as British (163). An overwhelming 89 per cent of Protestants want Northern Ireland to remain in the United Kingdom (167), and a comparable, large majority of Catholics want a united Ireland (56), though some 13 per cent think union with Britain would be preferable (65). The correlation here of religious allegiance and political identity and aspiration remains very strong, and is confirmed by the fact that both Protestant and Catholic respondents remain powerfully opposed to cross-community marriages. Only 26 per cent of Catholics describe themselves as willing, even in theory, to marry a Northern Ireland Protestant, whereas 28 per cent say they would be willing to accept a black marriage partner (47). Only 14 per cent of Protestant churchgoers say they would be willing to marry a Catholic, and again, statistics across the Protestant denominations indicate that an inter-racial marriage would be preferable to a cross-community one (87). Clearly, the ethnic divide between the "two communities" remains firm on certain basic issues, to which one's religious background is highly pertinent.

So far, I have suggested that religion in Northern Ireland is a marker of ethnic identity, but also that complex cross-currents run between a mature religious faith based on an understanding of Jesus's teachings, and the less fully personal enculturation into a community where religion signals tribal or ethnic allegiance. In such a situation, one's ethnic identity is protected by powerful taboos into which are built political aspirations and a conviction about the oppressive intent of the main enemy, the "other" community, the mirror opposite through which one's identity is shaped. The sad fact remains – perennial though it is in the history of religions – that elevated and liberating spiritual principles can all too readily be annexed to kinds of behaviour that these principles denounce. Christians should know that Jesus's crucifixion demands the end of crucifixions for ever, and yet Christians have gone on imposing the cross, not only on the many varieties of infidels through the course of history, but also on one another.

Sadly, then, it seems that the fighting in Northern Ireland is about religion if we accept that one meaning of religion is to signify ethnic identity inherited by birthright. It is depressing but not surprising to learn that strongly religious children from both communities are considerably more likely to condone violence for political purposes than their less religious peers.[17] Also, as I have already noted, overt sectarian opinions are frequently more open among Protestants than Catholics, and this is because the loyalist sense of identity is so directly dependent on religion. As Bruce[18] says, loyalists

> want to be British but the British do not want them. They are loyal, but loyal to what? The only coherent set of ideas which explains the past, which gives them a sense of who they are, which makes them feel justifiably superior to Catholics, and which gives them the hope that they will survive, is evangelical Protestantism.

Also, Protestantism is by definition, at least in its historical origins, anti-Catholic, and in Northern Ireland, as Bruce concludes, "what it comes down to is the fear, as old as Protestantism itself, that where the Catholic Church is dominant, as it would be in a united Ireland, the religious and civil liberties of non-Catholics would be eroded". By contrast, Catholics are likely to dissociate their nationalism from anti-Protestantism and to deny that their resentment against unionists is sectarian, claiming instead that it is based on resistance to British rule in Ireland. Yet, as is well known, Daniel O'Connell's campaign for Catholic emancipation in the early nineteenth century depended heavily on a marriage of nationalist sentiment and religious identity. Links between these elements had been forged especially by the penal laws of the 1690s, directed specifically against Catholics and connecting the dispossession and disenfranchisement of the native Irish with religion. That connection remains deeply implicated in modern Irish nationalism, but, as commentators notice, the Northern nationalist community is often unaware of how strong its Catholic ethos actually is – a fact that Protestants can find distressing and hypocritical.

This distinction between loyalist and republican attitudes to religion is interestingly – and again depressingly – confirmed by Boal and colleagues,[19] who discover that among Protestant churchgoers, the younger age group is more doctrinally conservative than older church members, and is drawn to the DUP. By contrast, younger Catholics are more liberal doctrinally than their elders, but have a more emphatic consciousness of themselves as Irish. In short, both groups insist on their separate identities, and Protestants find this first in religion, and Catholics in their Irishness. Yet, just as Protestant identity expresses itself politically, so nationalist politics are pervaded by Catholic tradition. As we have seen, the emergence of the Provisionals was precipitated when the IRA under Cahal Goulding was taking a strongly non-sectarian, anti-religious, Marxist line. By contrast, leading Provos such as Sean MacStiofain, Billy McKee, Seamus Twomey, Gerry Adams and Martin McGuinness are devout Catholics, maintainers of the old compact between Catholicism and republicanism, and as such they have managed to draw popular support when they needed it, especially at the crucial moment in 1970 when they broke ranks with the Officials, declaring themselves the best defenders of the Catholic community. The degree to which the Catholic Church and the government of the Republic colluded in this development remains controversial, but it is probable that anti-Marxist vigilance caused both to prefer, however tacitly, the republicanism of Christian Brothers-educated Catholic boys in the tradition of 1916, to the new communist and anti-religious aspirations of Goulding and company.[20]

One further, interesting indicator of how inter-involved are republicanism and Catholicism at the grass roots is the attempt by the IRA leadership in 1966 to stop the practice of saying a decade of the rosary at commemorations, on the grounds that this practice is sectarian, as it certainly is.[21] Roy Johnston, chief theoretician of the IRA's new Marxist direction, wrote an article in the paper *United Irishman*, pointing this out, but Sean MacStiofain, IRA organizer in Kerry, stopped the distribution of the paper in his area. He was then summoned to Dublin and suspended for six months. As former IRA member Des O'Hagan told Martin Dillon:

> Being in the IRA and being a Roman Catholic, somehow or other, fulfilled obligations which were handed down. The IRA wasn't a Catholic organisation though at yearly commemoration ceremonies decades of the rosary were said and there was other symbolism of that kind. It must have horrified any non-Catholic who wished to subscribe to the republican tradition.[22]

The hunger strikes of 1980 and 1981 also dramatically emphasize the tradition which O'Hagan describes, as is evident in the literature emergent from and otherwise describing prison conditions at that time.[23] Recitation of the rosary was a common practice in the H-Blocks, with prisoners joining in communal prayer from their cells. Likewise, attendance at Mass, the making of novenas and the possession of religious objects became part and parcel of prison culture, especially among republicans protesting against the removal of special-category status. This protest lasted some five years (1976–81), escalating through the blanket and no-wash stages, to the first hunger strike of 1980, and then the fatal hunger strike of 1981, in which ten men died.

In the fascinating record compiled and edited by Brian Campbell and colleagues, *Nor Meekly Serve My Time*, one prisoner, Peadar Whelan,[24] explains how "I got my rosary beads and prayed" while waiting for a riot squad to arrive to deal with a cell-wrecking spree. He goes on to explain that

> Being religious and being Republican went hand in hand, so I had a sense that religion and being religious made us better people and so gave an added sense of legitimacy to our struggle. . . . All the men who were doubled up with me prayed in the cell. They said novenas and rosaries all the time.

Whelan also points out that the conflict between prisoners and guards was heavily sectarian:

> Religion was also important to us as part of our identity because of the screws' contempt for us as Catholics, as much as Blanketmen and

Republicans. Often they would vent their bigotry by breaking rosary beads during searches and wing shifts. When we said the rosary out the doors at night, the night guard screw would turn on the vacuum machine . . . to drown out our praying.

The extensive iconographical representation of the hunger strikers by supporters and sympathizers outside the prison also clearly amalgamates Catholicism and the republican cause. Thus, the hunger strikers are like Christ on the cross, or like the dead Christ held by his mother, and scenes of bloody martyrdom, frequently invoking the Blessed Virgin (replete with rosary), are fully caparisoned with republican symbols and Celtic ornament.

Likewise, the funerals of IRA members show how closely involved is religion with the political cause. Yet republicans of the traditional school, such as McKee and Adams, claim to experience no essential link between the "armed struggle" and their religion, because they describe the conflict first and foremost in political terms as a just war against the colonizing British oppressors. Consequently, they deny that their actions are sectarian, and in some cases this might be so, but this explanation ignores the heavy influence of ethnic enculturation as I have described it, and leaves the way dangerously open for a return of the repressed, as became especially evident in the wake of the 1974 ceasefire, when IRA volunteers were drawn increasingly into sectarian tit-for-tat murders. Bishop and Mallie explain that "the violence previously directed towards the security forces was funnelled inwards into internicine feuding, sectarian murder and gangsterism",[25] all of which were corrosive of IRA morale. Dillon concludes that "the Provisionals were caught up in a sectarian war which they later described as their 'darkest hour'", and Brendan Hughes, a leading IRA figure, admits that "the whole machine slipped into sectarianism and a lot of us were very, very unhappy with that situation".[26]

Despite denials from within the ranks of the IRA and Sinn Féin, sectarianism therefore remains disturbingly at large within physical-force republicanism. One IRA source explains, simply, that some recruits "joined because they hated Protestants";[27] another concedes, "it's fair to say that in hating the loyalists I was hating Protestants. It was difficult to separate the loyalists from everything that was Protestant and anti-Catholic." Ruefully, another admits that "some volunteers took it upon themselves to hit Prods and that was bad".[28] The bombing of Protestant towns such as Cookstown (1991), Lurgan (1992) and Bangor (1992) – putatively as economic targets – as well as attacks on Protestant bars, such as the Bayardo Bar and the Four Step Inn, and attacks against "soft" targets – namely, Protestant civilians – at Kingsmills, Tullyvallen, and Darkley Pentecostal Church, remain all too clearly sectarian.

The return of the repressed: Padraic Fiacc and Billy Wright

When Gerald Dawe praises the poetry of Padraic Fiacc, he does so because "No other poet writing in Ireland today has been so forthright and committed in saying the uncomfortable thing,"[29] and among the uncomfortable things that Fiacc insists on dealing with directly is the connection between sectarianism and violence, observed mainly from a nationalist point of view. Especially, Fiacc is concerned with how the young are affected – whether his daughter, the children of his Belfast Catholic neighbourhood, the boy soldiers sent to Northern Ireland or the boy volunteers sent to kill the soldiers. This exploitation and destruction of innocence is laid at the feet of politicians who cynically disregard the desperation of ordinary people trapped in terrifying circumstances beyond their control.

Fiacc admits that his "fellow poets" have found his poems "cryptic, crude, dis / -tasteful, brutal, savage, bitter...",[30] and although there is more than this to be said, the fellow poets are not entirely wrong. Typically, Fiacc offers such a blunt and vehement assault on his subject matter – re-enforced by jagged rhythms, vernacular idioms, and terse narrative – that the result can indeed seem "crude, dis / -tasteful, brutal". Yet, one often feels also a counter-movement of discerning compassion beneath the tough carapace and fierce directness, so that the poems are frequently affecting, and are more carefully considered than might at first seem the case.

At one point, Fiacc recalls, in verse, a reading at which he questions his audience about a poem they have just heard:[31]

> I read my poem about
> The "icons and guns" and ask "Now is
> That 'sectarian'?"
>
> "We're all 'sectarian' here!"
>
> Some honest person replies.

This is plain – even banal – presumably to suggest the cadences of straight talk. But the meaning is in fact elusive and the tone carefully poised. Thus, the "honest person" might reply in such a direct way because insufficient reflection has been given to the poem just read, on the icons and guns. In that case, the honest person assumes a sectarian solidarity with the poet, suggesting either that the poem is sectarian or that it has fallen on deaf ears. Yet the honest person might have listened very well, and in light of the experience is able now to acknowledge a sectarianism that the poem has helped to disclose. A further possibility is that the honest person's reply is a wisecrack aimed at avoiding any real confrontation with the question, and partly voicing solidarity with the audience, who would recognize this ploy. The word "honest" is then the poet's ironic assessment of how the person's defensiveness is disguised as forthrightness, implying that we are not to take the admission seriously. These meanings jostle, forcing us to re-consider the apparent plainness, and giving us a glimpse of cross-currents that typically modulate and deflect the kind of direct question the poet has asked. But was the poem about icons and guns in fact sectarian? Let us consider the printed version, entitled *Credo Credo*.[32]

Here Fiacc addresses British soldiers who search and wreck Catholic houses. Although the soldiers seem to be in control, the poem warns them about the people's hidden power. The soldiers are accused of spitting on Catholic icons and of worshipping the instruments of violence; but their values are confused, and the people who bleed in solidarity will prevail.

The title "Credo Credo" is the first word of the Latin creed, repeated for emphasis: what we are about to hear is a commitment – an emphatic act of faith. The poem then engages and develops its central contrast between mechanical force and the further, spiritual reality that persists despite oppression and even because of it. The soldiers are merely a wrecking crew, locked into the mechanisms of violence, and they believe only in the instruments that they wield. The act of homage they pay to the guns as they get on their knees to examine the cache ("When you found our guns / You got down on your knees to them") is all the more idolatrous for being inadvertent. When they smash the holy pictures they do so out of contempt, but the poem suggests also that now, as in the Christian story, they know not what they do, and the people's faith, emerging from the depths, cannot be contained by force.

Yet the people's spiritual power is not straightforwardly Christian, but is a mixture of Christianity and something more archaic and ferocious: "We have the ancient, hag-ridden, long / -in-the-tooth Mother, with her ugly / Jewish Child." The Virgin Mary is conflated here with the Shan-Van-Vocht, the poor old woman of Irish mythology. In the shifting iconography of Mother Ireland, Celtic female figures and the Blessed Virgin may be combined in such a manner, and in Fiacc's version, the result is menacing rather than benign, atavistic rather than spiritually liberated. In the concluding lines we are assured that this daunting mother will win, paradoxically because, together with the people, she always loses. This might suggest the victory over the powers of this world won by Jesus's apparent defeat on the cross, mirrored in his mother's grief. But the images of a "richer dark" and a "hag-ridden, long / -in-the-tooth Mother" who is "swarthy / -faced" and seems herself to have fought in the wars suggest also a brooding ferocity that deepens because of persecution – an ethnic or tribal consciousness rather than the universalism of the perennial philosophy. The poem thus contains a powerful charge of resentment and threat, emergent from Fiacc's evocation of ancient loyalties that are dangerously under-estimated by the soldiers, who regard all this as superstition. The "dark / Secret" (with its echo of Blake's *The Rose*, wherein the "dark secret love" is corruptive and poisonous) is indeed linked to Irish Christianity, but the effect is ambivalent. On the one hand, we are reminded that Christianity enjoins us to transcend violence; on the other, that religion can be annexed all too easily to tribalism in a way that confirms the power of the iron circle of violent hatred. This annexation is basic to sectarianism, and Fiacc gives us a strong flavour of it even while suggesting that the antidote is offered by Jesus's patient forbearance.

The question, "Now is / That 'sectarian'?" is therefore entirely pertinent and suggests that Fiacc is aware of the ambivalent feelings with which "Credo Credo" might leave a reader. Just so, the wisecracking reply "We're all 'sectarian' here!" might register a discomfort at having to confront the ambivalence itself. In the upshot, we may find ourselves likewise hesitating to answer the question, but in that hesitation, as we prepare an answer that is not just evasive but is more complex than yes or no, we might feel that the poem has given us some further understanding of how difficult and testing the issues really are.

In so far as loyalist sectarianism tends to be less concealed than the republican variety, it can also give rise to experiences of strong contradiction between Jesus's central teachings and the conduct of violence, less open to the kind of uncertainty Fiacc explores. For instance, prison conversion experiences of the "twice born" variety are a peculiarly loyalist phenomenon, and reflect within the prisons the fact that for young Protestant churchgoers in general, conversion experiences are of much greater importance than for Catholics, as Boal and colleagues have discovered.[33] Still, however dramatic, conversion does not simply neutralize the effects of deeply rooted, lifelong prejudices, as a converted Protestant youth worker explains.[34] This man (who prefers to remain anonymous) tells how his prejudice against Catholics was at one time so intense that he would spit on the ground when he saw a priest or a nun. Then, he assures us, "My conversion experience changed me." However, his conversion also gradually undermined his confidence as he came to learn that many things he had previously believed were wrong, and also, he found himself continuing to harbour old resentments. Eventually, he was required to visit some Catholic families who had recently lost members to sectarian violence, and he was afraid "because I was aware that my tribe had done it". But he knew also that he wanted to follow Christ and not "tribal gods". In the upshot, he was heartened and moved by his encounter with the bereaved families, who did not want reprisals and who welcomed his willingness to share their pain. Still, the process was not straightforward, and the clear understanding that came with conversion remained in conflict with deeply set habits that did not simply relinquish their grip, despite a conviction that they were harmful.

This problem is also exemplified, though in a more complex and unsettling way, by Billy Wright, the hardline loyalist who founded the LVF and was dubbed King Rat by the press. Wright was born in 1960, and, as a teenager, was drawn to loyalist paramilitary activities in South Armagh. In 1977 he was arrested on a weapons charge and jailed for six years, but was released in 1980. Soon after, he was arrested again, and while being held in remand he studied the Bible. After yet a further arrest, he experienced a religious awakening, and in 1983 became a lay preacher. But Wright's new-found vocation was short lived, and eighteen months later, in 1985, he reacted in anger to the Anglo-Irish Agreement and returned to paramilitary activity.

Toby Harnden[35] describes Wright as "one of the most brutal terrorist killers of the Troubles", believed to be responsible for murdering more than a dozen Catholics. His unit allegedly operated "dial-a-Catholic" killings, in which taxi or fast-food-delivery firms were phoned and the drivers killed, religion being "the only criterion". In 1996, Wright founded the LVF (Loyalist Volunteer Force) and a death threat was issued against him by the UVF, who saw his activities as destabilizing to loyalism in general. In 1997, he was jailed for intimidating a witness, and in December of the same year he was shot and killed inside the Maze prison by the INLA – an astonishing and still controversial incident.

In 1996, Wright gave an interview to Martin Dillon, parts of which are printed in *God and the Gun*.[36] Dillon came away from this remarkable exchange impressed by King Rat's lucidity as an analyst of his own motivations and of Ulster Loyalism as a whole. Central to this lucidity is Wright's unflinching acknowledgement of the contradiction between devotion to Christ and paramilitarism.

When he reacted against the Anglo-Irish Agreement (1985), Wright says he was "emotionally torn in two". On the one hand, he experienced an overwhelming bitterness because "our people" were betrayed by the British; on the other, he knew "that was a contradiction in relation to trying to live the Christian life". Wright returns to the contradiction, and does not attempt to fudge it: "There's absolutely no way one could walk with Christ and align oneself to paramilitary activity" (63). He then admits that he was prepared to lose his faith and perhaps his soul because of his love of his "people", and, again, he proclaims that paramilitary activity is "a contradiction to the life God would want you to lead" (77).

Wright assesses this contradiction in two main ways. First, he points out that Protestantism teaches that state law must be obeyed, and the state has declared paramilitary activity illegal. That is clear, and Wright accepts the consequences. Secondly, he admits that he "found it very difficult to disassociate myself from my emotional feelings towards Northern Ireland and its people", adding that this "was later to be my downfall in walking with Christ" (62). In short, he explains that the "depth of my feeling about our own people" (66) together with fears that "the uniqueness within us as human beings is being attacked" (65) constitute a main justification of violence. He then goes on to argue that religious faith is central to this "uniqueness", and he strongly castigates the socialist politicians in the UVF for ignoring religion: "if you take out of the equation the faith and culture and hold only to politics, then you are no longer a loyalist" (70). By way of explaining this point, he suggests that there are two sorts of Protestants. The first "hold fervently to the faith"; the second maintain that "the land holds pre-eminence" (67). The political leaders of the UVF are of the second type, but they will not last because it is always a mistake in Northern Ireland to leave faith out of "the equation".

Wright's analysis of his depth of feeling, bitterness, and loyalty to his "people", whose unique way of life is threatened, is forthright and compelling, as is his unflinching acknowledgement that such feelings are contrary to Christianity. But he becomes unstuck when he seeks to explain his position in more detail, not least because the "uniqueness" he wants to defend by violence includes religious faith as the central component. The problem here is that Wright offers to justify violence to protect the people's uniqueness, which, in turn, is characterized by a religious belief that repudiates the kind of violence he indulges. This is not the same point as the acknowledgement that, for legal reasons, paramilitary violence and Christianity are contradictory. Wright makes the extra point that violence will protect the culture even if this means him not walking with Christ, and perhaps losing his soul. Then to add that the Christian faith from which he turns away is central to the culture he wants to protect, introduces a difficulty that he simply does not address. Throughout, it seems that Wright is unable to recognize the key distinction between Christ's spiritual teachings and how religion can be annexed to ethnic identity in ways that lead to violence. It is not just that the UVF political leaders in Belfast have abandoned the faith, but that faith, which is bound into the "culture" as an ethnic marker, is itself an abandonment of what is entailed by "walking with Christ". Although Wright's conversion was insufficient to contain his intense sectarianism, it did enable him at least to acknowledge the contradiction between violence and true Christianity. Like many others, Wright simply remains bound by habits of behaviour that his principles condemn, and in a remarkable conclusion to the interview, he imagines God saying to him, "You obtained what you left Me for and now it's turned on you" (80). As we have seen, that is the way with violence, and Wright's almost Augustinian severity and directness (though the comparison might not appeal to him) suggests a difficult self-knowledge. None the less, in turning to violence, Wright also entered a demonic world, and in turning his back on the religious understanding that might best have saved him from the worst in himself, he ensured instead that the same hatreds that he showed to others would indeed recoil on him.

Wright's admission of having turned from Christ is not shared, however, by all his supporters, some of whom produced a pamphlet entitled, *Is There Room in Heaven for Billy Wright?*[37] Here, the interpretation of religious conversion is pushed to an extreme – and extremely unsettling – limit, aimed to counteract Wright's own misgivings about himself. The anonymous authors begin by claiming that at the time of his conversion in 1983, "Billy was made a new creature in Christ, he passed from death unto life," and subsequently, his salvation "did not depend on what he did or did not do". The authors specifically repudiate the notion that Wright "might have in some way become unsaved again, or have lost his salvation", and they go on to propose that he "died as a martyr for our faith and fatherland". Because the British government has failed in its "God-given responsibility" to protect Ulster Protestants, citizens such as

Wright are released from obedience to the law; his "struggle for his beloved Ulster" therefore "in no way detracted from his personal standing in Christ", and the pamphlet (liberally supplied with Biblical quotations) ends with an appeal: "won't you make Billy Wright's Saviour your Saviour too?"

It is easy to treat this peculiar document with contempt, but it is just as easy to underestimate its persuasive power for those sympathetic to the cause. Certainly, to the authors, Wright remains a hero and a martyr, and the cause for which he fought and died when "he committed himself to the counter-terrorist struggle" is religious, and specifically sectarian. The pamphlet therefore stands as a counter-statement – presumably the reason it was written – addressing Protestants who feel that conversion entails giving up sectarian violence. On the contrary, we are assured that in this instance violence is justified because it is sectarian, and here we return to the fact that extreme loyalism is often willing to promote sectarianism as deliberate policy.

Dillon tells us that although he found Billy Wright to be charming and intelligent he "could not help sensing a dark side to his character" (80), which caused Dillon to re-experience a particular childhood fear of shadows in the night. Clearly, Wright did inhabit a nightmare world, and he is all the more sinister because in the light of day he could be agreeable and lucid. This contrast between daytime reasonableness and night-time horror is exactly the means by which the playwright David Rudkin also approaches the problem of sectarianism and violence in Northern Ireland in *The Saxon Shore*,[38] which I now want briefly to consider.

"Werewolves in Magherafelt": David Rudkin and Field Day

In 1982, The Field Day Theatre Company[39] commissioned a play from David Rudkin, but when a manuscript version of *The Saxon Shore* was submitted, Field Day refused to produce it, to the author's dismay. As we shall see, not just the play itself, but also the history of its reception can tell us a good deal about how difficult it is in modern Northern Ireland to be free from the contagion of sectarianism.

The Field Day Theatre Company was founded by the playwright Brian Friel and the actor Stephen Rea in 1980. It is a cultural and intellectual enterprise stressing literature and history, and is centred in Derry. It aims to produce plays, pamphlets, anthologies, translations and the like, shaping a cultural "fifth province" (unconfined by Ireland's four geographical provinces), and assessing the effects of various political dispensations in Ireland, with a special emphasis on the effects of colonialism. Friel and Rea stressed the importance of having representatives of both cultural traditions on the company board, which comprised three people from Protestant backgrounds (Steven Rea, David Hammond and Tom Paulin) and three from Catholic backgrounds (Brian Friel, Seamus Heaney and Seamus Deane). According to Field Day's best historian, Marilynn Richtarik, one distinctive feature of the company was that it offered a critique both of republican nationalism and of the Northern political establishment. It is easy to overlook this dimension of Field Day, not least because, as time went by, the company appeared increasingly nationalist, and by 1985, Richtarik says, it was "effectively regarded as a nationalist organization, albeit an enlightened one – a cultural analogue of the SDLP" (254).

One reason for this identification with nationalism is that the board of directors is less representative than it might at first seem, mainly because none of its members favours unionism: "it would be fair to say that each of the board members favours a united Ireland of one sort or another, although they have arrived at that position from very different starting points" (108). Consequently, Field Day's predominantly anti-colonial critique, combined with the pro-nationalist inclinations of its main organizers, made it virtually inevitable that Field Day would be seen as a traditional nationalist enterprise after all. Still, the board members do not admit that any such political allegiances in common have shaped the Field Day programme, and perhaps non-engagement with the topic enabled the practical tasks to be managed without undue hindrance. But Richtarik cites a writer for the *Derry Journal* who broke the code of polite avoidance and put the question bluntly to Brian Friel, asking why Field Day had not dealt with Northern Ireland's sectarian strife. Friel replied that the neglect was "not as the result of a conscious decision", and that, besides, many works are available elsewhere on this topic. He then pointed out that two Field Day plays – the South African Athol Fugard's *Boesman and Lena*, and his own *Translations* – "do have obvious modern references", but that Field Day has "no set policy on the question of dealing with the troubles" (214).

This answer is highly evasive. As we have seen, avoidance that is not "the result of a conscious decision" but rather of unthinking habit is itself symptomatic of how prejudice perpetuates itself. Then to add that there are plenty of other studies on the topic, and that Field Day has "no policy", suggests a discomfort even about facing up to the question. Friel does not mention the word "sectarianism" in his reply, but instead talks about "modern references" and "the troubles". Finally, in citing *Boes-*

man and Lena as an example that might satisfy the interviewer, Friel is being doubly evasive. *Boesman and Lena* was the play chosen as a substitute when David Rudkin's *The Saxon Shore* was rejected, and *The Saxon Shore* is very much about sectarianism, but Field Day did not want it. In short, sectarianism is not a comfortable topic for Field Day, and part of the reason may be that the favoured colonialist analysis is concerned to downplay the importance of religion in general. Yet, as we also see, repressed sectarianism is a staple in the diet on which the Troubles feed, and, reluctantly, Richtarik concludes that despite good intentions Field Day was unable for long "to transcend sectarian politics" (239). Certainly, Field Day's dealings with David Rudkin are suggestive of the malaise to which Richtarik points.

Initially, Field Day was interested in presenting the work of a Protestant dramatist to offset the large contribution made by Brian Friel's plays, with which the company was fast becoming identified. Consequently, David Rudkin, a Northern Protestant living in England and a distinguished playwright, was commissioned to write a play that would focus on Protestant experience. When Rudkin submitted *The Saxon Shore*, he expected that the company would take it on tour later in the year, but he was soon to discover otherwise.

Basically, *The Saxon Shore* offers a parallel between ancient Roman Britain and modern Northern Ireland. As Rudkin explains in an introduction to the printed text, the Celtic people north of Hadrian's Wall resisted Rome, "and when, toward the end of the 4th century, Roman power began to weaken" (vi), some of these northern Celts began to attack southward. One way in which the Romans helped to protect the area of "Lesser Britain" (v) against incursions over the wall and invasions from the sea was by deploying planter communities of Saxons, who were loyal to Rome and were prepared to fight the Celtic invaders. When Rome withdrew from Britain, these Saxons were left exposed and unprotected, and their predicament resembles that of Northern Ireland's Protestant (also planter) community, ranged against an indigenous population and loyal to an imperial power that is increasingly unwilling to protect it. The play also takes into account the spread of Christianity through the empire, and Rudkin's Saxons are Bible-quoting Christians with an evangelical streak that also evokes Ulster Protestantism. By contrast, the Celts practise a pagan religion dedicated to female deities who are repugnant to the Father God of the Saxons. Rudkin is thus able to contrast the imperial ideology of ancient Rome, which maintains civilization by the use of force, and the core teachings of Christianity about healing and reconciliation. He does this by telling a painful story of love destroyed by violent tribal atavism, and the play strikes clearly at the heart of Northern Ireland's sectarianism, disclosing its interwovenness with politics and its contradiction to the spiritual teachings of Christianity.

In a bold, though risky, imaginative stroke, Rudkin has a group of loyal, god-fearing Saxons turn into werewolves by night. Transformed, they hunt and kill whatever unprotected native Britons they can find, telling themselves this is "God's Work" (2). Killing a woman means "one woman less for Brit to breed by" (2), and killing a child means "One Briton less, to sow his rebel seed" (1). The familiar Northern Ireland stereotypes (Catholics over-breed and are rebellious) are invoked here to remind us of the indiscriminate savagery directed by loyalist extremists against any Catholic at all. The werewolves thus represent the murderous hatred of sectarian killers who, by day, can seem ordinary and even pious people.

A young man, Athdark, is one of this group of werewolves, but he receives a wound in his side from a flinthead which he thinks came from an axe thrown at him during a night foray. The wound causes Athdark to limp, and is also symbolic of his wounded nature in other respects. Eventually, new understanding comes to him, and he says, "God is good. He sent me this stone and wound to show me what I am" (13). Unlike the others in his group, Athdark now begins to realize that he is "of that company I've heard of. Those not of one skin. Man outward, wolf inside" (12).

As pain from his wound increases, Athdark comes upon the shrine of a young priestess, Ceiriad. She prays to her female deities, who, by analogy, suggest Catholic devotion to the Virgin Mary: "Lady of Mercy, Lady of Healing, Lady of Grief" (14). But Ceiriad is also a princess about to come into her inheritance, and to explain her situation, Rudkin supplies a set of references to *King Lear*. Thus, the dead king is called Llyr and his two evil daughters – Ceiriad's older sisters – cast him out into a storm, as a result of which he dies, saying "Look there . . . Look there . . ." (23). Like Cordelia in Shakespeare's play, Ceiriad is therefore a youngest daughter facing a tragic sacrifice for love. And, as with Cordelia, her innocence makes her vulnerable, but also enables her to take in and cure the suffering but alien Athdark, whom she finds in a faint.

Ceiriad is offset by an older priestess, Sulgwen, who warns against helping the Saxons – they are "your Kingdom's enemy" (21), thieves of the lost Britain, and Ceiriad must think instead of "The struggle" (23). Here Sulgwen repeats the familiar Irish nationalist clichés about dispossession and the armed "struggle", and her virulent opinions throughout stand in contrast to Ceiriad's conformity to Jesus's Great Commandment, even though Ceiriad is pagan: "We must heal this," she says, "We are sisters in Our Lady's Mercy" (21).

When Athdark discovers that his wound is healed, he is overwhelmed with gratitude and love. Consequently, he is full of admiration for the Celtic goddesses and rejects the Father God of his own tradition. He also thinks he has found paradise and is wholly enchanted by Ceiriad, with whom he has an exchange that transcends their different languages (a scene no doubt consciously paralleling the similar courtship scene in Friel's *Translations*). But when Athdark is allowed to see the actual hovels, bog and mire that constitute Ceiriad's kingdom, he is disillusioned and the pain returns to his side even though the stone is gone. And so he goes back to his mother's farm, which in his absence has been attacked and burned, and he finds her dead. Athdark is now convinced that he has sinned by having conversed with Jezebel in her "witches' mire" (37), and finds himself summoned once more by the werewolf within, as "a deeper deeper Athdark" (37) stirs and awakens. As "half wolf" (40), he sets out to track his lady, partly wanting to save her from the other wolves, but partly also to hunt her down for himself. In the upshot, the beast in Athdark prevails and he kills Ceiriad, returning then to his duty as protector of Lesser Britain as the Romans withdraw. At the end, he wonders, "How shall I be neighbour, who have been such fiend to these?" And as he continues to struggle with himself, the final line of the text – a stage direction – tells us, "He is standing now, the beginnings of a man" (49).

Athdark's *agon* is the play's emotional and moral centre, as Rudkin shows him torn between the werewolves' savagery and the enchanted vision of love that transcends traditional enmities. When his wound is healed and Athdark feels "a new stone" beating "like a baby" in his heart, and when he is entranced by "The lovely angel" (31) who has healed him despite the fact that she is an enemy, he glimpses a higher morality than the one by which he is accustomed to live. Likewise, when Ceiriad says "Man to me is him forever" (32), refusing Sulgwen's distinctions between friend and foe, she also transcends tribal differences and heals her enemy. Yet Rudkin wants us to notice how close the elevated moral vision is to wishful thinking. Thus, Athdark imagines that he is in paradise and expects to see the city of Jerusalem; Ceiriad believes that Athdark must really be a prince. Both are cruelly disillusioned, and the play suggests that high ideals and visionary experiences are likely to disintegrate when tested in experience. Still, the ideals themselves are not negligible, and the play manages to have us share in the elevated moral feeling and delight of the love scenes wherein healing is effected across traditional barriers, as the best earnest of a true Christianity in which paradise and Jerusalem combine. None the less, the fact remains that the hovels are not Jerusalem and Athdark is not a prince.

The love between Athdark and Ceiriad stands strongly in contrast to the sensationalism of the werewolves with their ghoulish recitations of tearing and rending. If the former is too much for humans to live up to, the latter is a debasement into violence which humans cannot sustain either. Between them is the play's ordinary world of farming activity, stray animals, bossy NCOs, manual labour, worries about inheritance and marriage, prejudices, politics, and family concerns of various kinds. In this everyday world, Rudkin's Saxons share a particular identity entailing obligations and goals that parallel the experience of Northern Ireland's Protestants. To clarify the parallel, Rudkin has a lay preacher give a sermon based on the Biblical story of Ahab and Naboth, focused on the importance of cultivating a "goodly garden" (7) which is the planter community's inheritance, despite the ill intent of rebellious natives. The idea that a special, quasi-Biblical covenant binds the loyal Saxon community to the ruling imperial power re-enforces the urgency with which the Saxons defend and repair the boundary wall between themselves and the natives. But the planters are uncertain of themselves, and as the pastor, Agricola, says, "We are Romans. We are Saxons. We are British" (7). That is, a covenant binds them to Rome; their stock is Saxon; they inhabit Britain. The analogy is plain: Northern Ireland's Protestants also are bound to the imperial power by contract (the constitution); they are planter stock; their dwelling place is Ireland where they defend an artificial border against Celtic people by whom they fear they will be over-run.

In this context, Rudkin makes clear also how religion functions as a tribal marker, confirming political loyalties. The pastor's sermon about how Naboth's garden is to be taken away by treachery is intended as a warning: in "Northern Britain have we our garden" (6), and if we "shield it well", we shall "never be forsaken" (7). Earlier, Agricola scores a cross on the ground to "bless this new land" (4) and he abjures "those older, darker British" who "scowl and mutter, hating us to death" (7). Thus, religion is linked to territory and confirms the identity of those who hold and defend it against the enemy group. Consequently, the were-wolves pronounce that they are doing "God's Work" by killing off women from the other community who might breed, and children who might grow up to rebel. By showing the link between religion and ethnic violence, Rudkin distinguishes between this deployment of religion and another, spiritual meaning briefly evident in the relationship between Athdark and Ceiriad. Not surprisingly, he insists on how destructive religion can be when annexed to ethnicity, as his sensationalist werewolves make clear. But he also suggests how, in the day-to-day world, this dangerous link between religion and group identity is commonplace, whereas the higher moral and spiritual vision is rare. As we saw, Billy Wright was unable to distinguish between these two senses of religion, and Rudkin could teach him how to do it by thinking and understanding more imaginatively and accurately, and by being less illusioned about the monstrosity of violence and the creatures of the night that it awakens.

Some aspects of Rudkin's historical analysis do not map exactly onto contemporary Northern Ireland, and the play is sometimes overburdened by the author's concern to pin down whatever parallels he can. Readers will discover a range of place names and events with dual application, and there is some interest in detecting these. Still, there is difficulty in having the ancient goddess religion represent Catholicism, and in making Latin Christianity of the late fourth century stand for post-Reformation Protestantism. The first might confirm a fundamentalist Protestant prejudice that Catholicism is pagan and not Christian at all; the second might be taken as an insulting confusion of the reformed religion with its chief enemy, the Latin church. Again, the werewolves might be a bit much to take, but Rudkin is also sympathetic to his Saxon loyalists, while also refusing to gloss over the abominations of sectarian murder. It is doubtful if the echoes of *King Lear* are helpful, and they may even diminish *The Saxon Shore* by calling to mind so directly Shakespeare's most powerful and disturbing play by way of comparison. In this light, we might notice all the more clearly that, despite (perhaps because of) the careful thought that has gone into Rudkin's text, his characterization is often flat, and Athdark's struggle with himself, for instance, is not given any memorable poetry.

None the less, *The Saxon Shore* is a compelling play, and Rudkin finds original ways to investigate the incommensurability of the Roman ideal – the city built to preserve peace by warding off barbarism – and Christianity, which claims that the cross shows us the way to a higher morality that civilized order must perennially suppress in order to avoid acknowledging its own violence. Within this dialectic, the subterfuges by which violence is justified or concealed are evident also in the dynamism of sectarian hatred and the all too human means by which it is promulgated, as religion is annexed to ethnic identity and tribal atavisms based on territory, heritage and group solidarity. One problem is that ethnic identity and heritage are good things in their place, providing security and nurture within which people can grow and thrive. But morality deriving from such identity alone cannot but depict others, the outsiders, as an alien threat, and then, all too easily, as scapegoats who are victimized to consolidate the cherished tribal unity. A higher morality, that would discover the scapegoat mechanism in order to dispense with it, inevitably comes into conflict with these acculturized habits geared to tribal preservation. As we have seen, this conflict remains central to the debate about religion in Northern Ireland, but it is not easy to analyse, partly because it is often promulgated by avoidance, a fact that might lead us now to wonder again about Field Day's rejection of *The Saxon Shore*, after having commissioned it.

Marilynn Richtarik has assessed the rejection and interviewed some of those involved in it. Basically, Rudkin received a letter from Friel saying that the script was unsuitable, and offering no further explanation. Rudkin felt "immensely betrayed", and "For him personally the decision was a devastating one" (197). He felt that because his views clashed with those of the Field Day directors, despite their professed liberalism, he was now being silenced.

Richtarik points out that the small amount of commentary on the incident implicitly assumes that Field Day's reasons were political, based on a concern about how nationalist audiences would react. But, as Lynda Henderson[40] says, this is unlikely, if only because Rudkin, though sympathetic to his Saxons, is also quite hard on them, and shows that both sides are savage to one another. Richtarik's collection of opinions gleaned from the directors themselves is largely unhelpful, but its very sparseness manages also to be eloquent. There is nothing at all from Friel, Heaney or Deane (the Catholic component). Hammond says, "I thought that the image of northern protestantism was a bit askew. . . . It was just that David Rudkin's northern protestants were not the people I knew." He then goes on to say that "from what I remember" the vote to reject was unanimous (200). Stephen Rea keeps insisting that Rudkin is "a fabulous writer", but he complains that *The Saxon Shore* "Somehow" didn't have "the same dramatic charge" as his other work, and it was "a bit over-stated" for Field Day. He then adds that perhaps Brian Friel, as a Catholic, would have been sensitive about showing "those people" as werewolves, though for Rea himself this didn't matter (200–1). Tom Paulin explains that he resisted the play's implication that Northern Protestants are colonial settlers, and besides, "I just didn't fancy the idea of putting werewolves on stage in Magherafelt" (201).

My own view of this sad episode is that Henderson is correct: the Field Day directors probably were not especially interested in the reaction of nationalist audiences. I find it more significant that only the Protestant directors offered opinions to Richtarik, and that all of them mentioned religion. Presumably, now that Rudkin has depicted sectarianism so boldly, it is better if members of his own community offer the corrective. The Catholics would be expected to remain silent, this being the best strategy for not giving offence. Indeed the potential for giving offence to Protestant audiences seems to me a quite likely concern of the Catholic directors, who might well be made to appear sectarian by letting loose against the Protestant community one of its own – a renegade member – all too willing to bite the hand that fed him. But the Catholic directors would hesitate to say this because it would let the sectarian genie out of the bottle, and moreover, such a concern on behalf of Protestants might itself appear as sectarian because it pre-judges how Protestants might react; in so doing, it assumes they might not be able to appreciate the play's complexity.

As Richtarik says, it "seems unfortunate" that Field Day did not produce *The Saxon Shore*, and if the company was indeed "serious about challenging its audience, this was certainly the play to do it" (203). Just so. But I also want to register something stronger. The failure of nerve by Field Day to some degree abets – however unconsciously – the sectarianism that Field Day abjures and publicly holds in contempt, and which, by a subterfuge all too familiar in the culture at large, it hopes to manage by avoidance. Rudkin knew better, but, as with others who also know better and try to say so, he found himself a scapegoat.

To summarize: The question of how central religion is to the Northern Ireland conflict is vexed and contentious. On the one hand, it is important to understand the oversimplifications and distortions that attend the labelling of the opposed factions as Catholic and Protestant; on the other, it is important not to miss the "crystal clear" differences that divide the communities despite their internal variety, and which are strongly marked as religious. Useful as liberal and socialist analyses are, by sidelining the religious issue they do not adequately account for the insidious staying power of sectarianism, which deserves careful attention. Much good work has now become available on the mediation of religious values to civil life in Northern Ireland, in light of which I have argued that religion is indeed central to the conflict, but also that the word "religion" is especially equivocal as a result of habits of enculturation designed to conceal the religious divide and to enable people to cope with prejudices they would rather not acknowledge. In turn, these prejudices are closely linked to ethnic identity, and one main function of religion in Northern Ireland is that it is the chief marker of ethnicity. Although cultural traditions and ethnic identities are valuable and nurturing, in so far as they engender a morality dependent on identifying the opposite, other, group as threatening and contaminating, they lead all too easily to representative violence and to dangerous fears and hatreds. This annexation of religion to tribal morality is exactly what Jesus preached against, and the spiritual principles emergent from the Great Commandment and exemplified by Jesus's life, death and resurrection remain also to inspire Northern Ireland's Christians to transcend the limitations of the herd instinct. But the conflict between the universal spiritual precepts of Christianity and engrained hatreds and habits of concealment (conscious and unconscious) is not easy to identify or resolve. Old habits and prejudices do not just go away under the influence of enlightened principles, but continue often to influence feeling-structures and behaviours, catching people up in contradictions of which they frequently remain unwitting, or which they contrive to fend off by a variety of stratagems.

In such a context, Padraic Fiacc, the converted youth worker, and David Rudkin provide examples of people attempting to deal with sectarianism and its connections to hatred and violence. They do so with varying degrees of insight and effectiveness, but, despite their differences, they can impress on us the importance of opening a space for the kind of critical re-evaluation that might bring our own contradictions to the surface. The resonant, contemplative hesitations with which literature especially leaves us, at once invite our participation in complex, imagined experiences, and also our understanding of these experiences in ways that will help us to reshape our habitual selves. As Coleridge says, imagination is the psychological equivalent of incarnation, and in so far as the process I have been describing shows flesh and spirit contending through language to enable new understandings that turn us away from violence, then we might say, that process too is incarnational.

5
Shoot the Women First

Subversion, incoherence and non-violence:
Medbh McGuckian and others

Here is a poem by Medbh McGuckian:

Apostle of Violence[1]

There is an extra gathering of snow
over the prisoner on the Roman triumphal arch:
his arms are bare, his legs crossed,
his lips wind-packed with snow, not twisted
in pain, his sixteenth-century eyes
are used all the more
breaking their snow-lids to the outer morning.

Windows higher on the outside
than on the inside lead his eyes upwards
to tabernacle corners, blind-windows belonging
in the ceiling's world.
A blend of morning's freshest hours
blows through his wind-clothes
till his right hand seems a brother by his side.

The rivers that are the companions
of the times of the day
reply with the gift of a day in his life
in the person of night,

> a day too heavy for one angel,
> like an empty throne, at the stair-foot door,
> open the length of the ice-veiled garden.

As is frequently the case with McGuckian, these lines are elusive, at once disconcerting and strangely haunting. Initially, a reader might respond to the shifts and contrasts in imagery and tone, as snow, ice and the monumental play off against "freshest hours", "rivers" and the waiting garden. Yet the suggestions of thaw and fluidity remain intimations only, a dream-like promise of deliverance longed for from within the stony precincts confining the prisoner, where a view to the outside is restricted by "blind-windows" slanting up and away, above eye level. This confinement in turn reflects something of the violence that produced it and which also freezes, petrifies and shuts off its apostles from the sources of life for which they none the less feel some poignant longing. The poem thus registers a sense of loss, and the prisoner's alienation is pervaded also by sadness.

Much of the captivating power of "Apostle of Violence" derives from the interplay among its images, but a reader seeking narrative or conceptual coherence soon feels frustrated and baffled. As commentators notice, McGuckian's poems typically provide suggestions or intimations of a narrative which dissolves just when we think we are on to it, and we find ourselves teased instead in some further, oblique direction. Consequently, McGuckian often leaves us feeling that a poem contains a secret which is withheld or melts away, eluding us. As Thomas Docherty[2] wittily remarks, reading one of these poems is like opening an envelope and finding no letter inside. Yet, if this were entirely the case, every poem would be reduced in the end to the same interior blankness. Perhaps sending envelopes with no letters is an amusing thing to do once in a while, but poetry (like other kinds of communication) cannot thrive for long on that kind of confidence trickery. Indeed, the future reputation of McGuckian's work as a whole might well depend on whether or not the critical consensus is that she provides mainly alluring enigmas (envelopes without letters), or that there is a key to these enigmas, releasing a coherence that readers find illuminating and not just arbitrary. Sometimes McGuckian herself is helpful in providing such a key, and from the author-as-oracle I learn, for instance, that "Apostle of Violence" addresses the plight of a political prisoner in contemporary Northern Ireland. Without this information I would have been less confident even about offering my brief, foregoing assessment of what the poem's imagery and tonal shifts might be getting at. Certainly, I would not have gathered what I now take to be the sequence of the poem's development.

In the opening stanza, the prisoner is confined by the state, exemplified by ancient Rome. Just as "the Roman triumphal arch" is adorned by the stone carving of a slave (enslavement and petrifaction being analogous), so the prisoner also is confined and objectified, frozen into immobility, suggested by the snow. There is perhaps also a hint in the title that an "apostle" might be a follower who condones violence without actually committing it, in which case the prisoner might be confined for being an advocate rather than for having committed a violent crime. This possibility is barely hinted, but it raises the question of wrongful conviction, and how readily a "triumphal" state seeks scapegoats to assuage public opinion and to maintain its own authority. This possibility may help in turn to explain the poem's complex attitude to the prisoner.

As the first stanza proceeds, the images of frozenness and immobility are counterpointed by a touch of sensuality ("his arms are bare, his legs crossed"), and by the prisoner's "sixteenth-century eyes" communicating mutely because his lips are silenced, "wind-packed with snow". During the sixteenth century, religious wars accompanied the Reformation and Counter-Reformation, and it is as if the prisoner looks upon the state with the eyes of one who has suffered religious persecution. The religious controversy which remains implicit in the Northern Irish political conflict is seen therefore as something for which the British state (like ancient Rome in relation to early Christianity) has little understanding or sympathy.

In the second stanza we move to the interior of the jail cell where the high, slanted windows admit daylight but provide no view of the outside. The words "tabernacle corners" are suggestive in several ways. Technically, a "tabernacle" is a particular kind of recess in a wall, and the phrase is architecturally precise. But a tabernacle is also a temporary abode or dwelling (like the jail cell), as well as a receptacle for the sacred host. The word derives from Latin (*taberna*, hut), and here its ecclesiastical use combines with the architecture of the cell to bring together again the Roman and Christian motifs, strengthening the suggestion that this apostle of violence is also a victim, in which case the state is in turn a perpetrator of violence.

In the final stanza, the rivers combine with the fresh morning to suggest fluidity and release, in contrast to the frozen statue. But the rivers remain on the outside and the prisoner is cut off from them, so that even his days seem like night. The peculiar use of the word "person" I take in the dictionary sense of "bodily presence", describing the prisoner's habitation. In the circumstances, such a "gift" as the rivers provide would be too much to bear, even if the prisoner's suffering had transformed him into an angel. Still, at the end, the kingdom stands open to be re-possessed, just as the frozen garden awaits the thaw. Promise and expectation therefore remain, even as the emptiness, the uncrossed threshold and icy serenity suggest a painful desolation, however beautiful. This is what violence does, turning day into night, gardens into ice, people into stone, and, as an apostle of violence, the prisoner has brought such a condition on himself. But the retributive act of punishment, the Roman triumphalism, is also deadening, and in so far as it cuts off the prisoner from the forces of life, the state also is an apostle of violence. Consequently, the proponents of violence on both sides confirm the life-denying consequences of their actions, represented by snow, stoniness, alienation and suffering.

Like much of McGuckian's work, "Apostle of Violence" catches us up in complex shades of feeling which critics frequently explain as the poet's attempt to subvert the traditional masculinism of Ulster politics and religion. Thus, Edna Longley[3] notices how McGuckian "aligns herself" with "flux", in contrast to the "patriarchal sublime", which is rigid, clear, and architectonic. Her "teasing subversions" effect a "dismantling of hierarchy and authority", indirectly disclosing "the repressive force of Ulster patriarchies". Clair Wills[4] argues that McGuckian resorts deliberately to enigma and secrecy partly to reveal but also to protect the repressed and occluded elements in women's experience. A wide range of critics likewise insist on McGuckian's feminism, her "struggle to subvert ... phallo-centric literature", as Molly Bendall says, or to undermine logocentrism in a manner "proclaimed by feminist critics", as is argued by Mary O'Connor.[5] McGuckian[6] herself sums up the main drift of these assessments by comparing her poems to the "sea and its flux", by which she means that they are "moody and menstrual" rather than "masculine". Yet if we followed the implications of these remarks we might easily find ourselves praising mere flux – mere incoherence – as an acceptable critique of excessive rationalism (which is what I take "logocentrism" to mean). Much therefore depends on how effectively McGuckian's writing thematizes the oppositions between "flux" and the "architectonic" to enable us to see masculinism in a fresh light. In what sense, then, should we describe "Apostle of Violence" as feminist?

Beginning with the criteria proposed by Longley, Wills, and McGuckian herself, we might suggest that the Roman arch and other representations of stoniness and confinement are masculine, and are the means by which violence is perpetrated. By contrast, the fluid female energy with which McGuckian "aligns herself" is evident in the imagery of fresh breezes and rivers, and in the elusive process of the poem itself. The effects of violence are therefore petrifying and patriarchal, and are opposed by a richer, more compassionate quality of perception and understanding. But does this mean that feminism and violence are incompatible? Here, we find ourselves moving to a consideration of issues that lie outside the immediate domain of the poem, but which might also enable us in due course to assess the implications of the poem more fully.

One way to approach these further issues is by noticing how often McGuckian's critics adduce French feminist theory to explain her work. Thus, the writings of Hélène Cixous, Luce Irigaray, Julia Kristeva, and the general phenomenon of *l'écriture féminine* are frequently offered as analogues of McGuckian's subversive and lyrically disconcerting discourse.[7] It does not matter that McGuckian herself is not much concerned about theory; only that her writing and the work of these French feminist thinkers seem to provide mutual illumination.

In her introduction to *The Second Wave: A Reader in Feminist Theory*, Linda Nicholson[8] explains the contribution of French feminism to the modern women's movement. She begins by stressing the importance of the Women's Rights campaigns of the 1960s in bringing into public debate the problems of discrimination experienced by women in the labour force (1). Slightly later, a more theoretically inclined Women's Liberation Movement emerged from the New Left and was especially concerned to explain why and how women's oppression had endured so persistently across the centuries (2). Much creative analysis emerged from this "second wave", and, not surprisingly, conflicting opinions soon developed and were keenly debated. The most contentious of these was the question of whether or not men and women are fundamentally different. On the one hand is the argument that everyone shares a common humanity, and men and women ought therefore to be respected equally and accorded equal rights. On the other hand is a view that differences between men and women constitute the firmest grounds for women's resistance to patriarchy, and difference ought therefore to be emphasized. Nicholson concludes that further discussion of such issues produced "what became perhaps the major theoretical debate of the 1990s", focused on "essentialism" (4) – that is, whether or not it makes sense to talk of such things as equality, or a common human nature. This debate is many-sided, but the contributions of a small number of French feminist thinkers have been central to it, and the ones most often cited are Kristeva, Cixous, and Irigaray.

In an illuminating essay, Ann Rosalind Jones[9] explains that these three authors share a conviction that Western thought is "based on a systematic repression of women's experience"; consequently, they stress that positing a distinctive "female nature" is the best means to "deconstruct language, philosophy, psychoanalysis, the social practices, and the direction of patriarchal culture as we live in and resist it" (361). Because Western culture is bent on dominating "through verbal mastery" (362), resistance can be effected especially through discourses that are fluid, non-linear, and gestural rather than controlling. The result is *jouissance* – "the direct re-experience of the physical pleasures of infancy and of later sexuality, repressed but not obliterated by the Law of the Father" (362). In this context, Kristeva makes her well-known distinction between the symbolic and semiotic. The first is authoritative, conceptual, normative, and controlling; the second is fluid, rhythmical, pleasurably unconfined, and returns us to our pre-verbal identification with the mother. Irigaray likewise recommends *jouissance* as a means of subverting "phallocentric oppression" (365), but she stresses that women's bodies are different from men's in ways that enable women to experience a diffuse and multiple libidinal energy to which phallocentric culture does not have access (364). Also, in locating the difference between men and women specifically in the body and in sexuality, Irigaray confirms the principle of opposition (as distinct from a homogenizing equality) basic to "gynocentrism" and, by extension, "gynocriticism".

Ironically, but not surprisingly, proponents of *l'écriture féminine* are sometimes criticized for re-introducing the very essentialism for which they often berate masculinist discourse. Also, *jouissance* is aligned with such a nebulous and indefinite set of criteria that it becomes impossible to link it to particular political goals without compromising its much praised and valued indeterminacy. Further examination of these difficulties by a wide range of feminist writers has produced much interesting argument on virtually every foundational issue – including, even, what the foundational issues are. Still, despite the complexity of this debate, it is easy to understand how McGuckian's critics could see her poems as examples of *l'écriture féminine* in action, offering a fluid, baffling and often erotically-tinged lyricism, teasingly subversive in a way that dismantles hierarchy and authority. Here we might also add that McGuckian is open to kinds of criticism similar to those directed against *jouissance*, on the grounds that she often comes close to identifying subversion with the merely incoherent. All of which can return us to the relationship between feminism and violence because, presumably, if phallocentric culture operates by power and control, then the *jouissance* opposing it must be unwilling to coerce or dominate. Thus, in "Apostle of Violence" the fresh breezes and thawing rivers offer to release the patriarchal from its Roman severity, and compassion rather than punitive judgement is its mode of operation. Understandably, feminists who associate phallocentric culture with violence are likely to want feminism to be pacifist. Certainly, women in Northern Ireland were central to the peace movement that captured world attention when Betty Williams and Mairead Corrigan were awarded the Nobel Peace Prize for 1976, and in a well-known essay, Edna Longley[10] argues that a proposed discussion of "Feminism and Physical Force" is "self-evidently a contradiction in terms". Provocatively, Longley also suggests that "As a general rule: the more Republican, the less feminist," and the antidote, she argues, is best imagined as a "web", which is "female, feminist, connective – as contrasted with male polarisation", and which admits "more varied, mixed, fluid and relational kinds of identity".

But not all women are willing to describe their feminist agenda in such terms, and the hostile confrontations with the Women's Peace Movement (later, Peace People) in 1976, orchestrated by Maire Drumm, among others, is matched in a different mode by hostile responses to Edna Longley by such writers as Geraldine Meaney and Sarah Edge. Meaney argues that women can indeed be Republican and feminist, as a good many are. Also, women in general are not "essentially more peaceable" than men, or "uninfected by bloodthirsty political ideologies",[11] but are implicated in a wide range of political endeavours, many of which condone the use of force. Edge[12] repeats some of these points, but focuses especially on "the tensions that arise between republicanism/nationalism/Catholicism and feminism" (217), and she warns against homogenizing such differences through an essentialist view of women's "sameness" (225). Edge then criticizes Longley for ignoring "the very real discrimination faced by Catholic/Irish people in Northern Ireland", and for "the assumption that there is only one true feminist position". Edge says that this assumption is "essentialist" (222), and concludes that "feminism needs to reject perceptions of female essentialism as a feminist strategy"; otherwise women "are ultimately placing themselves as the naturalised 'Other' to men" (225). Whereas Longley, then, finds feminism and violence incompatible, other women who also speak as feminists disagree with her. Still, the question remains whether or not women are in fact less violent than men, and by what criteria we could decide such a thing.

Representing violent women: stereotypes and hybrid fantasies

In her book *Deadlier than the Male*, Alix Kirsta[13] argues vigorously against what she describes as the "misleading and dangerous" notion that if women ran the world there would be no violence (1). On the contrary, she assures us that "We delude ourselves if we really believe women's cruelty or ability to revel in gratuitous violence to be any less than men's" (135). Kirsta then scornfully dismisses certain feminists of the "first wave" who "tended to deify the nurturing, pacific, Mother Earth image" in order to assert "women's 'natural' role as the custodians of peace" (53). Kirsta sees this kind of thinking as merely another tyranny bent on keeping women in their place, and instead she argues that "qualities such as anger, dominance, competitiveness and the killer instinct were always present in women" (8). A large amount of her book is given over to documenting this claim by cataloguing some of the appalling violence actually committed by women. There is plenty to document, and the enthused Kirsta goes on to cite the US criminologist Freda Adler, to the effect that the rise of feminism and an increase in violent crime by women are linked (23). Although women commit only a small percentage of homicides (Kirsta says 12 per cent, but it is unclear which group she is measuring [130]), none the less, she argues that violent crimes committed by women have risen by 250 per cent since 1973, and the main reason is that women are now more free "to marshal their existing potential for what was until recently deemed unfeminine and hence unnatural behaviour" (388).

Presumably, Longley would reply that such an increase in violence is a distressing example of women adopting men's oppressive behaviour and confusing it with liberation; such women are merely taking up the weapons that have been used against them, so that yesterday's oppressed become today's oppressors. In her study of politically violent women entitled *Shoot the Women First*, Eileen MacDonald[14] addresses this issue by focusing more closely than does Kirsta on the often complex inter-relationships between violence and liberation. MacDonald takes her title from a piece of advice allegedly offered by Interpol to European anti-terrorist squads, to the effect that, when confronted with terrorist groups containing women members, it is best to shoot the women first. MacDonald was unable to find anyone who had been offered this advice directly, but she found several seasoned anti-terrorist officers who thought that it made good sense. These officers agreed that terrorist women tend to be more ruthless, dedicated, likely to shoot first and unlikely to break afterwards under interrogation. If you love your life, confides Herr Christian Lochte, director of Germany's intelligence-gathering network, it is "a very clever idea to shoot the women first" (4).

Herr Lochte's "clever idea" seems at first to take Kirsta a step further – apparently, women who go in for violence are not just equal to men but are much worse. Yet MacDonald, whose book consists mainly of interviews with politically violent women, resists this conclusion. Like Kirsta, she begins by repudiating explanations that violent women are, somehow, "unnatural" as is often alleged (for instance, that they have more body hair, are evolutionary throwbacks, have a chromosome imbalance that makes them more masculine, and so on). By contrast, her interviewees "often look and speak much like the next-door neighbour or the woman behind you in the queue at the check-out" (3); indeed, these women are "disturbingly normal" (11). Why is it, then, a "clever idea" to shoot them first, or is this yet another masculinist fabrication?

MacDonald's answer is that in breaking out of traditional roles into a predominantly disapproving or sceptical male domain, some women feel they have more to prove. Certainly, the inherent sexism of violent male groups provides an arduous testing ground for women wanting admission, and who know they will easily be blamed if things go wrong, or if they show weakness. Consequently, they strive to outdo the men at their own game. MacDonald's interviews provide the raw material for this analysis, which leaves us now with a perplexed set of issues, about which I will venture some tentative observations before returning to representations of women and violence in Northern Ireland.

First, it seems that quite "ordinary" women can be violent, as MacDonald shows, just as quite "ordinary" men can be pacifist. Biological essentialism (and the mythology of the doubly-deviant "monster" women that goes with it) is therefore not a credible explanation of women's political violence, though it would certainly encourage those who think it a good idea to shoot "terrorist" women first. Still, a resistance to biological essentialism need not pitch us to the opposite extreme, namely, a homogenizing that discounts the ways in which women and men are different. Historically, women as a class have been oppressed, and women therefore are in an especially good position to understand how the mechanisms of subjection operate. This, I take it, is the point Edna Longley wants to make in asserting that feminism and physical force are contradictory. She does not necessarily espouse the kind of "essentialism" which Meaney and Edge ascribe to her, and she does not say that women are "essentially more peaceable"; only that women ought not to be co-opted into reproducing the kinds of control through force that have effectively oppressed them in the past. Yet, as we see also, if women are better advised to have no truck with the coerciveness of phallocentric culture, it might be difficult for them to engage it sufficiently to transform it, and, not surprisingly, feminists have addressed this difficulty from various angles.[15] For instance, Monique Wittig maintains that the idea of "woman" is a myth enabling the oppression of "women" as a class. Consequently, the "first task" of feminists is to "dissociate 'women' (the class within which we fight) and 'woman', the myth". But if the idea of woman is "an imaginary formation", so also is the idea of man, and because both terms are political inventions, both will disappear together, "for there are no slaves without masters" (268). Still, because each person is more than a product of the dominant ideology, we ought not to "suppress our individual selves", and there is no effective resistance unless "one can become *someone* in spite of oppression, that one has one's own identity" (269). Wittig therefore posits a pragmatic, historicized subjectivity as a position from which to protest, *en route* to the emergence of a humankind "beyond the categories of sex" (270).

Judith Butler agrees that individual human subjects cannot simply be reduced to the identity categories that regulate behaviour, and like Wittig, she insists that the subject is contingent (302), developing from our historical engagements rather than pre-existing them. Gyatri Spivak proposes the term "strategic essentialism" (318) to describe this kind of positioning, whereby women can engage with political issues to effect change that would result in the elimination of the categories that they are, in the meantime, willing to adopt. Along the same lines, Carol Gilligan argues for "contextual" (210) judgements to promote women's concerns and eventually to enable a "vision" that will "encompass the experience of both sexes" (211). Nicholson also concludes that it is useful to understand how subjectivity is "discursively constituted", so that "the meaning of 'woman' shifts over history". Feminism therefore evolves, as "men as well as woman, struggle over how gender is to be understood" (5), working towards a "new personal and subjective definition for all humankind" (270), as Wittig says. All of which suggests that, by accepting a strategic compromise with patriarchal values in order to change them, even women who deplore violence might find themselves condoning it, and the degree to which this is so is likely to vary in individual cases and situations. Certainly, in Northern Ireland, women's engagement with violence during the Troubles has been highly diverse, ranging from the academic and theoretical to the murderous and sensationalist.

On the murderous end of the scale, for instance, women have lured members of the security forces to their deaths – as Dillon explains, a "honeytrap" was fatal in the case of three young soldiers in 1971, and in 1973 two women invited four off-duty servicemen to a party where three of them were shot and killed; the fourth was wounded but survived.[16] Also in 1973, the Price sisters, Dolours and Marion, were part of a team that planted bombs at New Scotland Yard, the army recruiting office at Whitehall, the BBC building in Dean Stanley Street, and the Old Bailey. Two of the devices were disarmed, but two were detonated, resulting in one death and many injuries. In 1974, an Englishwoman, Rose Dugdale, in cahoots with the hapless Eddie Gallagher, hijacked a helicopter and dropped two milk-churn bombs (which failed to explode) on a police station. In 1988, Mairead Farrell achieved folk-heroine status after she was shot dead, along with Daniel McCann and Sean Savage, by an SAS unit in Gibraltar, in an incident that still raises unsettling questions.[17] Rita O'Hare, who became editor of *An Phoblacht/ Republican News* and now runs the Washington office of Sinn Féin, is wanted by the police in Northern Ireland, accused of the attempted murder of two soldiers (a charge she denies). She herself was shot in the head during the incident involving the soldiers, but fled to the Republic before her trial.[18]

These are well-known names, and they could easily be multiplied, but many women also have been involved in violence anonymously, along many fronts. For instance, we are told that explosives were routinely concealed in women's platform shoes,[19] and sensitive messages carried in tiny packages of cling film.[20] Bishop and Mallie claim that in the 1970s IRA couriers were "mostly women",[21] and Dillon points to the extensive use of IRA women in intelligence-gathering: "They carried guns and explosives and, in one instance, I saw several fire weapons during a gun battle with troops."[22] McGartland[23] reports how young unmarried mothers and widows would store weapons for small amounts of money, and O'Callaghan[24] describes how he travelled with a woman and two children who provided cover for him by making him appear a family man. Women might drive scout cars, clatter dustbin lids on the pavement to set up an alarm, or go on hunger strike. Women have also been informers, and Mark Urban[25] describes how Colette O'Neill was rescued by police in 1989 while being abducted by the IRA. There is some suspicion that she was implicated in the SAS ambush at Loughgall in 1987, when eight IRA men were killed. If so, she was lucky to escape with her life. Caroline Mooreland was not so fortunate, and in 1994 she was tortured before being killed by the IRA, again as an informer,[26] a charge also levelled at Jean McConville, who disappeared in 1972 and is believed to be buried in a secret grave, to the continuing distress of her family.

Violence committed by loyalist women is more difficult to assess, perhaps because fewer loyalist women are directly involved; yet, as with loyalist sectarian killings, it might also be that less effort has been made to document their involvement than is the case with the IRA. According to Rosemary Sales, a women's branch of the UDA was disbanded after the torture and murder of Ann Ogilby by other loyalist women in 1974. But it is not clear that this event did in fact put an end to loyalist women's paramilitary organization, and a recent UDA publication describes how a group called Women's Action was founded in 1971, containing an inner circle "who directly involved themselves in active service on behalf of the UDA. They were used as couriers to move weaponry; supply 'safe' houses and on many occasions, were directly involved in all aspects of paramilitary activity." Although the influence of Women's Action diminished from the mid-1980s, the group still functions, and further study is needed on the general topic of violent loyalist women.[27] To date, information is sparse but suggestive. For instance, a few months after Ann Ogilby's death, the newspapers were intrigued by the "Murderous and racketeering activities"[28] of the UDA as revealed by one Louise Brittania Davey, who claimed to have been a UDA captain. Davey and her teenage daughter Jacqueline (photographed, fetchingly, in a mini-skirt, high leather boots, and brandishing a pistol) apparently went on the run, claiming to be fearful for their lives and willing to tell all. Loyalist sources eventually settled for dismissing them as deluded, but no such clemency was evident in the horrendous killings of Anne Marie Smyth and Margaret Wright in 1992 and 1994. These women were victims of circumstance, finding themselves in the wrong place at the wrong time, among sectarian sadists who, in Margaret Wright's case, were mistaken in thinking her a Catholic.

As Stallybrass and White point out, mainstream culture often accords special significance to socially peripheral and marginalized figures or groups. This is because elements excluded at the overt level of identity formation can readily become objects of desire that are also, simultaneously, frightening or objectionable. Consequently, a "complex hybrid fantasy" emerges "out of the very attempt to demarcate boundaries, to unite and purify the social collectivity".[29] For instance, tramps, prostitutes, servant girls, clowns and bandits are socially peripheral figures, but a great deal of imaginative energy has been expended in probing their symbolic significance and how they bring into view unacknow-ledged conflicts of value concealed by the regulatory practices of normal society. Despite a wide range of individual differences, paramilitary women have evoked a good deal of this kind of "hybrid fantasy", especially on the part of mainstream commentators. For instance, a sampling of newspaper reports from the early 1970s quickly shows how ambivalent is the fascination exerted by IRA "bomb girls", "gun girls", "party-trap girls", "terror girls", "IRA girls in jail", and even a vampish IRA "Mini Skirt Brigade".[30]

In 1975, Scotland Yard issued a press statement together with a photo-graph of a young, attractive woman, Margaret McKearney, describing her as an exceptionally dangerous terrorist. The main British news-papers immediately took up the story, and the *Daily Mirror* published a photograph, supposedly of McKearney, dramatically labelling her "the most dangerous woman in Britain". The *Irish Independent* also published the photograph with a similar caption: "The face of the most wanted woman in Britain", and the *Express* ran an article advising readers to "Consider this female of the species" but to "keep well clear. For Margaret McKearney is certainly more deadly than the male."[31] Mean-while, McKearney herself lost no time filing suits of libel, as did a certain Goretti Amanda Kennedy, whose photo also had been published and wrongly identified as this "most wanted woman". In the ensuing controversy over the authenticity of the Scotland Yard photograph and how it was obtained, we can see with painful clarity how crass and sensationalist was the prettifying of this supposedly dangerous terrorist in order to vilify her the more effectively. Moreover – all too predictably – the problem soon extended beyond the war of words, and the McKearney family had to be given police and army protection after a threat to their lives by the UVF. A month later, two people called McKearney were shot dead in Co. Tyrone, evidently "mistaken for Margaret's family, who lived in the same area", as Liz Curtis says.[32]

Something of Stallybrass and White's "hybrid fantasy" has surfaced even in the venerable precincts of Mr Justice McDermott's courtroom, where the judge extended an avuncular warning to certain "terror girls" (as the *Daily Mail* says), announcing that "You will be punished just like men." This view was, soon after, confirmed by Lord Justice Jones, who confided to another group, with perhaps a hint of regret: "the fact that you are women cannot operate in your favour".[33] Some months later, the *News Letter* announced that the army was now prepared to "shoot women terrorists". By way of explanation, we are assured that "In poor light conditions", and with "winter evenings coming in, it would be impossible to tell the sex of an attacker", and although soldiers would be "naturally reluctant to fire on a target clearly identified as a woman", a "spokesman" explains that "they would do so if their lives or those of their comrades were put in danger".[34]

In these examples, a patronizing sexism masquerades as chivalry, all too unaware of its own assumptions. Why would it have occurred to these Justices that the women would expect to be treated differently? Likewise, the ponderous explanations invoking poor light and uncertainty about the sex of an attacker barely conceal the prejudice lurking in "naturally": soldiers through the ages have "naturally" shot the men and spared the women, but not out of chivalrous regard; rather, the reverse. In short, the assurances that women will be treated equally are based on an assumption that they are really different.

In a newspaper article on "The Frightening Cult of the Violent Woman in Northern Ireland", Jane Gaskell[35] cites a prison psychiatrist who expands on this notion that men and women behave differently when they engage in violence, and that women's nature, in contrast to men's chivalry, is part of the reason. Men, we learn, "are brought up more or less within a framework of the accepted codes of warfare – honour, the decent treatment of the enemy once he surrenders". But, "Once women bring their more intense emotionalism to any cause, they tend to go too far" – that is, they don't know how to behave or how to play fair. Although the psychiatrist does notice that the codes of honour and decency governing men's violence are socially produced, he pays no attention to the repressions involved and to the fact that soldiers might not be so "decent" once they have *carte blanche* and there are no restraints on them. Also, women's "more intense emotionalism" (which, we are assured, is detrimental to "any cause") puts them beyond the pale because women get out of control and "pull out all the stops" in a manner that the psychiatrist then assures us is "fanatic". Here, Stally-brass and White's "hybrid fantasy" is entirely on the loose, but such tendentious and ambivalent imaginings do not come just from establishment sources. They are evident also, for instance, in the iconography of Mother Ireland so favoured by many nationalists and republicans.

Belinda Loftus's[36] study of this topic provides a mine of fascinating information backed by careful scholarship, surveying the elements combined and re-combined within the Mother Ireland complex – for instance, Celtic goddesses, the Virgin Mary, Liberty, Hibernia, Cathleen-ni-Houlihan, the poor old woman, and a range of stylized, often submissive, sentimentalized or aggressive figures. Loftus concludes that this iconography in general is "highly ambiguous" (82), and Mother Ireland and her entourage are "two-faced, both beautiful and horrific, subservient and manipulative". In short, the "boundary figures" we encounter here "are not clear and clean-cut", but are "dangerous" and "dirty", "fascinating and fearful" (86), fuelling exactly the crisis of values that Stallybrass and White describe. Not surprisingly, there is some controversy about whether or not Mother Ireland encourages and affirms Irish women's liberation, or whether the symbolism is promulgated and manipulated mainly by men "for their own solace" (76). That is, by depicting Ireland as a vulnerable maid, men can cast themselves as heroic rescuers; alternatively, when the mother calls her sons to arms and to the final sacrifice, the sons prove themselves worthy by rallying to her cause. Mother Ireland then becomes also a *pietà*, mourning the blood sacrifice of these surrogate Christs, as is especially clear in the iconography of the hunger strike of 1981. The ambivalence so tellingly described by Loftus becomes evident also in the interesting film *Mother Ireland*,[37] directed by Ann Crilly, when Bernadette McAliskey describes herself as "very much a child of Mother Ireland", and, by contrast, Mairead Farrell is contemptuous: "Mother Ireland get off our backs." At the end of her study, Loftus recounts a striking vignette from a book by Tim Pat Coogan, about how, during the "dirty protest" in Armagh jail, women Republican prisoners "framed in excrement their holy pictures of the Virgin", and "Protestant members of the prison-visitors committee were appalled" (86). Ambivalence is central to our reaction here, as in the other examples. Was the Virgin blasphemed or celebrated? Were the women identifying with traditional values, or showing themselves contemptuous of them? In short, is Mother Ireland a conservative or liberating figure for Irish women?

Clearly, the actual involvement in violence of such "ordinary women" as those interviewed by MacDonald and catalogued by Kirsta cannot easily be separated from the biased depictions of women's roles in the press, the lawcourts, and in enduring traditions of symbol, myth and religious practice. Nor can women easily extricate themselves from a subjectivity shaped and infused by such cultural forces and influences. As we have seen, McGuckian's poetry is interesting partly because hers is, above all, a liminal art, designed to provoke a crisis of evaluation, encouraging readers to reassess conventional representations of women through an active process of re-imagining. With this in mind, I would like now to consider, in conclusion, some further literary representations of women's involvement in violence during the Troubles, as a way of enabling us further to assess the interplay between some feminist principles and women's "discursively constituted" subjectivity, as Nicholson says.

Dealing with it: women and violence in Maurice Leitch, Jennifer Johnston and Nuala O'Faolain

Maurice Leitch's *Silver's City*[38] deals with an ideological split within loyalism, pitting an ageing folk hero, Silver Steele, against a new breed of young hard-men who are involved in racketeering and are controlled from afar by a businessman, referred to only as Mr Wonderful. Silver has spent time in jail, where he was renowned for his success in maintaining military discipline among his fellow loyalist prisoners. He also became well-read in revolutionary socialist literature, and the subsequent radicalizing of his opinions put him seriously at odds with the narrower perspectives of racketeering loyalist paramilitaries on the outside. At the start of the novel, Silver is abducted from his guarded hospital bed by his loyalist enemies (he is suffering from what seems to be a brain tumour and he has six months to live but doesn't know it). Partly by accident, he manages to escape, but he is hunted down and is forced to kill his assailant before handing himself over to the police, who have fruitlessly been trying to find him after his abduction.

Broadly, Leitch portrays developments within loyalism that have pitted a socialist faction (as I explained in Chapter 4) against a body of traditional grass-roots opinion that regards socialist intellectualism as the thin edge of a wedge that will lead to compromise with the enemy (not least, socialist elements of republicanism). Also, it is not difficult to feel something of the presence of Gusty Spence, the UVF folk hero and inspirer of the socialist policies espoused by the PUP, behind Leitch's portrait of Silver Steele, though the novel develops Silver's character independently.

In short, Leitch skilfully evokes an actual political situation, even while keeping it in the background as he focuses on the interactions between the ailing (and ageing) Silver, and the young Scotsman Ned Galloway, the hired assassin who tracks him down. At the start of the novel, Galloway is put in charge of Silver's abduction, and when Silver manages to escape, Galloway is held responsible. He is badly beaten and given orders to return to Scotland, but decides instead to find Silver, and the novel ends with their violent confrontation.

Throughout, Leitch creates an intense, claustrophobic world filled with betrayals and narrow, thwarted hatreds reminiscent of Graham

Greene. At the centre, is the relationship between Silver and Ned, but
the crucial link between the two men is a prostitute, Nan Harding. The
despicable Billy Bonner – dapper, vain, and dangerous – has orchestrated
Silver's abduction as well as the doorstep shooting with which the novel
begins, during which Galloway riddles with bullets a Catholic doctor
suspected of IRA sympathies. Bonner also runs the whorehouse where
Nan is in charge, and he verbally humiliates her before forcing her to
attend to the ill and depleted Silver. This sadistic treat forced upon Silver
is designed to humiliate the ailing hero, whom Bonner now relishes
having in his power. But Nan is a confused and inept masseuse, and
Silver is ill and unreceptive. In their shared vulnerability and humiliation, a moment's mutual sympathy passes between them, and on the
strength of it, Silver calls Nan for help when he escapes from Galloway.
She hides him, partly because she has "a lot of revenge left in her" (101)
and many scores to settle with the likes of Bonner. For his part, Silver
counts on what he takes to be her sentimentality – "soft, giddy bitch
that she was" (98) – but as their relationship develops, it is he who
softens, and he eventually trusts her enough to weep in her presence.
By contrast, she takes charge, and at one point makes an impassioned
feminist argument against violence, blaming it on men: "If you must
know, we're sick and tired of the lot of you, and all you stand for!" (142).
In response, Silver feels a sudden vindictive "urge to inflict hurt" (143),
but he also realizes that something new has been released in him by
Nan, and he reflects: "let that tap flow long and freely". At last, he puts
himself in her hands: "I'll take my chances – with you, Nan" (145).

   Ned Galloway is the counterpoise to Nan, and their eventual meeting
decides the story's outcome. Like her, Ned has been humiliated and
violated by Billy Bonner and his hirelings, and Ned also savours "dreams
of revenge" (132). Especially, he singles out a girl, Sharon McElwee,
for "the worst punishment of all" (115). Initially, along with two
young men, Sharon had been Galloway's accomplice in the abduction
of Silver. Galloway chose her partly because being a woman enabled
her "to move and act independently" (20), and partly because of her
dedication and resolve. When the policeman guarding Silver's room
is disarmed and bound by the kidnappers, they set about beating
him as Galloway watches, letting the youngsters get it out of their
system. He notices that the girl "was particularly vicious", but then,
he reminds himself, "they always were". Galloway eventually tells
them to lay off, but Sharon continues "in spite of him" (25), and he
slaps her to get her to desist, so that the group can make good its
escape.

Later, when Galloway is subjected to a "rompering" (150) for having let Silver get away, Sharon is among those who assault him, and she has a score to settle: "*That fucker hit me once!*' she shrieked, clawing at his cheeks, before the others threw her aside, for she interfered with their own careful workmanship. Towards the end, however, just as in the movies, the squaw was to have her way with him. While the others passed a bottle, she went for his face again" (114). When he is released, Galloway's hatred of Sharon combines with a ferocious misogyny (" he hated women, all women, and their ways" [115]), the consequences of which become all too evident in his threatening behaviour towards Mandy, the prostitute from whom he forces Nan's name, and also in the crude perfunctoriness of his sexual congress with the anonymous woman who is the mother of his child. When at last Galloway breaks into Nan's flat, eventually binding and torturing her into betraying Silver's whereabouts, the full, thwarted contempt fuelling his hatred flares obscenely. Afterwards, when Silver learns that Nan has betrayed him, he imagines he hears her laughter, and his own anger so enrages him that he musters the strength to kill Galloway, whose dying words are, "Not worth it. A huer....All of them...huers..." (179). As the novel ends, we leave Silver reflecting on the fact that "He had killed a man because of that laugh" (180).

The principal women in *Silver's City* are, then, a prostitute and a paramilitary fanatic, and throughout the novel men's attitudes to women are hostile and contemptuous. Here, presumably, Leitch wants to show how a violent male paramilitary culture entails the subjection of women. Admittedly, in Silver and Nan the beginnings of some better possibility faintly stir, but Nan is violently degraded yet again, so that she betrays Silver, who returns to his old macho resentment. Likewise, Sharon's competence and reliability are soon overwhelmed by her violence, and the mixture of hardness and vicious rage makes of her the cliché female terrorist so favoured by tabloid journalism. She is not imagined at all outside this narrow compass, and her main function in the novel is to intensify Galloway's sadistic misogyny through her own excessive, violent hatred.

Although the soft-hearted whore and the hard-hearted "terror girl" might at first seem equally stereotypical, Leitch gives Nan more complexity than Sharon, and the way in which the characters of Nan and Ned mirror one another is skilfully developed. By comparison, Sharon remains two-dimensional, reproducing the cliché characteristics of women terrorists and causing us hardly at all to re-examine these, or to imagine her as a person in the manner in which, for instance, Mac-

Donald has sought to show us is the case with her interviewees. Yet, as a whole, Leitch's gritty story of violence, betrayal and revenge does suggest that the sub-cultures of paramilitarism, thriving as they do on racketeering, intimidation and exploitation, are likely to reproduce the worst elements of violent male dominance. Certainly, there is no liberation for women in the world of *Silver's City*, but rather the reverse. Indeed, this point is made so unremittingly that we might detect in it a simplification of how complex the lives of violent women are in fact likely to be. And so in leaving us with a strong distaste for the way in which these bullying paramilitary gangsters treat women, Leitch may also leave us wondering whether or not other kinds of women, besides whores and fanatics, are likely to be engaged at all with the likes of Silver and his associates.

Jennifer Johnston's novel *Shadows on Our Skin*[39] has in common with *Silver's City* an older male character, now a burnt-out case, whose glory days as a paramilitary activist are all too readily romanticized, especially by himself. But whereas Leitch focuses on loyalist Belfast, Johnston deals with republican Derry, and whereas Silver Steele remains an imposing character despite his illness and vulnerability, the partly disabled, sentimental, bitter, manipulative, whining and self-indulgent father of young Joe Logan and his older brother Brendan, never manages to be more than pathetic. Unfailingly, he is reminded of just how contemptible he is by his embittered wife, who works outside the home to keep the family going and who is fiercely protective of her younger son, fearful that he might become involved in "the Movement" (18). By contrast, Brendan is a willing listener to his father's heroic stories of the IRA during the civil war, in which he was wounded. Partly in consequence, Brendan, who has just returned from England, soon gets involved with the IRA, in a capacity which remains unclear but which is hinted at in the repeated references to his new job as a lorry driver.

The sibling rivalry between Joe and Brendan is insightfully managed by Johnston as the older brother returns, usurping Joe's bed (as Joe knows he will) and otherwise polarizing the family. We never learn Joe's age, but he seems to be somewhere in his early teens, still at his mother's beck and call and dutifully performing domestic tasks to assist her, yet also independent enough to make friends with an older girl, for whom he feels a nascent erotic attraction though he does not quite identify it as such. Kathleen Docherty has been hired on a one-year contract as a teacher at a nearby school, and she is lonely. As she sits on a low wall and smokes, she strikes up a conversation with Joe, and they develop a friendship, eventually going on a picnic together. But

Brendan interferes, and is soon interested in Kathleen in a more mature way than his younger brother can manage.

Kathleen confides in Joe that her loneliness is caused partly by her separation from her fiancé, Fred Burgess, a British soldier stationed in Germany. She hopes to leave Ireland to marry him, but she is well aware that soldiers are hated by many people in Derry, and she asks Joe to keep her secret. In turn, as Brendan becomes increasingly soft on Kathleen, he tells her about his IRA activities. But Brendan has also discovered that he doesn't have the stomach for killing and is unable to use the gun with which the IRA has supplied him. Consequently, he plans to return to England, and he confides in Joe that he will perhaps take up with Kathleen there. Joe is upset, and angrily tells Brendan that Kathleen is already engaged, and, what's more, to a British soldier. Brendan lashes out at Joe, who then taunts him, knowing that the fear of being branded an informer makes Brendan vulnerable. Brendan wastes no time in leaving the country, but first he visits his IRA friends, who in turn visit Kathleen. How much Brendan tells them is unclear, but it would be enough if they knew of Kathleen's relationship to a British soldier, in whom she confides about her life in Derry while having a special friendship with a young boy from a republican family. Kathleen is beaten and her hair is cut, as Joe discovers when he goes to visit her in a panic of concern and remorse. She is in the final process of packing when Joe arrives, and before she gets into the taxi with her few belongings, she gives him a book of poetry, and kisses him. Then she is gone, and Joe returns home.

The contrasts and similarities between the victimization of Kathleen and the tribulations of Mrs Logan are central to the novel. Mrs Logan is bitter, partly because she is trapped – as she doesn't hesitate to proclaim, again directing her withering sarcasm at her husband's romanticized heroism: "Sit up above like Lord Muck with your stout and your betting slips telling us all what a great hero you were. You say you're crippled. What about me? With you chained round my neck for life?" (136). She is confined, that is, not just by the institution of marriage, but also by the violent ideology of a traditional republicanism that she never tires of condemning as escapist, contemptible and dangerous, and which she rejects as "fairy tales": "It's old buggers like you should be shot," she declares, "with your talk and your singing of glory and heroes" (154). Her beleaguered husband is no match for her: "Always the witty word" (15), he laments, lamely, as she rounds on him, and she is caustic even when he is silent: "Is he dead? Where is the hero's voice that should be calling my name?" (28).

Throughout, Mrs Logan is undaunted in her conviction that the violence and high-minded duplicities of republicanism have brought nothing but misery, not least to women like herself who must struggle to keep their families together in a world where the men are besotted by self-indulgent and destructive fantasies. It is no wonder that she wants to protect Joe and to save him from his father's ways, but also, we learn, she needs Joe's company "all the time", so that she "wouldn't have to be alone with his father. He was some sort of protection for her" (20). Joe's hatred of his father (blatantly declared in the first page of the novel) is therefore partly an expression of an unhealthy closeness to his mother, which in turn fuels the sibling rivalry that has such painful conse-quences. Mrs Logan, however, remains unremittingly formidable and hard: " 'She's a hard woman all right,' said the old man. 'I always told you that. A hard one. It's the only word for her. Hard' " (68). He is right, and his opinion is confirmed by the narrator, from whom we learn that "Her voice was as cold as the sleet outside" (18), and "The wind that blew across the Foyle in the winter was no colder than her voice" (78).

By contrast, Kathleen is to all appearances fragile and naive. She is alone in a culture in which she feels alienated, and she is in such need of companionship that she befriends a schoolboy. Her rootlessness is con-firmed as we – along with Joe – learn more about her. Her parents are dead, and she has no brothers or sisters. At one point, Joe finds himself wondering if she is a Protestant, and when he asks her she laughs: "My mother was. So how clever you are" (54). Her father, we are to assume, was Catholic, so that she is the product of a "mixed marriage". Even-tually, we learn that she is from Wicklow and with no experience of the North, drawn there merely by an obscure feeling that she might do some good. But her engagement to a British soldier ensures that she will be uncomfortable in a place where British soldiers are shot at and some-times killed. At the end, she is the innocent victim of a brutality she neither understands nor expects.

At first sight, Kathleen's vulnerability and powerlessness seem to com-plement and parallel the different kind of powerlessness represented by Mrs Logan. Yet, Mrs Logan's evident strengths notwithstanding, the parallel shows us also that the deepest virtues are Kathleen's. This is because Kathleen offers to cross so many of the boundaries confirming traditional enmities, and her status as mediator is to some extent impli-cit in the circumstances of her life. She has no particular family or tribal allegiance. Her parents are dead, but she has inherited from them the example of their mixed Protestant and Catholic marriage. She was born in the Republic but lives in Derry, a strongly nationalist city, even though she is engaged to marry a British soldier. In a non-dogmatic way she transgresses against traditional taboos and she is brutalized for doing so; none the less, she forgives Joe with some show of cheerfulness and sends him away with a gift, which is likely also to be a remembrance of the gift of herself. Joe, who is a budding poet, we are asked to believe will seek the words to express what Kathleen's friendship has really offered him. By analogy, Johnston has already found the words to force us to address this same question, and to place a high value on Kathleen's generosity and willingness to effect the liberative transgressions that involve crossing traditional boundaries that the violent are all too ready to re-confirm.

Still, one problem with Kathleen's characterization is that her function as mediator and scapegoat is developed at the expense of the kinds of detail that would enable us really to know her. We are given hardly any access to her inner life, and, for instance, at no point is it clear what she thinks she is doing when she befriends a schoolboy, inviting him to her flat and on a secret picnic. When they get soaked, she brings him home and tells him to go to the bathroom and take off his clothes so that she can dry them. Brendan also is present, and Kathleen gives Joe an overcoat to wear when he removes his wet clothes. She herself is by now clad only in a dressing gown. An erotic component here is hard to miss, but Kathleen seems unaware of it, and we wonder how she could be so naive as to think nothing is awry, or whether she does perhaps have a crush on the boy. If we decide the former, then Kathleen looks silly; if the latter, the novel should give us some insight into this complexity in her character. As it is, her attitude to Joe is oddly indefinite, and is matched by a peculiar uncertainty in how he also is depicted. Indeed, a teenager might oscillate between adult and childish kinds of behaviour, but too often Joe seems like two different people, not because his teenage volatility is convincingly depicted, but because the plot needs him to appear sometimes as a schoolboy and at others as a young adult on the edge of his first love affair. In short, Johnston's design is often intricate, and the moral complexity of the situation at the end of the novel is compelling, but the inner life, especially of these two central characters, is thinly developed. This is a point of some significance, not least because a close personal knowledge of individuals is the very means of the mediation for which Kathleen stands, and which the novel sees as exemplary.

All in all, in *Shadows on Our Skin* Johnston provides a telling critique of a violent male culture and of women's subjection within it, and she shows how women resist on two main fronts. The first is Mrs Logan's clear-headed criticism of her husband's false heroics and her determination to protect Joe from the influence of the IRA. The second is Kathleen's unselfconsciously brave mediation, which would destabilize traditional oppositions, and her generosity of spirit. Each woman perhaps needs something of what the other has, but together they make a difference to Joe, who, as we leave him, has developed under their influence a conscience that we feel will enable him to grow, and also prevent him from following in the violent footsteps of his father and brother.

The reconciling efficacy of personal knowledge and how it challenges the simplifications on which prejudice thrives, is central also to Nuala O'Faolain's autobiographical memoir, *Are You Somebody?* [40] This bravely confessional, intellectually bracing book manages to be at once rebellious and conformist, catching the ethos of a repressive mid-century Irish culture as it changed rapidly in the 1960s, and then again in the 1970s under the influence of the feminist movement.

O'Faolain's education (convent school, University College Dublin, Oxford), and her employment (BBC, RTE, *Irish Times*) mark a conventional path to a successful and admirable career. Partly because she shaped this career in such a fashion, her story mirrors some ways in which public institutions have come (however unevenly) to acknowledge the right of women to participate, whereas a generation previously, this would not have been so. Yet *Are You Somebody?* is also the record of an emotionally chaotic life, frequently painful, confused and unstable, and O'Faolain struggles throughout to find some adequate containing form – work, love, books, writing – to stabilize or at least make manageable an ever-threatening chaos. One unexpected consequence of the book for O'Faolain herself, as she tells us in an erratic but interesting "Afterwords" added to the 1997 edition, is that many readers saw their own experience reflected in her sheer struggle with loneliness and in the emotional duress about which she was willing to be honest and which she is able also to express convincingly.

As one of nine children raised by an alcoholic mother and an often absent father who had an eye for other women, an inclination to domestic violence, and not much conscience about providing consistently for his family, O'Faolain grew up under considerable stress. At puberty she rebelled, resorting to petty theft to enable her to go to dances and to meet boys, and at thirteen she discovered, "I was supposed to be bad" (30). Her father sold his car and sent her to boarding school, an event that she credits with changing her life, but the insecurities, emotional deprivation and dysfunctional elements of her early upbringing left marks that were not to go away, and with which she wrestles throughout her story. Her embrace of feminism then becomes part of the difficult process of dealing with fears and insecurities that had already shaped her in ways beyond her control. In short, her personal confusions, together with the ideological complexities of feminism (or a range of feminisms), ensure that no straightforward transformation occurs, but rather a process of re-evaluation conducted on several fronts and in particular contexts, themselves often fraught and unstable. O'Faolain catches this sense of tentative advancement when she suggests that "unconsciousness was the condition that allowed the culture I grew up in to exist. When change did come, about a decade later, the fog I had been wandering in was so dense that it took me ages to make my way half-out of it. Which is where I am now" (92).

Such a condition of complex pre-involvement and uncertain progress is registered throughout by a re-creation of experiences densely enough realized for us to understand the exigencies of her struggle, as well as its achievements and incompleteness. Like McGuckian, O'Faolain therefore resists simplifying her encounter with feminism, acknowledging herself to be inconsistent and at times expedient. Thus, at one point she explains how two liaisons with men were "almost case studies in the limitations of my supposedly raised and feminised consciousness" (146), and about one of these relationships she admits, bluntly: "I didn't want to respond to the feminist call to self-respect. I wanted to know Harry, and the conditions of knowing him were not negotiable" (149). Yet, elsewhere she is equally blunt in denouncing the sins of patriarchy, whether the "ingrained" misogyny that has refused properly to acknowledge Katherine Maloney's care of Patrick Kavanagh (76), the ignoring of women academics at University College Dublin (89), the alarming objection to her proposed marriage (which didn't occur) in the form of a letter – a "document from the patriarchy" – written by her grandfather (120), the neglect of women in the *Field Day Anthology of Irish Literature* (111), the lack of equality between men and women even in the bohemian environment of her student days (63), and so on. Clearly, feminism is important to O'Faolain, but the means by which feminist principles infuse and change an individual are also represented as subtle and indirect.

This indirection in turn is reproduced in the style by which O'Faolain describes and deals with her emotional volatility, evident not least in the welter of difficult and broken relationships through the course of her life. She recognizes how, at convent school, she was already "a confused and emotional exhibitionist" (23), but even at the end of her story this early confusion and exhibitionism are not entirely expunged: "What can I do, when everything is so various, and so beyond me, but cling on, and thank the God I don't believe in for the miracles showered on me?" (238). This sentence – the final one of the "Afterwords" section – holds something still of the exhibitionist "creeping self-pity" (197) that elsewhere O'Faolain realizes she needs to fend off, and which she mentions as a special liability of hers (216). Yet her writing is at its best when she encounters and struggles with this very liability – that is, when she manages simultaneously to catch us up in her emotional turmoil while also correcting its excess, so that the book itself achieves (however intermittently) the equilibrium between feeling and understanding that has been so elusive in her life.

An example is the wonderful early section about "dafties" – as junior girls at the convent school were called when they had crushes on admired seniors. The emotions experienced by dafties were "volatile and exaggerated", but, O'Faolain insists, "they were not trivial. They were a grounding in the affective dimension that was to matter most to us all our lives" (33), and they entailed "learning appropriateness, learning control, learning to differentiate our selves from the other selves around" (34). As an adult, O'Faolain resents the stigma attached to these intense but innocent sublimations, and she is also aware that the perspective provided by critical reflection after the passage of years can sometimes intensify rather than diminish the poignancy of what happened. Thus, she describes how on two occasions she stole from other girls' cubicles to bring gifts to "my heroine". She did so because "I had to. I had no money. I didn't take them for myself – just to give to her. And I think that she may have known. And that the nuns knew, and never came out with it" (35). When she left the convent, she harboured "furtive resentments against it" (36), but when she returns after 30 years, hoping to pay a brief anonymous visit, she is immediately recognized and welcomed by the nun whom she had once seen as especially formidable, and who now remembers her name and age exactly and without hesitation. When Mother Dorothea kisses her goodbye, "I ran out and got into the car, and bent over the steering-wheel, crying too hard to drive." Later, she phones a friend, Marian, to unburden herself of her new-found understanding of her old teacher. "Our first revisionist" (37), Marian replies.

A lot is going on here, and this is O'Faolain at her best, struggling as she does throughout the book to order but not anaesthetize an emotional excess which is itself a symptom of a profound woundedness. The learning of "appropriateness" which she commends at a later time clearly did not come to her easily, because, as a daftie, she stole from other girls. The "appropriateness" here was on the part of the un-named heroine and the nuns who let the matter pass, a delicate decision, the fruits of which were borne only much later when O'Faolain came to suspect that these people had saved her embarrassment, probably because they recognized her own selfless intentions. Yet even as an adult, she is not proof against the torrent of emotion that overwhelms her as she leaves the nuns, and her sensitivity here is not unadmirable, even if it duplicates the excess of her feelings as a young girl. At this point, Marian provides the required "appropriateness", with the wry remark about revisionism, but O'Faolain the author has seen fit to let Marian have the last word, so that the writing manages to contain the emotional excess it describes, and in a manner that heightens the charge for a reader of this interesting episode.

Throughout her book, O'Faolain struggles repeatedly to find this kind of balance, whereby an emotional energy on the edge of chaos is quenched and given form by the writing. Thus, she describes how, on her return to Ireland, she "was a walking swamp of emotion" in contrast to the "ironic people" (160) around, whose perspective helps to put her right, and the corrective offered by the ironists is duplicated in the description itself by her own ironic estimate of what was going on. Again, she is moved and excited when she visits Derry, where she is to make a film: "I had never been anywhere so exotic" (137). But when a knowledgeable colleague later laughs at the film (without further comment), "that laughter", she says, "was the beginning of real watchfulness in me" (139). Later, when she visits Nell McCafferty's family home, also in Derry, she again cannot help an initial, sentimental reaction, which is soon followed by disenchantment: "At first, I sentimentalized it all. Then I felt an outsider to it" (191). The event that did much to check the initial sentiment occurred when she participated in a debate at the Guildhall on the topic of feminism and nationalism. Her position, in the name of feminism, was against violence: "I said feminism was about human development and was therefore incompatible with killing." She went on then to argue that the armed struggle had impeded the progress of women's rights in Ireland, and while she spoke, Bernadette McAliskey "prowled up and down on the platform behind me, rolling pieces of paper into balls and flicking them sharply at my back" (191). She was soon attacked verbally by the partisan audience, and was spat on as she left the building. But when she returned to the McCafferty house, the family "were the soul of tact" (192), and did not pursue her on a point about which, we are led to suppose, Nell must have felt something the same as the riled Bernadette.

I conclude with this example because it brings us back to feminism and violence, and to an understanding of how the antagonisms on which violence thrives are inevitably oversimplifications of real and complex human relationships. Nell McCafferty is likely to have had a good deal of sympathy with the Guildhall crowd, but in the circumstances she chooses to put this difference aside in the interests of another kind of human concern. The picture remains mixed, and the writing renders a sense of intricate connectivity, neither too much sentimentalized nor too clearcut. The discernment evident here is itself part of a continuing case of feminism against violence, the topic of the debate, in which intense emotion led to outright antagonism. The writing therefore does better than the Guildhall crowd because O'Faolain's disarming circumspection breaks the chain of mutual recrimination, thereby making particular sense of the way in which the personal is indeed political.

In broad terms, I have no difficulty accepting that feminism and violence are incompatible, if only because violence destroys human happiness and impedes human development through the mechanisms I have described in previous chapters. But one main point of this book is that, within history, none of us is entirely free from complicity in violence if only because we are always already compromised and pre-involved in political situations that entail the use of force, and which are, consequently, a mark of our imperfection. By and large, feminists point out that women ought especially to understand the means by which oppressive controls are exercised, and to suggest strategies of resistance and of transformation that would liberate women and men alike. It will not do to insist on essential differences between men and women in a manner that would naturalize male dominance, nor will it do to stress the sameness of women and men in a manner that would encourage women merely to join the men's world and to "compete on equal terms", especially when these equal terms entail violence.

Still, as I have argued, women who turn to political violence are far from being a homogenized group, even though they are often depicted in stereotypical ways. Not surprisingly, the stereotypes may in turn have a shaping force on the subjectivity of women themselves, and the results, in individual cases, can be complex. As Nicholson says, the self is "discursively constituted", reflecting the multi-faceted realities of actual people in real situations. It seems, therefore, at the very least to be prudent to posit a historically situated subjectivity in order to avoid the extremes of logocentric arrogance and of a merely incoherent *jouissance*. Such an understanding of the subject might then, as Butler says, enable the assumption of particular critical positions aimed at destabilizing the normalizing categories by which hegemonic control is perpetuated.

As I have suggested, literature is a highly effective agent in this kind of destabilization, undermining the architectonic clarities of the "normal" by an imaginative displacement that allows the intimacies of personal knowledge to envelop, enmesh, and deconstruct the stricter simplicities by which control is regulated. Not surprisingly, feminist theorists have looked especially to literature as a means of challenging patriarchal culture, and I have offered a selection of literary examples to explore some different relationships of women to political violence. With varying degrees of success and from a range of perspectives, these examples can in turn show how imagination is a means by which we might come both to know the grounds of an implicit incompatibility between feminism and violence, while also acknowledging the compromised subject positions actual women occupy, so that this incompatibility is not always clear, or the way forward obvious. As if in reply to Nuala O'-Faolain's question, "Are you somebody?" Monique Wittig offers the assurance that "one can become *someone*," but not without difficulty and compromise. In conclusion, it is worth noting that the iron circle by which violence effects its continuance – as, for instance, in *Silver's City* – is challenged by Kathleen's generosity and forgiveness in *Shadows on Our Skin*, and also, at the end, by O'Faolain, who finds herself addressing herself spontaneously about her parents:

> "Forgive them," I heard myself saying to myself, "the same way you forgive yourself, for the same reasons you forgive yourself."
> And with that – a tiny moment but a true one – something inside me, that had been agitated for as long as I could remember, went quiet.   (237)

McGuckian's compassion, and the injunctions to forgiveness in Johnston's novel and in O'Faolain's memoir point us in the same direction, towards a leap of faith, confirming a higher morality that alone can break the entail of the iron circle. But forgiveness is a difficult notion and easily misunderstood, as we shall see in the next chapter.

6
Breaking the Circle

"Pardon like rain": John Hewitt, Gordon Wilson and others

John Hewitt, whose poem "The Iron Circle" helped us in Chapter 2 to describe the core mechanisms of violence, elsewhere provides an account of how the cycle of revenge and recrimination might be broken. He does this especially in *The Bloody Brae*, a dramatic poem for six voices written in 1936, broadcast in 1954 and published in *Threshold* magazine in 1957.[1] In a manuscript poem dated 1969, Hewitt remarks that although he wrote the piece "over forty years ago", still "Four decades on, the heartbreak's relevant."[2]

The Bloody Brae deals with the consequences of a "legendary and largely fictitious event" at Islandmagee in 1642, in which Cromwellian soldiers massacred Catholics. Hewitt imagines that one of the soldiers, John Hill, now an old man, seeks the ghost of a young woman he killed and from whom he wants to ask forgiveness. At first, Hill is dissuaded from his search by another ghost – that of his erstwhile fellow soldier, Malcolm Scott – who feels no remorse about his own part in the killing and is dismissive of Hill's self-recrimination. But Hill persists, and at last he meets the ghost of Bridget Magee, to whom he expresses sorrow and regret. She offers him forgiveness, but reminds him also of his continuing responsibility, exhorting him to the difficult task of conveying his hard-won knowledge to others, who in all likelihood will be disinclined to accept it.

Hewitt's treatment of the mechanisms of violence in *The Bloody Brae* clearly recalls "The Iron Circle"; thus, he has John Hill protest that "Hate follows on hate in a hard and bitter circle" (408), and, in a Girardian moment, Hill explains that the stratagem of justifying violence by blaming others for starting it – thereby "seeking the primal wrong" (407) – is seductive but treacherous. Scott, however, thinks otherwise, and accuses Hill of negligence for forgetting "who began the murder" (408), going on then to state his own preference for "swords and stirrups" (410) over what he takes to be Hill's foolish sentimentality.

Much of this will strike us as familiar: violence is circular; it depersonalizes the victim, who becomes a representative of a hated outsider group; it hardens the perpetrators, who point to a prior wrong to excuse their search for a scapegoat. Yet the antidote is set out simply and directly in Hill's response to Scott: "we should have used Pity and Grace to break the circle". Predictably, Scott is contemptuous – "This talk of circles is like a juggler with rings" (408) – but Hill insists, recommending forgiveness as a "golden light" which is also "the water of life" (409). When Scott at last leaves, thinking Hill crazy, Bridget Magee appears and Hill again moves swiftly to the point: "I only ask for pardon," he says, and then confesses, "I murdered pity when I murdered you, / and reason and mercy and hope for this vexed land." He realizes that mercy and kindness should have had a chance "to weave together the broken halves of this land, / to throw his shuttle across the separate threads, / and make us a glittering web for God's delight", but instead, a "sword-thrust" has "made our opposition for ever" (411). On hearing this, Bridget feels pity, explaining in turn how her initial anger faded through time, and how she also has come to realize that bitterness stunts life and growth. She assures Hill that "Pardon like rain must fall on every face / that's lifted up towards it" (413), but she reminds him that he must take his message to the world, "till, here and there by chance, one turn from his place / among the living to beg your strength and aid" (415). She warns also against the excessive introspection induced by Hill's solitude ("you should have stormed singing through this land, / crying for peace and forgiveness"), and she reminds him that "every moment is the time for mercy" (414). As she leaves, she tells him, simply: "John Hill, as the woman you murdered, I forgive you" (415).

The solution then is clear: the iron circle is broken by forgiveness, which enables reconciliation, and the consequent experience of release is depicted in language suggesting spontaneity ("every moment is the time for mercy"), fluidity ("water of life"), and radiance ("a glittering web"), all of which stand opposed to the hardness of the stones, swords and military accoutrements recommended by Scott. The images here carry the burden of Hewitt's judgement, but the value of Bridget Magee's forgiveness lies also in the poignancy we feel, the rightness, after all, of this higher morality that Scott correctly says is "over my head" (408).

Yet, the poetry convinces us, not least because it also reminds us that the inclination to revenge does not yield easily to appeals for mercy, and although Bridget Magee says that anger and hatred are debilitating, it must be left to her to say this, and if she had continued to be unforgiving about the murder of her child, we would understand. It is natural that she should feel anger, and we would be likely to feel it ourselves, or at least we could not be sure that we would not. In short, there is something incalculable (and uncalculating) about forgiveness, which is part of its mystery and challenge, and because this is so, we cannot prescribe it. As Charles Williams says, it is impossible for a writer to lay down the rules either for himself or for others on this topic; rather, "The only safe place to find it is in those writers who have been able to put it in undeniable phrases – especially the poets." For Williams, "Great poets" write effectively about forgiveness because "they understand everything", and so do the saints because "they are united with everything".[3] Certainly, in *The Bloody Brae* Hewitt confirms Williams's point about the difficulty of prescription, even as he also seeks to render imaginatively the cleansing and life-enhancing energies that are released when forgiveness is sought, extended and accepted.

Hewitt therefore does as Williams suggests, appealing for our assent to the liberation brought by forgiveness and reconciliation, which are elusive to prescription and which he shows us through imagery and narrative. Still, there is a significant omission in Hewitt's account. The fact that John Hill is repentant from the start leaves open the difficult question of whether or not his victim might have forgiven him had he not shown remorse – a matter of no small relevance to victims of violence in general. What, then, can we say about forgiving the unrepentant, or those who have caused great harm anonymously, and whom we cannot meet or confront?

When ex-Sergeant McConkey, who was maimed by an IRA bomb and whose plight I described in Chapter 2, says, "If I was put face to face with the people who did it I would shoot them. . . . I'm not religious and can't forgive,"[4] I, at any rate, am inclined to say, fair enough. I would hope the ex-Sergeant would not in fact shoot anybody, and I believe that doing so would not help, for the reasons John Hewitt (among others) provides. But ex-Sergeant McConkey was all-but destroyed by the bomb designed to kill him, and no one should expect him to forgive – least of all those who believe in forgiveness and who hope that he might discover its benefits. So also with Ethel Allen, whose son Philip was killed by loyalist extremists in 1998, possibly because he had a cross-community friendship with Damien Trainer, who also was killed in the same attack. One year after her son's death, Mrs Allen made clear how she feels about the killers: "No, I could never forgive them. I hear people talk of forgiveness, but I could not forgive them. I hope to see them suffer the way they made us suffer."[5] Again, no one should expect this bereaved mother to think otherwise. Yet the most famous case in Northern Ireland's recent history of a person in fact thinking otherwise is that of Gordon Wilson, whose 20 – year-old daughter Marie was killed at the Enniskillen Remembrance Day ceremonies in 1987, when an IRA bomb collapsed a wall near the War Memorial, killing 11 people and injuring 63. The atrocity and its aftermath have been chronicled by Denzil McDaniel,[6] who provides a compelling account of the reactions and coping strategies by which the victims, their families, and the broader community strove to manage this shocking and traumatizing event.

Gordon Wilson was a local draper who had attended the ceremony with his daughter. When the bomb exploded and the wall collapsed, Marie was buried under the rubble. Gordon also was trapped, but was soon released, sustaining some minor injury to his left shoulder. Marie fared less well, and after she was freed from the rubble and transported to Erne hospital, she died.

Enniskillen quickly became the centre of international attention, and in the turmoil following the death of his daughter, Gordon Wilson was interviewed by Mike Gaston of the BBC. Gordon's wife Joan recalls how bravely he "gathered himself" (63), and how simply he told his story, not realizing the effect it would have. He recounts how, as he lay under the rubble, his daughter grasped his hand:

It was Marie. Marie said, "Is that you, Daddy?"
I said, "Yes."
"Are you all right, Daddy?" she asked.
I said, "I'm fine."
    Three or four times I asked her if she was all right and each time she replied, "I'm fine, how are you?" I said, "Hold on. They will be coming to have us out soon". Then she said, "Daddy, I love you very much." That was the last thing she said. I have lost my daughter, and we shall miss her. But I bear no ill will, I bear no grudge. Dirty sort of talk is not going to bring her back to life. She was a great wee lassie. She was a pet and she's dead. She's in Heaven and we'll meet again. Don't ask me, please, for a purpose. I don't have an answer. But I know there has to be a plan... it's part of a greater plan, and God is good. And we shall meet again.   (64)

One feels in the simplicity and directness of these words a distillation produced by an all-but intolerable pressure. The opening exchange in direct speech is spare, suggesting lucidity, quiet urgency and tender concern as father and daughter hold on, carefully yet in great peril. Then come the words which he now knows are her last. But the change of register, as she switches from the repeated "I'm fine, how are you?" to the avowal of love, suggests also that she knew then that something very serious was happening to her, and she was saying goodbye but without wanting to alarm him. This opening part of the interview is plain and dignified, unselfconsciously tender and unflinchingly direct.

The words that follow, in which the bereaved father reflects on his loss, contain the striking and challenging statement that lies at the heart of the matter: "But I bear no ill will, I bear no grudge." Wilson's self-consciousness and clarity are not in question, as we can judge from the preceding part of his statement, and this is no febrile outburst, no momentary idealism or heroic pose. The following sentence, "Dirty sort of talk is not going to bring her back to life," indicates a deliberate refusal to speak hatred, which he knows will only mire him further in the thing he already abhors. Instead, he offers further words expressing familiarity and restraint ("great wee lassie", "a pet"), and his final sentences turn to religion, but he admits a bewilderment that prevents complacency: "Don't ask me, please, for a purpose. I don't have an answer."

Gordon Wilson did not offer the media its usual fare, but his interview was described at the time as a "world stopper" (64) by Gerry Burns, the Clerk and Chief Executive of the Fermanagh District Council. Wilson's words were indeed so powerfully moving that he rapidly became a minor celebrity. In 1993 he accepted a seat in the Irish Senate, and he lectured widely and worked energetically to promote peace and non-violence. In 1993 he met secretly with the IRA leadership, and Joan explains that he, like herself, "just wanted to confront them face to face, to show them what they had done and ask them to stop" (151). But, as Joan goes on to say, this meeting exhausted him, and he seemed "deflated and defeated" (152) when he returned, realizing that he had made little impression on his interlocutors. In 1995, Gordon Wilson died at home, alone, of a heart attack.

I have offered some account of this now famous interview partly because from the printed version alone it is initially hard to see what made it a "world stopper". The simplicity and unaffectedness are cer-tainly admirable, and the combinations of lucidity and tenderness, familiarity and restraint, dignity and tact, are moving. But the power of the interview cannot be adequately assessed without taking into consideration Wilson's unselfconsiousness in a moment of great suffering and vulnerability. In this context, his declaration that he bears no ill will and harbours no grudge is as luminous as it is unexpected, expressing an immense integrity and magnanimity. Consequently, we respond not only to the words, but to a quality of the man that the event as a whole brings out. If, as Williams says, poets and saints can best tell us about forgiveness, then Gordon Wilson's saintliness is what strikes us rather than his poetry, and the contrast with John Hewitt's *The Bloody Brae* is easy to see. But, as I have mentioned, a complicating factor within this contrast arises from the fact that Hewitt has his guilty soldier seek forgiveness, whereas the IRA members whom Gordon Wilson met face to face remained dedicated to violence. Also, we might notice that Wilson did not exactly forgive his daughter's killers; he said only that he bore no ill will, no grudge. In short, even in this exemplary instance, forgiveness is not unproblematic, as becomes increasingly clear the closer we look.

As Alf McCreary explains, Wilson was deeply troubled by the problems and complexities attendant upon forgiveness, deciding eventually that human beings can only try to do their best while acknowledging that "the last word rests with God". But even though Wilson himself did well in the famous BBC interview, he did not find much peace of mind, and seven weeks afterwards he became so distraught that he lost his memory for a period of approximately 24 hours, and was hospitalized.[7] Something of his perplexity is evident also in his repudiation both of those who said he forgave the IRA ("I did not mention the word 'forgiveness' ") and also of those who stressed that he had held back ("the press have produced headlines suggesting that Gordon Wilson is unforgiving, which I'm not").[8] Although his carefully worded statement to the IRA, printed in *The Times* on 21 March 1993, is unambivalent ("when I expressed my forgiveness for my daughter Marie's killers"; "What I meant to do in expressing forgiveness"; "in extending Christian forgiveness"),[9] we might feel that Wilson is bent here on claiming the high moral ground in preparation for the meeting that he hoped would occur with the IRA.[10] Certainly, taken together, these painful vacillations can suggest how difficult and imperfect the process of forgiveness might be, shaped and experienced in unpredictable ways according to circumstances, and despite the best intentions.

Understandably, for some of those bereaved or injured at Enniskillen, the attitude exemplified by ex-Sergeant McConkey and Mrs Allen predominated, and for some, Gordon Wilson's speech, together with his celebrity, were offensive. One of the injured, Jim Dixon, admitted: "It annoyed me badly to hear that he forgave the IRA. What right had he? It was obnoxious" (131). Likewise, on hearing that Wilson had met with the IRA, Aileen Quinton's initially cautious judgement about the interview (she pointed out that "He never said he forgave" [124]) hardened considerably: "I felt nauseous, that somehow I had been contaminated" (150). Denzil McDaniel notices that "A number of people around Enniskillen also privately belittle" (131) Gordon Wilson, but few will say so publicly. It is not surprising that some of those who did make their opinions known latched on to the idea that forgiveness cannot be extended to a person who does not repent. Thus, Joe Kennedy repeats Aileen Quinton's point that you cannot forgive someone who is not sorry: "Don't ask me about forgiveness – it's not relevant. I believe there is no forgiveness without repentance" (124). Partly in response to opinions like these, a local Presbyterian minister, the Reverend David Cupples, preached a sermon on forgiveness five weeks after the bombing, and he faced the issue squarely:

> The debate also rages in the Christian Church about whether you can forgive people before they repent. I believe if we are to follow the example of Jesus, we must offer forgiveness unconditionally. But the person who has committed the injury cannot actually have an experience of forgiveness unless they admit that they have done something wrong.   (124)

That is surely correct, if the challenge of Christ's cross is to be taken seriously. Indeed, as Williams also says, pardon cannot fully exist until there is mutual acceptance, but the injured party must none the less extend forgiveness, "waiting for the second's opportunity"[11] to make it perfect through reciprocation, in the lightning flash of truth that Hewitt describes. Otherwise, the iron circle maintains its grip and within its confines the spectres of resentment, fear and loathing remain, as always, hungry for blood.

A recent publication edited by Paddy Monaghan and Eugene Boyle, *Adventures in Reconciliation: Twenty-Nine Catholic Testimonies*,[12] confirms what we have so far seen about forgiveness as a means of liberation, and provides also a useful complement to McDaniel's book on Enniskillen. Among other things, these testimonies confirm that Gordon Wilson – his singularity and celebrity notwithstanding – is not alone in refusing to hate those who harmed him.

In 1996, soon after he had graduated from Queen's University, Michael McGoldrick was shot dead by loyalist paramilitaries in the aftermath of the "Drumcree Standoff" (37). His father, also Michael, describes the shock, anger and suffering that followed upon his son's murder, and how those overwhelming feelings were at last released when he found himself able to forgive. "I felt that, despite the agony we were going through, God had given me a message of peace, forgiveness and reconciliation" (38), and with this came "freedom and release" (39). Yet the way ahead was not easy for Michael McGoldrick, and he fell into a depression, a "deep despair" (39) which in turn was alleviated as he came to realize that God forgave him as he forgave others. McGoldrick then immersed himself in volunteer work, collecting and shipping food and clothing to the Ukraine and Romania, happy to "give my life to loving God and serving His people" (41).

A similar story is told by Harry McCann, who had both legs blown off by a car bomb. McCann's first words on recovering consciousness were, "May God forgive the people who did this to me," and he describes himself as "finding myself saying" these words as if the utterance were not entirely within his control. As the ambulance rushed him to hospital he again heard "in a faraway, almost objective kind of way" some further words: "Father, forgive them for they know not what they do" (134). Once more, the impulse to forgive seemed to come from a source outside himself, and he continued to live in the conviction that people who have been hurt are easily "eaten up with thoughts of revenge" (135), but that forgiveness alone liberates. Like Michael McGoldrick, Harry McCann subsequently directed his energies back to the community, volunteering to chauffeur elderly people and becoming active as a lay Catholic leader with a cross-community commitment.

Tom Kelly is unlike McCann and McGoldrick, both of whom were innocent victims. Kelly is a convicted IRA activist who spent 10 years in jail. In a brief account of his paramilitary career, he explains how, when he fired his first shot at the British Army, he experienced for the first time in his life a sense of "absolute power", and "The adrenalin raced through me." He then became so "consumed" by violence that his friends "began to see a psycho on the loose" (121). Kelly describes himself as fearless, detached, and bitter, setting his course on "a self-destruct journey of retaliation" (123). After he was released from prison in 1982 he got a job as secretary of a Republican Club, but felt he was "being handled like a puppet" (125), under constant supervision by the IRA.

The combination here of sudden intoxication, dramatically narrowed horizons, and increasing psychological derangement will strike us as familiar, and Kelly describes himself as feeling like a puppet – a simplified, mechanized thing – as long as he remained associated with the paramilitaries. Eventually, his wife invited him on a pilgrimage to Mount Mellaray and he agreed to go, but only after he had accompanied her there several times did he seriously ask himself why he was doing this. The answer came through a conversion experience as a result of which, Kelly says, his "old ways of thinking were completely obliterated" (125). This experience was partly penitential, and subsequently he felt "all the bitterness and resentment" leave him (126). Afterwards, he began working to promote interdenominational and cross-community reconciliation, and by and by he met and befriended an ex-UVF man, with whom, some time later, he was invited to the House of Lords and to the making of a documentary for Dutch television.

These testimonies are provided by what are sometimes known as "Evangelical Catholics"; that is, Catholics who are part of the Charismatic Renewal Movement which occurred in the wake of the Second Vatican Council (1962–5). In the words of Cardinal Daly, this movement has given many Catholics "a new love for and familiarity with Holy Scripture, a newly-felt personal experience of Jesus Christ as their Lord and Saviour, a new experience of the presence and power of the Holy Spirit in the Church and in their personal lives" (12). By and large, the 29 stories collected and edited by Monaghan and Boyle conform to Daly's general description, bearing witness especially to the liberating effects of forgiveness. Certainly, there is no reason to disbelieve that the lives of Michael McGoldrick, Harry McCann and Tom Kelly were changed as they say, as is confirmed by the kind and quality of work that each undertook subsequently. As the mystics insist, a claim to special spiritual experience is substantially judged from the works that flow from it. The "lightning flash" – the moment of higher understanding that seems spontaneous because it is inexplicable and somehow unmerited – is therefore a breakthrough also to a higher morality, a new way of behaving that could not be deduced from its antecedents. As Williams says, poets and saints tell us important things about forgiveness, and, as with Gordon Wilson's interview, the Catholic testimonies come from saintly rather than poetic sources. These people's lives become, as it were, the poem; by contrast, poets may all too easily relapse into an unsaintly worldliness, having achieved the perfection of language which is a writer's chief goal, rather than the perfection of life. But what, then, might poets give us that saints do not (except in rare cases where the saint is also a poet, as, say, with John of the Cross)?

True complexity of experience in the form of words is one answer: as George Steiner[13] says, poetry – like literature in general – records the particularity of our meetings with others, catching especially a sense of the "alien which we come up against in the labyrinth of intimacy"; the mystery, that is, of "the *terra incognita* of our own selves" and the "inviolate enigma of the otherness in things" even as we are drawn into communion with them. "All aesthetics, all critical and hermeneutic discourse", is then an attempt "to clarify the paradox and opaqueness of that meeting as well as its felicities". Indeed, as Steiner says, we are not to ignore the alien and opaque, but through the "felicities" of art we can also discover an affinity for what we thought was different, a reconciliation with the alien and a compassion growing from our experience of the plight of others as partly our own. Thus, "Without the arts, form would remain unmet and strangeness without speech in the silence of the stone."

In previous chapters I have argued that the stoniness of our mute separations from one another is effected and confirmed especially by violence; here I want also to suggest that this stoniness can be alleviated by the "felicities" of which Steiner speaks, not just in the aesthetic realm, but in the kinds of moral renovation to which, for instance, Hewitt points us. Yet, Steiner is correct in reminding us that our reconciliations are never final in the vast complexity of the world, and in our meetings with one another, however intimate, some strangeness persists, some opaque residue that ensures our discontent, moving us to seek some further communion and understanding. Even the saints who have had special experiences of the oneness of all things in God cannot dwell there for long, but must return to the complexities and sufferings of a recalcitrant world. The saint's life therefore shows us what the poet tells us, that we are, in Steiner's words, "answerably peregrine in the unhousedness of our human circumstance".[14] In this context, I would like briefly to consider Frank McGuinness's play *Carthaginians*,[15] which is much concerned with forgiveness and reconciliation as both necessary and imperfect in the "unhousedness" of our condition.

Forgiveness and injury: Frank McGuinness and Robert McLiam Wilson

Carthaginians was first performed in 1988, and is set in Creggan graveyard in Derry, where an ill-assorted group of people keep a vigil, waiting for the dead to rise. The title and the *mise-en-scène* bring together Vergil's depiction of Carthage in the *Aeneid* and the Christian belief in the resurrection of the dead. As the action unfolds, we learn that Bloody Sunday is the central, traumatizing event that has driven the main characters to the graveyard and, as in Heaney's "Freedman", McGuinness merges ancient imperial Rome with Roman Catholicism: "The British Empire is dead," says Paul, and Greta replies, "The Roman Empire?"

> Paul: Roman Catholic Empire. This city is not Roman, but it has been destroyed by Rome. What city did Rome destroy?
> Greta: Carthage.
> Paul: Correct. Two points. Carthage.
> Greta: How are we in Carthage?
> Paul: Tell them you saw me sitting in the ruins, in the graveyard. I live in Carthage among the Carthaginians, saying Carthage must be destroyed, or else – or else –.   (310)

The conflation here of the Roman and British Empires extends to include the Catholic Church as another kind of imperialism, and Carthage is not only the ancient city destroyed by Rome, but also the place to which the characters resort in shock and disorientation after Bloody Sunday. But Paul's despair and resignation also carry a note of rebellion ("I'm no slave. I am Carthaginian. This earth is mine, not Britain's nor Rome's. Am I right?" [311]). Throughout the play, the fact that Carthage does not finally capitulate to Rome despite great suffering is a token of the human power of survival: "How's Derry? Surviving. Carthage has not been destroyed" (379).

The analogies between Carthage and Derry are developed throughout, and, although he does not make the point explicit, McGuinness may allude here to an eighteenth-century theory, based on a supposed analysis of the Irish language, that after their defeat by Rome, the Carthaginians came to Ireland. At any rate, we keep being reminded that the two cities are linked; thus, the play opens with music from Purcell's *Dido and Aeneas*, and a central character – a homosexual who also makes an appearance in drag – is named Dido. In one of the play's several pub-style quizzes, Paul asks: "Which Queen of Carthage ruled there until deserted by Aeneas?" and Dido replies, "Dido, Queen of Carthage," to which Hark responds caustically, "Dido, Queen of Derry" (364). In an earlier exchange, Paul asks who wrote the *Aeneid* and who guided Vergil through "the city of hell" (309). Paul assures Hark that "An Irishman" (311) wrote the *Aeneid*, and there is a reference also to the story of Dido retold in *The Merchant of Venice* (361).

The quizzes that break into the dialogue at intervals to introduce these questions provide also a mixture of bizarre amusement and energetic *contretemps* distracting the characters' from their problems. Yet, the quizzes function at the same time as a sort of association exercise drawing the characters' attention to the very things which, by means of distraction, they hope to avoid. Throughout, an atmosphere of disorientation prevails, and as this zany congregation of damaged people wait for the dead to rise, their anxieties and neuroses pass over intermittently into outright derangement. Thus, the former teacher, Paul, thinks of himself as building a pyramid out of assorted rubbish, through which the dead will come back to life. "Why do you go mad, Paul?" Greta asks, and he replies, "I go mad when I have to" (367), believing that only the resurrection will heal his pain.

Paul's delusion is matched by Maela's fierce denials that her daughter is dead. In fact, the child died of cancer at the age of 13 (the same number as those killed on Bloody Sunday), and her death occurred also on Bloody Sunday. The distracted Maela has subsequently refused to acknowledge that either event happened, imagining instead that her daughter is resting in the grave and will soon awaken. Sarah also is haunted by her past and struggles to come to terms with the fact that she spent time as a drug addict and prostitute in Amsterdam, following a painful disillusionment with the Northern Irish civil rights movement. In turn, Greta has had an operation for "a woman's problem" that leaves her "not a woman anymore" (373), and her disturbed childhood has laid the ground for the onset of a neurosis that now overwhelms her, as she feels herself already one of the dead. Seph remains mute for much of the play because he has been an informer, and the IRA have let him live with his guilt instead of shooting him. By contrast, Hark has been jailed for IRA activities, and now has a job as a gravedigger. Sarah waits to renew an old relationship with him, but he suffers from self-loathing because, as an IRA operative, he found he was unable to kill.

Dido provides supplies and a modicum of entertainment for this ill-starred group. He is tolerant of their eccentricities and feels at home among them, being a fringe-dweller himself. He also supplies the typescript of a farcical play, *The Burning Balaclava*, which is performed, impromptu, by the other characters, and is a terminally gauche send-up of all the main sacred cows and clichés of the Troubles: Catholic piety, the RUC, the Army, mixed marriage, bigotry, education, the civil rights movement, and so on. These are the targets of a farcical satire re-enforced by dismayingly bad jokes and a ludicrous, all-but non-existent plot. Throughout *Carthaginians* as a whole, farce and dirty jokes represent the sordid tricks of fate and circumstance that have reduced the main characters to a pathetic indigence, and at one point the unfortunate Greta describes her life simply as "A dirty joke" (373).

Clearly, McGuinness is no complacent advocate of conventional pieties, and *Carthaginians* throughout is abrasive, combative, irreverent, funny, satirical, coarse, compassionate, absurd and aggressively provocative. Pretensions of all kinds are dismantled and ridiculed, as are the high seriousness of the epic theme ("Dido Queen of Derry" [364]) and the Christian doctrine of resurrection ("Well, here they all are. The lunatics" [313]). And yet, *Carthaginians* is not nihilist or cynical, and the idea of raising the dead is taken seriously, as are the closely allied ideas of reconciliation and forgiveness. This becomes clear when we realize that the dead are not just those in their graves; they are also the people forced to the graveyard through trauma, neurosis, and damaged self-esteem. These walking dead especially need to be made fully alive again, and in their extremity they provide help and consolation to one another. But the process of coming back to life is not easy, taking place as it does through an *agon* that the characters engage when they reach the limits of themselves, at which point the truth can be discovered and told. As we see, each of them is driven to the graveyard as a result of a trauma that cannot properly be faced. In the opening scenes we are given hints as to what is wrong, but no certain information, and the play itself operates like one of the quiz shows it features throughout, providing clues and urging us to guess the answers. Why does Maela talk to the grave? Why does Greta keep repeating the jingle about the lost "wee ducks"? Why does Sarah sing about Amsterdam? Why is Seph so conspicuously silent? What is the meaning of Paul's pyramid? Why does Hark tell Sarah not to call him by his first name? The characters do not want to reveal their secrets, and they are often at odds with one another, thrown together in the fantastic expectation of a miracle that in fact happens in a way they don't expect, through the truth-telling by which, *in extremis*, they reveal themselves to one another. Something of Carthage, the "new city", therefore indeed survives, presided over by the homosexual and occasionally transvestite Queen Dido, whose camp humour, pain, humiliation, feistiness, and open admission of his feelings make him exemplary if unconventional, an anti-epic and unlikely hero, an agent of reconciliation who is also an outsider.

At every turn, McGuinness prevents us from lapsing into cliché in assessing the effects and consequences of violence, and his strategies are paralleled in his earlier, better known play, *Observe the Sons of Ulster Marching Towards the Somme* (1985), in which, again, a homosexual is a catalyst for reconciliation and truth-telling, this time among a tragically doomed group of young soldiers. McGuinness's achievement in representing the experience of young men from Protestant Ulster balances his imaginative investigation of the effects of Bloody Sunday in *Carthaginians*, and each of these plays gains by being seen in relation to the other. Still, despite their different subject matter, both focus alike on the idea that painful self-revelation is often necessary to find peace and reconciliation. Thus, in *Carthaginians*, by various, often tortuous indirections, the main characters disclose themselves to one another. Hark has done time in jail, but was a failure as an IRA killer; Maela realizes "My wee girl's dead" (351) and then pours out her grief, recalling how she wandered in distraction through Derry in the midst of the Bloody Sunday killings; Seph admits he was an informer and gives his reason: "They said after Bloody Sunday they wanted to avenge the dead but they wanted to join them," and by informing "I'd save them from the dead" (370); Paul explains that his mad fits are caused by seeing the dead carried in plastic bags, "like a pile of rubbish through Derry on Bloody Sunday" (368); Sarah recounts her disillusionment with the civil rights movement, and her addiction and prostitution; Greta explains the lost "wee ducks" by disclosing her terror, being orphaned and alone and without hope of children.

Although, in all this, the violence of Bloody Sunday is central, it is also linked by association to the child's cancer and to the social ills of drug addiction and prostitution, as well as to the fears and terrors of our existence and our aloneness. In short, Bloody Sunday represents in concentrated form the violence inherent in our condition, and the play causes us to think about the questions of epic heroism and religious hope at which McGuinness looks askance, but which he engages seriously after all. Thus, Dido oversees the heroic survival of a group of damaged people, a small victory of civilization, properly understood, in this "new city" at the edges of the old, in which the grip of the iron circle is loosened and the dead are revived. Hark admits to Sarah that he has failed as a man of violence, and his words speak to all those who would make violence their cause: "I cannot kill to avenge you. All I could have killed was myself. And I couldn't. I can't. Come back to me, Sarah. I'm dead. Come back and raise the dead" (372). She replies, calling him at last by his first name.

Although McGuinness's imagined world is a far cry from Hewitt's, their conclusions about breaking the iron circle are similar, in so far as both insist that violence seals people off from one another, committing them to a spectral reality which can be redeemed and given new life only by forgiveness and reconciliation. Yet McGuinness's exploration of the process of redemption is fiercer, more entangled, agonized and also funnier than Hewitt's, coming to grips especially with the recalcitrance and pain that impede our truth-telling, and with the difficulties of reconciliation as well as the need for it. As George Steiner says, art shows us the "alien in the labyrinths of intimacy", but the reverse also is true and is at the centre of McGuinness's achievement – we can discover intimacy in the labyrinths of alienation, and another name for that intimacy is compassion, which laughter might help us to know and better understand.

As I have indicated in Chapter 1, the absurdity and grotesquerie of some kinds of violence can also evoke laughter of a very different kind – mocking, terrified or cruel – and it is as well not to forget how laughter contributes to the scapegoating process. Still, laughter can be a reconciling agent, as we discover not only in McGuinness but also, for instance, in Robert McLiam Wilson's increasingly celebrated novel, *Eureka Street*,[16] where comedy operates in many different registers to confirm the virtues of good nature, especially against the justifiers of violence. It is as if Henry Fielding here finds his way to Belfast, promoting in the form of a rollicking narrative the broad Enlightenment view[17] that laughter helps people to preserve a sense of proportion, avoiding the extreme kinds of behaviour that arise especially from over-rigorous adherence to abstract principles.

Eureka Street describes the fortunes of Jake Jackson, an ex-tough-guy who is about to give up his job as a repo man, and who has just been dumped by his English girlfriend. Jake's adventures parallel and intersect with those of his cross-community Protestant friend Chuckie Lurgan, whose utterly unselfconscious and entirely dubious entrepreneurial wizardry make him a great deal of money as he also (successfully) pursues a beautiful and rich American girl. The story is set in Belfast just before the 1994 ceasefires, and its boisterous, foul-mouthed, preposterous and winning characters are the vehicle of a frequently topical, gob-smacking satire in which no partisan position or established institution remains unbruised.

As one result of his several adventures, the blithely unreflective and none-too-bright Chuckie comes to realize how "The frail and the harmable had to be loved" (377), and this point of understanding lies close also to the novel's moral centre. The pathos and beauty of ordinary people and their fascinating stories everywhere evoke Wilson's solicitude and protection against the callousness of the self-important, the official spokespersons, the celebrities and idealists who commit themselves to causes but ignore their own and others' common condition. At one point, the bigoted Ronnie Clay tells his workmate Rajinder that all black people look the same, and Jake reflects: "It was an ugly moment but, in fairness to Ronnie, I had to admit that black people all looked the same to me as well. But then white people all looked the same to me too. To me, we all looked pretty awful" (162). Jake doesn't recoil from Ronnie's bigotry by way of the expected liberal reflex, but by an indirection that co-opts Ronnie's "ugly" opinion to strengthen and toughen Jake's own brand of liberalism in a way that acknowledges common failings while avoiding a too-simple binary oposition.

There is a vigilance, here, about the dangers that can attend excessive clarity in human moral judgements. Thus, in a later episode when Jake announces that "Violence is wrong. That applies in all situations," he is challenged by the redoutable, over-serious republican Aoirghe Jenkins, on the grounds that she recently saw Jake punch someone at a peace rally. Jake replies, a tad lamely, that he is "an imperfect follower of my own theories", then adding, "And, yes, it was wrong" (294). Although the novel as a whole is strongly opposed to violence, Wilson is aware that a zealous pursuit of ideals or principles is itself a major cause of violent behaviour. Consequently, Jake, like many other characters in the book, is richly inconsistent though not unprincipled: he admits that he was wrong, and Wilson invites us to expect similar contradictions in people's behaviour generally. Indeed, during the conversation with Aoirghe, Jake is perturbed that she is not at all amused, and he ruefully describes their exchange as "comedy-free". The implication is that laughter helps people to avoid some dangers attendant upon high-seriousness – violence chief among them – as Aoirghe has yet to learn.

Eureka Street thus recommends the virtues of a benign disposition, tolerance and good nature. In this respect, despite his intellectual limitations and general amorality, Chuckie Lurgan basically has what it takes, as when he refuses to enter a bar decorated with memorabilia of loyalist killers: "Double-chinned double-Protestant Chuckie could barely have pronounced the word integrity but there was no place in his big gut for the hatred and fear they peddled there" (55). For Wilson, Chuckie's humane discernment is an irreducible value, but although Chuckie comes by it naturally, to some degree it can also be acquired. Thus, Jake confesses that he had once found it easy to hit people "because I had no imagination", going on then to explain that "The human route to sympathy or empathy is a clumsy one but it's all we've got. To understand the consequences of our actions we must exercise our imaginations", because then "violence or harm becomes decreasingly possible for you" (62). Although Chuckie himself, like Jake's admirable foster parents Matt and Mamie,[18] has little imagination, these good-natured people do not need the kind of correction that Jake does, and for which imagination is indispensable. Still, how does one deal with the harm committed before imagination reveals the futility of violence? The answer comes by way of a one-word letter from Jake's English girlfriend. He reads it towards the end of the novel, discovering that "The one word in Sarah's letter was *Forgive*" (368). For Wilson, redemptive laughter and forgiveness go together, and imagination is the means by which we might learn how this is so.

In their depiction of the pain and generosity that enable reconciliation to occur, Wilson and McGuinness confirm what Gordon Wilson and the Catholic testimonials also tell us about the intimate links between forgiveness and injury. In a challenging statement, Kierkegaard says we can truly love only those who have hurt us, and here he has in mind the crucifixion as the central model of how forgiveness emerges from the heart of suffering and victimization; only those who have suffered injury are in a position to forgive. Yet, as we have seen, in a violent world such as we inhabit, everyone is complicit with violence, and for the same reason, everyone has suffered injury. To greater and lesser degrees, that is, we are all victimizers and victims; no one is innocent, and no one is unhurt. It follows that forgiveness and reconciliation are a necessary part of the fabric of ordinary life if only because none of us can withstand rigorous scrutiny, and we constantly need the forbearance of others, just as others need our forbearance. At the very least, then, there are strong practical reasons for offering forgiveness and seeking reconciliation, as Francis Bacon long ago pungently explained: "This is certain, that a man that studieth revenge keeps his own wounds green, which otherwise would heal and do well."[19] That is, by refusing to let go and move on we make ourselves again victims of the same injury; by contrast, as John V. Taylor[20] says, we become free, through forgiveness, to make responsible decisions.

All of this makes good sense, and, faced with the burden of a history in which tribal enmity, hatred, bitterness and prejudice are deeply engrained, politicians and others in Northern Ireland not infrequently recommend "reconciliation". Yet they usually do so less out of a Kierkegaardian sense of the existential dilemmas of love and suffering than out of a pragmatic understanding that societies work better when people are not intent on settling old scores by violence. In such a context, the efficacy of reconciliation is easy to see, though the politicians who praise it by and large balk at recommending forgiveness as the prior condition from which it springs. One consequence is that much political talk about reconciliation remains superficial, proposing more or less that internicine violence be tranquillized and re-channelled within the mechanisms of the state under the rule of law, and calling the result "reconciliation". By contrast, the challenge posed by forgiveness offers a critique of the means by which the state itself confuses peace with the mere enforcement of law and order.

Moral imagination and the rhetoric of reconciliation: John Hume, David Trimble and Bernard MacLaverty

As is well known, one major result of the Good Friday Agreement is that the Nobel Peace Prize was awarded to John Hume and David Trimble, acknowledging their part in the peace process. In their acceptance speeches in Oslo in 1998,[21] both men had a chance to describe the significance of the prize for Northern Ireland, and it would be gratifying to report that they found language to do so convincingly, commenting, for instance, on the kind of reconciliation that their joint acceptance of the prize might entail. But alas, they do not.

John Hume begins by praising the "ordinary people" of Ireland, to whom he says the peace belongs. He draws attention to the fact that he is speaking on the 50th anniversary of the landmark Universal Declaration of Human Rights, which is soon to be incorporated into domestic law in Ireland through the Good Friday Agreement. He goes on to say how his own efforts for peace have been inspired by his experience of Europe, and how, one generation after the war, a new Europe is emerging as "the best example in the history of the world of conflict resolution". The key to this remarkable success is "agreement and respect for difference", which Hume recommends also for Northern Ireland where "both sections of our people" must learn to respect one another, so that "there will be no victory for either side". Hume then thanks the many non-Irish politicians who also helped to bring about the Agreement, and he goes on to admire the "quiet heroism" of those who have suffered violence with fortitude. In this context he suggests that because Britain and Ireland are bound by "countless ties", they should be able to live in friendship. Certainly, in Ireland, people are determined to achieve a peace that will "remove the underlying causes" of violence, and Hume praises the "foresight and courage" of the paramilitaries who have maintained their ceasefires and entered the political process. He then returns to the fact that the Universal Declaration of Human Rights is 50 years old today, and ends by citing Martin Luther King: "We shall overcome".

Repeatedly in this speech, Hume reaches for the universal: "the fullest respect for the human rights of all its people"; "the best example in the history of the world"; "all sections will be working together"; "Ireland and all its people"; "all of their skills", and so on. Yet, all too conspicuously, he avoids acknowledging any let or hindrance to the realization in Northern Ireland of the broadly admired rights that are to unite "all the people" equally. Throughout, an almost reckless lack of concern for the problematic and particular not only conceals the difficulties attending the peace process, but also implies that Hume's own generously all-encompassing good-will gives him the moral high ground. Who, after all, would oppose such sweetness and light? Still, Hume's rhetoric papers over cracks that, on inspection, criss-cross his speech.

At the start, he says that the Peace Prize offered to himself and David Trimble is a recognition "of the tremendous qualities of compassion and humanity of all the people we represent between us". Well, all the people represented by Hume and Trimble are not tremendously compassionate, and it is fantastical to suggest otherwise. Hume then proposes that the "Two major political traditions" in Ireland are "destined by history to live side by side" (peacefully, that is), and Ireland and Britain "are two neighbouring islands whose destiny is to live in friendship and amity with each other". But it simply is not clear that "friendship and amity" will characterize British–Irish relationships, if only because a considerable number of people are disposed otherwise. As for "destiny" – well, we only have Hume's word for it. Again, he tells us that in light of the Agreement, "No one is asked to yield cherished convictions or beliefs," and "All of us are asked to respect the views and rights of others as equal of our own." In fact, the Agreement came about because people *were* asked – compelled, even – to "yield cherished convictions or beliefs", and this yielding has often been truculent and resentful (as a brief look at the history and proceedings of the Assembly will soon confirm). Also, people do not respect others' views as "equal of our own." Catholic nationalists don't respect the anti-Catholicism of the Orange Order; many Protestants resent the Catholic Church and deplore the Catholic ethos of much traditional nationalism.

At one point, Hume mentions the "extraordinary courage and fortitude" shown by many victims of violence, and he commends "a quiet heroism" that "has borne silent rebuke to the evil that violence represents, to the carnage and waste of violence, to its ultimate futility". This is a considerate statement, but it is also a missed opportunity. Hume's victims are "quiet", and their rebuke is "silent". By implication, they remain passive, and in many cases this might well be true. But as we have seen with Gordon Wilson and Harry McCann (among others), victims of violence often actively seek reconciliation, and they often encounter difficulties in doing so. Frequently, they attempt to build bridges even to those who want to remain cut off, and against the wishes of many on their own side. In short, the kinds of evidence and testimony I have cited in the earlier pages of this chapter, and the kinds of personal struggle and anguish we see in McGuinness's *Carthaginians*, remain wholly absent from Hume's assessment. I do not suggest that he should have developed his speech in a manner inappropriate for the occasion; only that his language provide some indication that he is conscious of the complexities and trials of finding the peace and reconciliation he so willingly advocates. The fact that Hume's language is almost totally lacking in such circumpsection is hardly a consolation to his interlocutors from the "other tradition". Indeed, for those who have ears to hear, a sub-text in the speech confirms well-tried biases in a manner likely to be disconcerting to the fair-minded universalist for whom Hume putatively speaks. For instance, when he talks about the "two neighbouring islands" Hume does so in the context of the apparently destined friendship between "Irish and British people". But he avoids mentioning that Northern Ireland's unionists are also British, and in the previous paragraph he had simply lumped the people of Northern Ireland with everyone else "throughout the island of Ireland". In the one place where he does mention "British people", Northern Ireland's unionists are conspicuously excluded. This is hardly respecting "the views and rights of others as equal of our own", but Hume seems oblivious to the difficulty.

David Trimble also begins his Oslo speech by noting that many people in Northern Ireland deserve recognition, and he links their achievements to the work of "millions of peacemakers" across the globe, especially in troubled areas. Still, he assures us that he will not fail to pick up his medal or his cheque: in Northern Ireland, if John Hume gets a medal, it is important for David Trimble to have one too. Also, now that they have been singled out, both he and John Hume must "sing for our supper" because there "is no such thing as a free lunch", and Trimble then considers what kind of speech he ought to make.

One possibility is to offer "vague and visionary statements", but the "tradition from which I come", and which insists on "the precise use of words" will not let him make this kind of speech; he wants instead to discuss a "normal and decent" society, rather than a visionary "Utopia".

Another possible speech might discuss some recent lessons learned in Northern Ireland, but Trimble will resist this option too because every conflict is unique, and none is a model for any other. In this context, he presents Edmund Burke as a "role model for politicians everywhere" because he insists on practical matters rather than "visionary vapours". Especially, Burke opposes "abstract virtue, the urge to make men perfect against their will", and when people ignore this advice and pursue false doctrines of perfectability, the result is fascism. Plato's *Republic* is the start of such a "savage pursuit" in the West, leading to the French and Russian revolutions and then to the Nazis and communism. Rousseau also is especially to blame because he "regarded man as perfect", and "Rousseau's road" led to Stalin, Mao and Pol Pot. In Northern Ireland, we have our own fanatics who want utopian states (Irish or British); these fanatics must be resisted, and we ought not to indulge the "appeasing strand in western politics", even though, likewise, we should avoid being too rigorous and precise. In short, because we are all flawed, some degree of inconsistency is necessary to get along. Consequently, Trimble has not pressed the paramilitaries in Northern Ireland for details on decommissioning; only for some "credible beginning" to the process. However, Sinn Féin must decide whether they "are drinking from the clear stream of democracy, or still drinking from the dark stream of fascism".

Trimble now returns to "the vision thing", and to allegations that he lacks it. But vision, he tells us, has to do with clear sight, and to show this he develops an extended metaphor about driving and keeping your eyes on the road. By means of this metaphor, he suggests that "historical sectarianism" is a shadow that we can now leave behind. He points out that unionists in Northern Ireland "built a solid house, but it was a cold house for Catholics", and nationalists "seemed to us as if they meant to burn the house down". There are faults on both sides, but good politics "grounded on reality and reason" show us the best way ahead. In conclusion he assures us that the people of Northern Ireland "are no petty people", and they did good work in constructing the Agreement.

The main problem with Trimble's otherwise sensible appeal for a practical and democratic politics is that the points he makes are frequently at odds with the principles he espouses. For instance, he insists that "the tradition from which I come" is characterized by a "precise use of words", deployed "with circumspection" and with a "passion for precision". These admired qualities are then approvingly linked to Burke's avoidance of the abstract and visionary. Yet Trimble's speech is full of imprecision and is frequently uncircumspect. On points of detail, there are grammatical errors, masculinist language persists throughout ("to make men perfect", and so on), and the two literary figures whose works are cited are quoted inaccurately. The opening jokes about picking up the cheque and no free lunches are crass (Burke would have blenched), and there is much tendentiousness. Thus, Trimble asks, "are not vague and visionary statements much the same thing?" The answer is no; many (perhaps most) vague statements are not visionary (for instance, "I'm feeling sort of peculiar today"). When he says, "I am personally and perhaps culturally conditioned," what does "personally" mean if it is separated from "culturally"? Why say "Previous precedents" as if there is another kind. We are asked to "put aside fantasy and accept the flawed nature of human enterprises", as if fantasy cannot reveal such flaws (the novels of George McDonald might remind us otherwise).

I would not feel pressed to isolate these points, were it not that Trimble's self-description as someone who has a "passion for precision" is, in the circumstances, a provocation; besides, the difficulties evident in these details pass seamlessly into larger and more significant lapses. For instance, the lineage of fascism is oversimplified to the point of parody. To describe Plato's *Republic* merely as the beginning of a "savage pursuit of abstract perfection" ignores the best of Plato's genius – among other things, how, in the *Republic*, Socrates is everywhere aware of the insufficiency of his own arguments (including the possibility of an ideal Republic on earth), and how seriously Plato takes the problem of violence throughout. Likewise, Trimble offers no hint of Rousseau's teachings on how moral autonomy can and ought to free us from the entanglements of opinion, especially of the kind that results in civic humanism becoming corrupt. I am not suggesting that Trimble offer a fine-grained analysis of such ideas in a speech like this. A sentence or two would suffice to move the argument away from the crude binaries and simplifications that we in fact get, so that Trimble's own final judgements might be modified accordingly. For instance, when he tells us that Sinn Féin must choose democracy or fascism, he again offers a careless oversimplification, a false binary that cancels the very complexity that Trimble elesewhere recommends that we acknowledge in the name of a viable politics.

The liabilities of these imprecisions become especially evident when Trimble turns to his extended metaphor whereby driving represents the political process. He tells us that we need to attend to the road and to the next bend rather than to "the mountain beyond". He then says that decommissioning and policing are hills (not mountains), and that "the mountain" in fact is not in front of us "but behind us, in history". Although this mountain casts its shadow ahead, it is merely a "dark sludge of historical sectarianism" which we can leave behind "if we wish". Trimble then goes on with the remarks about a "cold house for Catholics" and Protestant fears that nationalists would "burn the house down".

As a moment's reflection discovers, this entire comparison founders when we are told that the mountain we seem to see before us is really the shadow of a mountain behind. A shadow (which lies flat along the land), is not easily mistaken for a mountain ahead, though Trimble might well wish otherwise because it is convenient to suggest that sectarianism is, somehow, "historical" – a thing of the past. In fact, as many studies show, sectarianism is very much alive in Northern Ireland, and the mountain is far indeed from being scaled. But this confusion is really a preface to Trimble's admission that Northern Ireland has been a "cold house for Catholics". This is as close as he gets to acknowledging anti-Catholic discrimination, which he quickly consigns to that mountain now behind us. Although the acknowledgement is creditable, the botched metaphor betrays a desire to avoid admitting too much responsibility in too clear a fashion, and plain statement is confounded in unhelpfully muddled figurative language, neither precise nor circumspect, but merely evasive.

As he works to a conclusion, Trimble announces that "there is only one true moral denomination" (not pausing to consider how much such a pronouncement about moral universals might owe to the despised Plato), and he then offers the peculiar reassurance that "the people of Northern Ireland are no petty people". Who would have thought they were? An answer may be found in John Hume's book *Personal Views*, which, in a truculent moment (not the only one in that book), does indeed dismiss Northern Ireland's unionists *en bloc* as "a petty people".[22] I am inclined to think that Trimble's closing words are a shot at John Hume, fellow laureate, under the table, as it were, while the pronouncement about the one true morality is being publicly displayed.

As statements about peace in Northern Ireland, these speeches are disappointing, and their main failure is one of moral imagination. Trimble is correct to admire circumspection, precision, and magnanimity, but there is no place in his speech between "vision" and the "practical" for the discernment of complex moral issues that imagination enables. Likewise, Hume's anodyne gestures offer no sense of the human complexities that in actual experience qualify the generalizations he so easily pronounces. Such rhetorical defects are not just formal; they also blind the speakers to their own biases and mutual hostilities, borne unconsciously in a sub-text that continually disturbs the glibly reasonable surfaces. It makes little difference that Hume notoriously seems to have a single transferrable political speech of which the Oslo address is a further variation, or that Dublin journalist Eoghan Harris seems to have helped compose Trimble's address,[23] and that Hume and Trimble were too busy on this occasion to do better, and that political speeches usually are full of cliché anyway. When one considers, for instance, the intense parsing of the Good Friday Agreement and the accompanying, heated political rhetoric about IRA decommissioning, it becomes all too clear that how one chooses one's words does matter. Consequently, I am claiming here that it matters also to consider how Hume and Trimble chose to speak on this august occasion when peace was the main topic and the Good Friday Agreement the main reason why they were being honoured.

I am not so much interested, however, in suggesting that these speeches represent some typical shortcomings of political discourse in Northern Ireland, as in noticing how they draw attention to the difficulty of bridging the gap between private testimony about reconciliation and political approaches to the peace that only reconciliation can effect. I am claiming that the morality needed to bridge this gap partly depends on an actively engaged, educated imagination, without which compassion does not properly exist, in so far as compassion entails a participatory understanding of the lived situation of the other. The fraught process of reconciliation through truth-telling so vividly imagined in *Carthaginians* therefore needs to be understood alike by the twice-born who testify about God's immediate, renovating forgiveness in a world filled with complexity and obduracy, and by politicians seeking to legislate the conditions within which reconciliation might take place. In this context, I want in conclusion to consider briefly Bernard MacLaverty's novel *Grace Notes*,[24] which is much concerned with reconciliation, and also with art as a figure for how private experience and the concerns of the public realm are perplexingly interwoven.

The central figure in *Grace Notes* is Catherine McKenna, a young composer who is estranged from her family in Northern Ireland. She returns from Glasgow for her father's funeral, and, with difficulty, admits to her mother that she now has a baby daughter and that she is separated from the baby's father, whom she had not married. As Catherine departs for Scotland after the funeral, some tentative but imperfect reconciliation occurs between her and her mother. The novel then backs and fills, recounting Catherine's relationship with David (her baby Anna's father). There is a description of Anna's birth and of a devastating depression that Catherine suffered afterwards. Later, as Catherine becomes increasingly alienated from the violent and hard-drinking David, she walks on a beach with the one-year-old Anna, and the beginnings of a musical composition stir within her. She is able then to leave David and find lodgings with her friend Liz. During this time she composes her important work, *Vernicle*, continuing to struggle with depression but triumphant in her art.

    Grace Notes is full of broken and disrupted human relationships. Catherine's father, Brendan, dies unreconciled with her, and the relationship with her mother remains strained and uncertain. David is an alcoholic who beats her, and she leaves him while he is recovering in a clinic. Her childhood music teacher, Miss Bingham, offers some relief from the tense family scene when Catherine returns for her father's funeral, but Miss Bingham is dying of cancer. Catherine's revered mentor Anatoli Ivanovich Melnichuck, whom she visits in Kiev on a scholarship, has a heart attack while she is playing for him, and she does not see him again. Depression causes her to feel overwhelmingly alienated even from her beloved baby, and she offends her friend Liz, though she apologizes and Liz understands that the offence is partly due to the depression. These are the main relationships with which the novel deals, and they are all fractured or damaged, though not without moments of joy and shared understanding.

    A sub-theme throughout keeps us aware also of the Troubles. Thus, when Catherine arrives home she discovers the town centre devastated by an IRA bomb, and her mother explains how angry Brendan had been when the event occurred: " 'It's our own kind doing this to us.' That's what he kept saying" (15). Brendan's partisan feelings are made clear early in the novel when Catherine recalls how bitterly he denounced a group of lambeg drummers to her as a small girl ("This is their way of saying the Prods rule the roost" [8]), going on then to assure her: "The whole problem, Catherine, is racist," and "It's the Protestant side's bigoted. The Catholics are only reacting to being hated" (9). Lambeg drums remain important in the novel because Catherine incorporates them into her musical composition, *Vernicle*, and in so doing manages to exorcise something of the crude prejudice and fear imparted to her as a child. Certainly, the remark about "our own kind", and Brendan McKenna's strong feelings about the drummers, express familiar Catholic nationalist sentiments, and, despite her estrangement, Catherine is not exempt from the complex claim that her family background makes on her. Thus, when she hears of a British soldier killed in Northern Ireland, she feels some obscure responsibility: *"Mea culpa, mea culpa, mea maxima culpa"* (203). Throughout, we continue to be reminded of Northern Ireland's pervasive sectarian divide; for instance, Brendan's friends "wouldn't be seen dead in a house where the rosary was being said" (55), and Miss Bingham notices the unusualness of "A Roman Catholic using Protestant drums" (105). In turn, the Orangemen (who perform on their drums in *Vernicle*) complain about "Roman Catholic propaganda" aimed "to make us look like fanatics" (259). And when she meets these Orangemen, Catherine, despite herself, feels old fears and resentments well up within her (262).

These reminders of violence and prejudice are extended also throughout the novel in various ways beyond Northern Ireland. Thus, Catherine has a conversation in Kiev about Babi Yar; David's alcoholism leads him to violence; Catherine herself has upsettingly violent thoughts caused by her depression. One implication is that illness, social maladjustment, bigotry and persecution are endemic, and we are all caught up in a tissue of alienations and half-understood antipathies that are, in turn, the difficult testing ground of our desire and need for reconciliation. In so far as music in the novel both symbolizes and effects the kind of reconciliation that answers a deep human desire, it stands opposed especially to mechanical repetition, which symbolizes and effects the alienations confirmed by violence. As Catherine explains to a class of schoolchildren, there is a difference between the rhythms of the sea and waves produced mechanically: "That's like techno. The same beat. Boring – like listening to a machine" (208). One main problem with her depression is the "Endless loops", the "Endless repetition" (199) of thoughts that afflict her, and at the funeral she complains about the sound of recorded church bells: "Taped bells are like dogma. Always the same" (59). The "herd instinct" (73) of the congregation rising and kneeling in unison is likewise a result of the deadening effects of rote repetition, and, at the end, Catherine's music is contrasted to the training of soldiers: "The purpose of training an army is to dehumanise, to make a machine of people" (276). By contrast, music – though also disciplined – expresses a personal vision, both patterned and affecting. Like Melnichuck's playing, it is "architectural, controlled – but it also cut at the heart" (226), and at one point Melnichuck says, "I can see music as the grace of God," as "a way of receiving God's grace" (125). Catherine does not believe in God, but she weeps at the music she hears in a monastery in Kiev, all of which leads us to the significance of the novel's title.

Catherine explains to her shocked and upset mother that she is no longer a believer, and in response to a question about whether or not baby Anna is baptized, Catherine is dismissive and impatient: "Nobody in their right mind believes that kind of stuff nowadays..." (117). None the less, Catherine wants to compose a Mass, and she understands that the religious music she heard in Kiev gave the people "something which satisfied a deep spiritual need" (122). Predictably, in Catherine's secularized world, art takes the place of religion, and in so far as her music brings joy and communion into the world, it also is a vehicle of grace. Religious language therefore remains significant for Catherine when it is aestheticized, and she looks especially to the theological idea of transubstantiation to explain what happens in her music. The key here is a reconciliation of opposites: "The same thing could be two things. Transubstantiation. How could the drum battering the first movement be the same as the drum battering the second movement – how could the same drumming in a different context produce a totally opposite effect? The sound has transformed itself" (275). The transformation of a Rose of Jericho (a dry, fern-like plant that flowers when hot water is poured on it) causes Catherine to say, admiringly, "Transubstantiation" (130). Melnichuck turns to the same idea in explaining the relationship between musical form and tone, taking his cue from his wife, who has left to put salt in the potatoes: "Form – potatoes. Tone unt texture – salt" (225). In short, form and tone, like colour and substance, interpenetrate, and attempts to separate them destroy the subtle miracle of their new unity.

In some such context, we are invited to think of how grace notes also go between and are "neither one thing nor the other." Rather, they are "Ornaments dictating the character of the music.... This is decoration becoming substance," and we are reminded again of transubstantiation and the reconciling of opposites: "East and West. Male and female" (133), as the Chinese composer Huang Xiao Gang points out, introducing Catherine in her student days to this mysterious process and asking her the question, "Where are the notes between the notes? Graces, grace notes" (33). His question echoes later in Catherine's meditation on how decoration becomes substance, and in a similar fashion she thinks, "The thread of the single voice meshes with the next voice and its neighbours to become a skein which weaves with other skeins of basses and tenors and altos and sopranos to make a rope of sound, a cincture which will girdle the earth so that there is neither East nor West.... *Credo*. I believe" (133).

The skein woven here with other skeins might remind us of Hewitt's "glittering web", and the broad idea of a redemptive joy and delight countering the world's stoniness, mechanical violence and alienation is much the same in both works. MacLaverty, however, is more concerned than is Hewitt with the aesthetic itself as a means of grace, and throughout the novel he puts Catherine's theory about art into practice in his own writing as he crosses from the world of words to the world of music, and also, as a male author, into the mind and experience of a single mother who suffers a profound, post-natal depression.

MacLaverty's verbal imagination has always been alert to sound, and *Grace Notes* is full of the music of things, closely attended to: headsets sizzle and tish (5), a cat purrs like a distant motorbike (10), a piano lid opens with a sound like scissors (22), a dog's claws clack on the hard floor (71), a train comes chuntering in (77), crows caw and click (83), a stick chatters on a fence (99), there is a drubbing of tyres on cat's eyes (104), rubber shoes squidge (166), salt splishes on bath water (177), wind whistles and tweeters (218), rain crackles (233), violas are like violins with a cold (270), and there is much else throughout of the same kind, culminating in those passages – especially in the concluding pages – where the sounds of music are described. But as the book moves to its own crescendo, describing the performance of *Vernicle*, we are offered more than a display of MacLaverty's auditory imagination. The description of the music also picks up several of the novel's key themes and motifs: the bells of Kiev, the Rose of Jericho, transubstantiation, homophones and other kinds of doubles, lambeg drums, and the secularization of religion. Through the interplay of words and music, MacLaverty thus attempts to have his novel do what music also does, effecting a transubstantiation, a transfiguration and reconciliation of opposites in a new synthesis that delights and enhances understanding. The value of this is authenticated by the experience itself, as we have seen is the case also with the other kinds of reconciliation we have discussed.

I have dealt so far with *Grace Notes* mainly to show how it depicts art as a reconciler of opposites in which something new is made. Still, as Catherine reflects on the death toll in Northern Ireland she reaches a disconsolate conclusion: "It was awful to think that if she wrote the most profound music in the history of the world it would have no effect on this litany" (127). Although art might provide solace, political violence is not directly affected by it, and, on the whole, MacLaverty is pessimistic about the extension of art's "transubstantiations" into the realm of alienated human relationships. Consequently, he turns the novel back on itself: Catherine's music is "her faith" (276), just as the book, reproducing in words something of what she values in music, is also his. Yet MacLaverty does offer some indications of how human relationships outside the realm of the aesthetic can be touched also by the moral equivalent of grace notes. Thus, Catherine apologizes to Liz in a painful moment in which distress, imagination and kindness come together; Melnichuck and his wife Olga unwittingly provide a dimension of parental solicitude and understanding that Catherine's actual parents lack; Miss Bingham finds Catherine's music helpful because it enables her to appreciate an extended community of human feeling and response: *"I am where you have been"* (112); by incorporating the lambeg drums into *Vernicle*, Catherine transforms the fears and residual bigotry inherited from her father, not by taming their power to excite strong feelings, but by placing them within a further set of relationships where that power communicates joy and celebration. In short, the novel suggests a pattern of interlacements, a "co-inherence", as Charles Williams says, whereby art becomes the type and pattern of redeemed relationships. What happens to the lambeg drums in the musical composition is what might happen also in a polity marked by a reconciliation of old and violent differences.

   As we see, the grip of the iron circle is loosened in many ways and by different kinds of meeting and encounter. Yet it might be all very well to say that forgiving our enemies sets us free; the fact is that we cannot expect simply to prescribe forgiveness and to have it produce an immediate, cleansing flow of beneficence and reconciliation, and Williams correctly asks how writers could hope to lay down rules on this topic, even for themselves. Still, he also points out, correctly, that without the "appalling diagram of integrity" that great writers manage to provide, there would be no adequate understanding of "the interchange of love".[25] As a Christian, Williams directs us here to the challenging fact that Jesus offered forgiveness from the cross, even to his tormentors. As Jürgen Moltmann says,[26] the resurrection is the meaning of the cross – that which makes the cross something other than a brutal atrocity – and the resurrection is implicitly bound up with forgiveness, as the scattered and guilty disciples were the first to discover. In turn, the challenge of the cross is the challenge to love our enemies, and when this occurs the stone sealing the tomb is moved, and life returns. As I have noted in Chapter 1, Jesus's intervention in history as bearer of this message – this higher morality – directs us especially to the transfiguring significance for human life of breaking the iron circle of revenge and scapegoating. In so doing, Jesus offers a value that cannot be proved before we commit ourselves to it, but which, as with all moral values, must be accepted first, on a hunch, as it were, as an act of faith. Just so, we cannot force others to forgive, even if, as Williams correctly says, our lives depend on it.

To summarize: John Hewitt depicts the mechanisms of violence as stony, circular and depersonalizing, in contrast to the liberating effects of forgiveness, which is the water of life and a "glittering web for God's delight", at once intricate, spontaneous and variously patterned. But reading poetry about forgiveness and actually forgiving our enemies can make very different demands on us, and here the testimonials of people who are not primarily writers but who have experienced the liberating effects of forgiveness and reconciliation have been useful to consider. These unelaborate, straightforward accounts claim as a matter of fact what Hewitt's poetry centrally proposes, and also what the saints and mystics would have us understand: that forgiveness and reconciliation liberate, as becomes evident from the deeds and actions that follow in consequence.

In this context, we have noticed that it is pragmatic to seek reconciliation if only because we are unable to make responsible decisions if we harbour resentment and bitterness. Politicians tend to stress this pragmatic advantage, but it is all too easy for political rhetoric to elide the difficulty of finding reconciliation in the teeth of profound alienations, confirmed as these often are by defence mechanisms of many kinds. Frank McGuinness allows us to see something of this painful reality and the recalcitrance and craziness that impede the kind of truth-telling that might enable us better to understand one another compassionately. In so doing, he reminds us, as does Robert McLiam Wilson, of the importance of imagination in moral discourse, a point to which politicians need also especially to attend. In short, an educated imagination entails, as MacLaverty points out, a change in the substance, mentality and language of those seeking reconciliations that are both politically viable and which also engage the actual complexities of experience. This kind of change is central in *Grace Notes*, wherein art represents and embodies the pattern of reconciled relationships in a "skein" or "cincture which will girdle the earth". But such a "transubstantiation" is realized in art in all too depressing contrast to the actual realities of politics, religion, and the many ordinary human relationships compromised by violence, bitterness and alienation. None the less, forgiveness and reconciliation remain central to the process by which the iron circle is broken, even though the means by which we might be moved to such a conviction are incalculable.

It seems, then, that in the diversity of our meetings, in our encounters with the alien within the labyrinths of intimacy, as Steiner says, the incandescence of our mutual recognitions, the life-giving power of compassion, and the reconciliations that produce something new that is also rich and strange, are known immediately with a shock of recognition that this is the meaning also of freedom – a freedom that is to be pursued through the entanglements of our fraught history with a tact, discernment and unsentimental clarity in which the educated imagination operates as an indispensable moral force.

7
Conclusion

In the previous chapters I have argued that the reasoning by which people convince themselves that violence solves any problem of real human interest is always oversimple and, if pushed to extremes, entails the obliteration of human interest itself. This is because violence reduces human agency to a mechanized process in which the combatants become depersonalized, resembling one another in the mirror hate and symmetrical rationalizations by which their reciprocal enmity is sustained. Even when the exchange of force is unequal and a helpless victim or weak opponent is damaged or destroyed, that victim becomes a token, a non-person, a slave or chattel deprived of interiority by the wielder of a superior force which, in turn, all too readily and ironically manipulates and enslaves the conquerors themselves, despite their illusion of autonomy. Once the sword is taken up it is difficult to set down, for the way of the sword opens as if by prestidigitation upon further sequences of retribution, treacheries and expedient alliances born of resentment and fear. A hydra of enemies grows newly ferocious heads at every fresh violent stroke, with a predictable unpredictability, as the chamber of horrors which is history abundantly shows. Clearly, such cycles of retribution are better curtailed, as they often are in the tranquillized force relationships of a "balance of power" among contending states or factions, each of which maintains order within its own jurisdiction through a rule of law guaranteed in turn by the threat of force.

Much of this is easy to see, but many questions are begged, not least because violence continues to thrive luxuriantly, and in ways that might win the approval even of those who denounce it in theory. For instance, most of us can imagine intervening forcefully to stop some outrage against a defenceless group or family member or child, and even if we cannot imagine ourselves feeling indignant to the point of violence, most of us will understand that others might well do so, confronting their brutalizers or the brutalizers of those close to them. In short, violent hatred is a common fact of life, and even the most cherished of civil liberties remain by and large under the protection of those prepared to defend them by force. Thus, nation states maintain their armies and police, and the violence performed by such agencies is no different from the violence performed by anyone else, in so far as the violent deploy instruments to inflict pain or fear on another person, treating that person as an object or thing deprived of interiority.

The advantages of regulating violence by law are of course considerable; internicine rivalries, blood feuds, petty jealousies and resentments are prevented from escalating and disrupting civil life and social productivity. Here it is crucial that considered judgement and due process inflict punishment thoughtfully and in a manner that safeguards the law's transcendent integrity while also satisfying the desire for retribution. Justice must be seen to be done, and those who cannot wait upon its processes will be judged and condemned in turn by those processes. Clearly, the peace maintained by such means is a shadow image of the real, non-coercive peace that passes understanding. And even though, in its many varieties, civil life may well offer examples of better, freer kinds of society among sub-groups of various kinds, such cells of good living are contained in turn by the state within which they reside, enjoying a protection from the very structures they offer to criticize.

In an imperfect world – however regrettably – we are, therefore, complicitous with violence if only because a state-sanctioned use or threat of force helps to keep day-to-day life stable. By such means civilization fends off the worst nightmares, preventing a mere regression to blood feuds and the atavisms of our pre-history, which were once necessary for survival and are light sleepers even now. Certainly, we owe much to the civilized, and yet we also need to understand how violence is managed and contained by the various strategies constituting ideology, including not least a preparedness for war against some scapegoat or other, some actual or imagined object constituted as fit to receive the effects of the state's own repressed violence, and that of its dutiful citizens. Sometimes, indeed, a designated enemy might deserve condemnation, and it is easy, for instance, to support the use of force against genocide. Still, I am claiming that it is wrong to think that violence solves even this problem. Although armed intervention might prevent hideous cruelty being done to others, the lesson then is that superior force wins, not that genocide is wrong. Next time, those bent on genocide may only have learned from history that their army needs to be stronger than those who will resist it.

The many-sided conflicts and difficulties attendant upon the advantages of civilization in relation to the dangerous repressions that are also part of the price of being civilized remain very much at the heart of the present study. Yet how have I decided such things, and on what grounds do I base such an argument? As I make clear in Chapter 1, my main models are the epic tradition and the gospels, and my claim is, again, simple: these are strong sources which are foundational to Western literature and culture and they have much to say about violence. Within the epic tradition, I focus on the *Aeneid* because of its proximity in time to the New Testament, and because it is the main vehicle for transmitting Homer to the Latin West. Also, as Christianity adapted the cultural riches of the ancient world, Vergil became a semi-prophetic figure and the Christianized empire placed a new value on the earthly city as an instrument for maintaining order in an imperfect world until the coming of the heavenly kingdom. The civilized values recommended and embodied in the epic, and the critique of civilization made imperative in the scandal of the cross, thus found themselves in continuing debate, which remained formative also in the emergence of modern nation states from the historical process that delivered the Reformation, Enlightenment and French Revolution. But I am less interested in this larger history than in relationships between violence and society in the key texts themselves. From these, I derive a set of criteria describing what I refer to as the economy of violence, and offering also a critique of the dangerous oversimplifications that I began this chapter by noticing.

Although epic heroism has a value – cultivated and sustained by ennobling stories, mythologies and aspirations – in its martial aspect it also bears a seductive gilding which readily splits and peels under the impact of the actual forces unleashed by warfare, driven by fury, anguish and terror. Such violence depersonalizes, reducing human agency to the level of an automatism whereby enemies are locked into a cycle that is endless until it plays itself out or a cessation is called – some word being given, some rule applied. Meanwhile, through the conduct of violence the violent become hardened to death in the double sense of treating their enemy not as a person but as a representative, a token, an object of hatred, contempt and ridicule, and also in the sense that this hardening towards the other perpetuates the mechanism of exchange whereby violence is accepted as the best means of settling differences. Unwittingly, the violent then stalk themselves (a point on which Vergil and Jesus agree); moreover, they conceal this unsettling truth about violence from themselves not only by means of heroic ideals, but also through propaganda and theatrical display. Consequently, violence can all too easily seem an intoxicating game, a stirring or carnivalesque perform- ance. In turn, such strategems of self-delusion produce an intoxicated, narrowing intensity under the protection of which the monstrosities of sadism, cruelty, and criminal psychopathy are released and have their day. The disjuncture here between theatrical self-aggrandisement and the sordid facts of the matter is often grotesque, a kind of cruel absurdity emergent from how people devote themselves to starry ideals while wading in blood. The theatricality, pathos, absurdity and putative lega- lism of the passion narratives show this all too clearly, reminding us in so doing of the intimate, often unconscious connection between vio- lence and scapegoating – the projection, that is, upon some outcast individual or group, of our own secretly harboured resentments and frustrations. In turn, the oversimplifications that enable scapegoating are sustained by lies and propaganda, disguising how violence in fact takes hold of us.

One central claim throughout this book is that literature stands at the opposite pole to propaganda, giving us access – however unevenly – to the actual, complex realities of violent behaviour. The educated imagin- ation therefore is a powerful moral agent, providing an antidote to the means by which violence is perpetrated. Yet, as I have also suggested, our choices in this matter are often not so much between violence and non-violence as between a lesser and a greater violence, and although (as Ellul says) we might never agree that violence offers a proper solution to human problems, we may find ourselves condoning it in certain circumstances.

Literature and its critical evaluation are not of course the only means by which the moral imagination is educated, but they do provide a privileged forum for such a process to occur. Certainly, as we have seen, in Northern Ireland a war of words is conducted along many fronts, and relationships between "literary" and "non-literary" writing (and the various ways these interpenetrate) are richly inter-involved and asymmetrical, as language about violence comments on, explores and meshes unevenly with the kinds of thinking and behaviour that pro- duce actual violence. With this in mind, I derive my main criteria from the overlapping yet incommensurate insights and instructions provided by the epic tradition and the New Testament, going on then to notice how surprisingly direct is the engagement with these texts and trad- itions among the Northern Irish writers I have discussed. In this light, the enquiry engages a number of key problems and issues, beginning with how the "iron circle" takes hold of human agency, and what kinds of language enable and resist such a process, including, especially, the means by which equivocation, disinformation and propaganda corrupt civil life and contaminate politics. Likewise, the annexation in Northern Ireland of religious language and principles to tribal loyalties and identities disastrously inflames the violence of ethnic conflict, another consequence of which is a gender stereotyping that further conceals and distorts how violence actually operates. Still, the entail of the iron circle can be broken by the advent of a moral insight higher than that which demands mere violent reciprocation and retribution. Yet reconciliation and forgiveness are not simply biddable and are neither predictable nor uniform in their begetting or their efficacy. Their value lies rather in the freedom they bring, always personal and providing an earnest also of a social interchange unconfined by the iron mills of necessity.

As I suggest throughout, in awakening readers in new and compelling ways to the interplay of freedom and necessity in our manifold meetings with one another, literature especially challenges the depersonalizing strategies on which violence thrives. Art thus suggests a pattern of redeemed relationships, and is the bearer of a myriad of "felicities" counteracting the "stoniness" of our separateness, as Steiner says. Literature then may give us pause, inducing a contemplative hesitation in which a moral sense might grow, bright with the compassion out of which understanding is born. It is a fragile plant, this compassionate knowledge, seeded in a harsh landscape, but like the flower saxifrage, it also can break rocks. As we have seen, the means by which we might come to know and value such a thing are patient and indirect, negotiated through a flickering, quixotic interplay within language itself of presence and absence, in which the strangeness and threat of our mutual separations and rivalries contend with another kind of immediacy, a communion and transfiguration in and through which we might discover an intimation of the kingdom among us, still in the making. We might hope to discern that difference carefully, for by unfreedom we perpetually imprison ourselves, but by freedom we discover ourselves always anew, again, in one another.

Notes

Chapter 1 Introduction: at War with Words

1 The debate between Eric Weil and Emmanuel Levinas is described in detail by Hent de Vries, "Violence and Testimony: On Sacrificing Sacrifice", in Hent de Vries and Samuel Weber (eds), *Violence, Identity and Self-Determination* (Stanford, Cal.: Stanford University Press, 1997), pp. 14–43. I draw on this article for the following account.

2 Jacques Derrida, *Writing and Difference*, trans. Alan Bass (Chicago: University of Chicago Press, 1978), pp. 146–7, cited by de Vries, "Violence and Testimony", p. 25.

3 Jacques Ellul, *Violence*, trans. Cecilia Gaul Kings (New York: Seabury Press, 1969), pp. 133ff.

4 Simone Weil, "The *Iliad*, or The Poem of Force", trans. Mary McCarthy, in *Simone Weil: An Anthology*, ed. Sian Miles (London: Virago, 1986), pp. 182–215.

5 For Hannah Arendt, the distinguishing feature of violence is that it uses instruments. See her *On Violence* (New York: Harcourt, Brace and World, 1969), pp. 42, 46.

6 Edna Longley, *The Living Stream: Literature and Revisionism in Ireland* (Newcastle upon Tyne: Bloodaxe, 1994); Jonathan Hufstader, *Tongue of Water, Teeth of Stones: Northern Irish Poetry and Social Violence* (Lexington: University Press of Kentucky, 1999). This book appeared when a first draft of the present study was complete. The author also applies the theories of René Girard to Northern Ireland, as I do in the present study and in *Breaking Enmities* (1999), which no doubt in turn was published too late for Professor Hufstader to refer to it, and in which I notice further applications of Girard to discussions of Northern Ireland, and especially to the sectarian problem.

7 Peter McDonald, *Mistaken Identities: Poetry and Northern Ireland* (Oxford: Clarendon Press, 1997), pp. 46, 56.

8 In the following account I refer to *The Aeneid*, trans. Frank O. Copley (New York: Bobbs-Merrill, 1965). Line numbers are cited in the text.

9 See René Girard, *Things Hidden since the Foundation of the World*, trans. Stephen Bann and Michael Metteer (Stanford, Cal.: Stanford University Press, 1987).

10 The following account summarizes some points of an exceptionally complex scholarly debate. I have dealt at greater length with such issues in *Reading the New Testament* (London: Macmillan, 1989). The following remarks draw especially on the magisterial, succinct account by Raymond E. Brown, *The Birth of The Messiah: A Commentary on the Infancy Narratives in Matthew and Luke* (New York: Doubleday, 1977), pp. 29ff.

11 Jürgen Moltmann, *The Crucified God*, trans. R. A. Wilson and John Bowden (London: SCM, 1974), p. 41.

12 See Charles Taylor, *Sources of the Self: The Making of the Modern Identity* (Cambridge, Mass.: Harvard University Press, 1989).

13 Conor Cruise O'Brien, *God Land: Reflections on Religion and Nationalism* (Cambridge, Mass.: Harvard University Press, 1988). The quotations are from pp. 12 and 14.
14 See Malachi O'Doherty, *The Trouble with Guns: Republican Strategy and the Provisional IRA* (Belfast: Blackstaff, 1998), p. 68.

Chapter 2   The Iron Circle: on the Core Mechanisms of Violence

1 *The Collected Poems of John Hewitt*, ed. Frank Ormsby (Belfast: Blackstaff, 1991), p. 142.
2 See *Collected Poems*, ed. Ormsby, pp. 537, 539.
3 See *Collected Poems*, ed. Ormsby, pp. 76–9.
4 See *Collected Poems*, ed. Ormsby, p. lxii.
5 Allen Feldman, *Formations of Violence: The Narrative of the Body and Political Terror in Northern Ireland* (Chicago: University of Chicago Press, 1991), pp. 46ff.
6 See Chris Ryder, *The RUC: A Force Under Fire* (London: Mandarin, revised edition, 1997; first published, 1989), p. 411.
7 Peter Taylor, *Loyalists* (London: Bloomsbury, 1999), pp. 4–5.
8 See Tony Parker, *May the Lord in His Mercy be Kind to Belfast* (London: Harper Collins, 1993), pp. 323–7, for the interview with "Eddie Boyle". Page numbers are cited in the text.
9 See Marie Therese Fay, Mike Morrissey and Marie Smyth, *Mapping Troubles-Related Deaths in Northern Ireland* (Derry Londonderry: INCORE, 2nd edition, 1998; first published, 1997), p. 30.
10 Malachi O'Doherty, *The Trouble with Guns: Republican Strategy and the Provisional IRA* (Belfast: Blackstaff, 1998), p. 193. For the commentary on Canary Wharf, see pp. 6 and 98, and on the two policemen, pp. 184–5.
11 On the relationship between power and violence, see Hannah Arendt, *On Violence* (New York: Harcourt, Brace and World, 1969), pp. 10ff.
12 See Patrick Bishop and Eamonn Mallie, *The Provisional IRA* (London: Corgi, 1997; first published, 1987), pp. 182, 195.
13 Michael Asher, *Shoot to Kill: A Soldier's Journey through Violence* (London: Penguin, 1990), p. 120.
14 Eamon Collins (with Mick McGovern), *Killing Rage* (London: Granta, 1998; first published, 1997). Page numbers are cited in the text.
15 See Martin Dillon, *God and the Gun: The Church and Irish Terrorism* (London: Orion, 1997), p. 27.
16 Martin Dillon, *The Shankill Butchers: A Case Study of Mass Murder* (London: Arrow, 1990; first published, 1989). The account of Joseph Donegan is on pp. 297ff.
17 See Feldman, *Formations of Violence*, p. 64.
18 Dillon, *The Shankill Butchers*, p. 319.
19 See Taylor, *Loyalists*, p. 101.
20 Collins, *Killing Rage*, p. 158.
21 See Ryder, *RUC*, pp. 3–5.
22 I deal with the above issues in detail in chapter 1 of *Breaking Enmities: Religion, Literature and Culture in Northern Ireland, 1967–97* (London: Macmillan, 1999).

23 Ryder, *RUC*, p. 330.
24 See Ryder, *RUC*, pp. 203, 243, 246, 265 and 449.
25 See Ryder, *RUC*, p. 328.
26 See Bishop and Mallie, *The Provisional IRA*, p. 186. This and the following paragraph also draw on Bishop and Mallie, pp. 186ff.
27 Dillon, *God and the Gun*, pp. 163 and 161.
28 Mark Urban, *Big Boys' Rules: The SAS and the Secret Struggle against the IRA* (London: Faber, 1992), p. 18.
29 The following account draws on John Lindsay (ed.), *Brits Speak Out: British Soldiers' Impressions of the Northern Ireland Conflict* (L'Derry: Guildhall Press, 1998). Page numbers are cited in the text.
30 Asher, *Shoot to Kill*, pp. 154, 120, 101, 196 and 95.
31 For the "pitchfork killings" see Martin Dillon, *The Dirty War* (London: Arrow, 1991; first published, 1990), pp. 124ff. On the "Lisburn lie machine" see Urban, *Big Boys' Rules*, pp. 180, 204, 246, et passim. The European Court's decision (1978) on the "interrogation in depth" of prisoners in 1971, and the events of Bloody Sunday are succinctly described in W. D. Flackes and Sydney Elliott, *Northern Ireland: A Political Directory* (Belfast: Blackstaff, revised edition, 1994; first published, 1980), pp. 151 and 99–100, and are frequently dealt with in commentary about the Troubles.
32 Parker, *May the Lord in His Mercy be Kind to Belfast*, p. 323.
33 The *Wreaths* group, from the collection *The Echo Gate* (1979), are cited from *Selected Poems* (London: Jonathan Cape, 1998), pp. 60–1.
34 The poem commemorates Magistrate Martin McBirney, who was killed in 1974.
35 "In Memoriam", from the collection *No Continuing City* (1969), in *Selected Poems*, p. 18.
36 "Wounds", from the collection *An Exploded View* (1973), in *Selected Poems*, p. 36.
37 See Bishop and Mallie, *The Provisional IRA*, pp. 177ff; Dillon, *The Dirty War*, pp. 234ff.
38 Examples are "Master of Ceremonies", "Mole", "Last Requests", "Second Sight", "Bog Cotton", "The War Poets", "Poppies", "The Ice-cream Man", "The Kilt", "Behind a Cloud".
39 John Lyon, "Michael Longley's Lists", *English*, vol. 5, no. 183 (Autumn 1996), p. 233.
40 "The Butchers", from the collection *Gorse Fires* (1991), in *Selected Poems*, p. 101.
41 "Self-heal", from the collection *Echo Gate* (1979), in *Selected Poems*, p. 68.
42 Jonathan Hufstader, *Tongue of Water, Teeth of Stones: Northern Irish Poetry and Social Violence* (Lexington: University Press of Kentucky, 1999), p. 4.
43 Brian Friel, *The Freedom of the City*, in *Selected Plays* (London: Faber, 1984). Quotations are from this edition, and page numbers are cited in the text.
44 Don Mullan (ed.), *Eyewitness Bloody Sunday* (Dublin: Wolfhound Press, 1997).
45 Flackes and Elliott, *Northern Ireland: A Political Directory*, p. 99.
46 Mullan, *Eyewitness Bloody Sunday*, p. 257.
47 Asher, *Shoot to Kill*, p. 109.
48 Peter Taylor, *Provos: The IRA and Sinn Fein* (London: Bloomsbury, 1998; first published, 1997), p. 114.

49 Asher, *Shoot to Kill*, p. 167.
50 Taylor, *Provos*, pp. 125–6.
51 "The Man from God Knows Where", interview with Fintan O'Toole, *In Dublin*, 28 Oct. 1982, p. 22.
52 Cited by Mullan, *Eyewitness Bloody Sunday*, p. 26. On Widgery's military background, see p. 43.
53 For the above points, see Mullan, *Eyewitness Bloody Sunday*, p. 96; photo caption between pages 192 and 193; pp. 21 and 183; p. 63.
54 See Flackes and Elliott, *Northern Ireland: A Political Directory*, p. 99.
55 Cited in Mullan, *Eyewitness Bloody Sunday*, p. 27.

Chapter 3   Equivocations of the Fiend: Self-Deception and Poetic Diction

1 Fionnuala O'Connor, *In Search of a State: Catholics in Northern Ireland* (Belfast: Blackstaff, 1993), pp. 139 and 136.
2 "Place and Displacement: Recent Poetry of Northern Ireland", a lecture delivered in 1984, in Elmer Andrews (ed.), *Contemporary Irish Poetry: A Collection of Critical Essays* (London: Macmillan, 1992), p. 130.
3 Edna Longley, *Poetry in the Wars* (Newcastle upon Tyne: Bloodaxe Books, 1986), p. 142.
4 "An Afterwards", in *Field Work* (London: Faber, 1979), p. 44; "Station Island", in *Station Island* (London: Faber, 1984), pp. 80 and 83; "An Ulster Twilight" is also in *Station Island*, pp. 38–9.
5 "The Golden Bough", in *Seeing Things* (London: Faber, 1991), pp. 1–3.
6 "Whatever You Say, Say Nothing", in *North* (London: Faber, 1975), pp. 57–60.
7 "Freedman", in *North*, p. 61.
8 Frank Wright, *Northern Ireland: A Comparative Analysis* (Dublin: Gill and Macmillan, 1992; first published, 1987).
9 Clare O'Halloran, *Partition and the Limits of Irish Nationalism: An Ideology Under Stress* (Dublin: Gill and Macmillan, 1987). The quotations appear on pages 95, 157, xvii.
10 Duncan Morrow, Derek Birrell, John Greer and Terry O'Keeffe, *The Churches and Inter Community Relationships* (Coleraine: Centre for the Study of Conflict, 1994; first published, 1991).
11 John Whyte, *Interpreting Northern Ireland* (Oxford: Clarendon, 1990), p. 4.
12 Brian Lambkin, *Opposite Religions Still?* (Aldershot: Avebury, 1996), pp. 53 and 48.
13 Tony Parker, *May the Lord in His Mercy be Kind to Belfast* (London: Harper Collins, 1994; first published, 1993), pp. 204–8.
14 Reported by Joy Rolston, "Cardinal Calls for a Unity of Hearts in Ireland", *Irish News*, 3 January 1989.
15 See Patrick Bishop and Eamonn Mallie, *The Provisional IRA* (London: Corgi, 1997; first published, 1987), p. 195.
16 Jim Cusack and Henry McDonald, *UVF* (Dublin: Poolbeg, 1997), p. 286.
17 Eamon Collins (with Mick McGovern), *Killing Rage* (London: Granta, 1998; first published, 1997), pp. 134, 180 and 243.

18 See Martin Dillon, *The Shankill Butchers: A Case Study of Mass Murder* (London: Arrow, 1990; first published, 1989), p. 254.

19 For more information on Brigadier, later General Sir Frank Kitson, see Richard Davis, *Mirror Hate: The Convergent Ideology of Northern Ireland Paramilitaries, 1966–1992* (Aldershot: Dartmouth, 1994), pp. 197–219; Mark Urban, *Big Boys' Rules: The SAS and the Secret Struggle against the IRA* (London: Faber, 1992), pp. 35ff; Martin Dillon, *The Dirty War* (London: Arrow, 1991; first published, 1990), pp. 27ff.

20 Frank Kitson, *Low Intensity Operations: Subversion, Insurgency and Peacekeeping* (London: Faber, 1991; first published, 1971). Page numbers are cited in the text.

21 See Marie Therese Fay, Mike Morrissey and Marie Smyth, *Mapping Troubles-Related Deaths in Northern Ireland 1969–1998* (Derry Londonderry: INCORE, 2nd edition, 1998; first published, 1997), p. 30.

22 See, for instance, Martin Dillon, *The Dirty War*, chapter 17, "Killing for Profit: Criminal Alliances and Terrorism", pp. 443–58.

23 See Chris Ryder, *The RUC, 1922–1997: A Force Under Fire* (London: Mandarin, 1997, revised edition; first published, 1989), p. 294.

24 See Chris Ryder, *The RUC*, p. 308.

25 Martin Dillon, *The Dirty War*, pp. 73–4.

26 See Mark Urban, *Big Boys' Rules*, p. 74.

27 See Mark Urban, *Big Boys' Rules*, p. 245. See p. xx for Tom King's address to the Commons.

28 See Tony Parker, *May the Lord in His Mercy be Kind to Belfast*, p. 203.

29 Bill Rolston and David Miller (eds), *War and Words: The Northern Ireland Media Reader* (Belfast: Beyond the Pale, 1996).

30 George J. Mitchell, *Making Peace* (New York: Alfred A. Knopf, 1999). Page numbers are cited in the text.

31 Malachi O'Doherty, *The Trouble with Guns: Republican Strategy and the Provisional IRA* (Belfast: Blackstaff, 1998), p. 64.

32 John Lindsay (ed.), *Brits Speak Out: British Soldiers' Impressions of the Northern Ireland Conflict* (L'Derry: Guildhall Press, 1998), p. 118.

33 See Tony Parker, *May the Lord in His Mercy be Kind to Belfast*, pp. 294–5.

34 The Stalker affair has generated a large amount of commentary. It is conveniently summarized in W. D. Flackes and Sydney Elliott, *Northern Ireland: A Political Directory 1968–1993* (Belfast: Blackstaff, 1994), pp. 312–13. For further information, see especially Peter Taylor, *Stalker: The Search for the Truth* (London: Faber, 1987); and John Stalker, *Stalker* (London: Harrap, 1988).

35 This event is discussed frequently in commentaries on the Troubles. See, for instance, Jim Cusack and Henry McDonald, *UVF*, pp. 161ff; J. Bower Bell, *The Irish Troubles: A Generation of Violence, 1967–1992* (Dublin: Gill and Macmillan, 1993), pp. 451ff.

36 The enquiry, headed by Cambridgeshire deputy Chief Constable John Stevens, is summarized by W. D. Flackes and Sydney Elliott, *Northern Ireland: A Political Directory 1968–1993*, p. 314. In the following brief account I draw especially on Chris Ryder, *The RUC*, pp. 412ff.

37 See Chris Ryder, *The RUC*, p. 415.

38 Elmer Andrews, "The Poetry of Derek Mahon: 'places where a thought might grow'", Elmer Andrews (ed.), *Contemporary Irish Poetry: A Collection of Critical Essays* (London: Macmillan, 1992), p. 236.

39 "The Sea in Winter", in *Selected Poems* (London: Viking, 1991), p. 115. Tim Kendall argues that window imagery leaves Mahon's poems after "The Sea in Winter", and is connected to his resolve not to live again in Northern Ireland. See " 'Leavetakings and Homecomings': Derek Mahon's Belfast", *Eire–Ireland*, vol. 29, no. 4 (1994), p. 116.

40 "Rage for Order", in *Poems 1962–1978* (Oxford: Oxford University Press, 1979), p. 44.

41 "Afterlives", *Selected Poems*, p. 50.

42 "Everything is Going to be All Right", *Selected Poems*, p. 111.

43 "A Refusal to Mourn", *Selected Poems*, p. 60.

44 "A Garage in Co. Cork", *Selected Poems*, p. 152.

45 "The Window", *Poems 1962–1978*, p. 108.

46 "A Disused Shed in Co. Wexford", *Selected Poems*, p. 62.

47 "Preface to a Love Poem", *Selected Poems*, p. 14.

48 "Van Gogh in the Borinage", *Poems 1962–1978*, p. 14.

49 "Courtyards in Delft", *Selected Poems*, pp. 120–1.

50 "The Hunt by Night", *Selected Poems*, p. 176.

51 "The Spring Vacation", *Poems 1962–1978*, p. 4; "Rathlin Island", *Selected Poems*, p. 122; "A Disused Shed in Co. Wexford", *Selected Poems*, p. 62.

52 "Rage for Order", *Poems 1962–1978*, p. 44.

53 Peter McDonald, "Louis MacNeice's Posterity", *Princeton University Library Chronicle*, vol. LIX, no. 3 (Spring 1998), p. 396.

Chapter 4   The God of Battles: Violence and Sectarianism

1 Oliver P. Rafferty, *Catholicism in Ulster 1603–1983: An Interpretative History* (London: Hurst, 1994), p. 270.

2 Simon Lee, "Unholy Wars Need Holy Solutions", *Fortnight*, 293 (March 1991), p. 13.

3 See Liam Clarke, "Punishment Beatings May Stop Release of Prisoners", *Sunday Times*, 24 January 1999.

4 See Jim Cusack and Henry McDonald, *UVF* (Dublin: Poolbeg, 1997), especially pp. 126, 143, 254 and 274; Martin Dillon, *God and the Gun: The Church and Irish Terrorism* (London: Orion, 1997), pp. 189ff.

5 The following summary is based on Patrick Bishop and Eamonn Mallie, *The Provisional IRA* (London: Corgi, 1997; first published, 1987), pp. 93ff.

6 *Violence in Ireland: A Report to the Churches* (Belfast: Christian Journals, 1976).

7 John Whyte, *Interpreting Northern Ireland* (Oxford: Clarendon, 1990), pp. 48ff.

8 See John Hickey, *Religion and the Northern Ireland Problem* (Dublin: Gill and Macmillan, 1984); Eric Gallagher and Stanley Worrall, *Christians in Ulster, 1968–1980* (Oxford: Oxford University Press, 1982); B. K. Lambkin, *Opposite Religions Still? Interpreting Northern Ireland After the Conflict* (Aldershot: Avebury, 1996).

9 John Dunlop, *A Precarious Belonging: Presbyterians and the Conflict in Ireland* (Belfast: Blackstaff, 1995); Robin Eames, *Chains to be Broken: A Personal Reflection on Northern Ireland and its People* (Belfast: Blackstaff, 1992); Cahal B. Daly, *The Price of Peace* (Belfast: Blackstaff, 1991).

10 Duncan Morrow, Derek Birrell, John Greer and Terry O'Keeffe, *The Churches and Inter-Community Relationships* (Coleraine: Centre for the Study of Conflict, 1994; first published, 1991); Inge Radford, *Breaking Down Divisions: The Possibilities of a Local Church Contribution to Improving Community Relations* (Belfast: Community Relations Council, 1993); Johnston McMaster, *Churches Working Together: A Practical Guide for Northern Ireland* (Belfast: Community Relations Council, 1994).

11 *Sectarianism: A Discussion Document* (Belfast: Department of Social Issues of the Irish Inter-Church Meeting, 1993); Frank Wright, *Northern Ireland: A Comparative Analysis* (Dublin: Gill and Macmillan, 1992; first published, 1987).

12 Paul Doherty and Michael A. Poole, *Ethnic Residential Segregation in Belfast* (Coleraine: Centre for the Study of Conflict, 1995), p. 95.

13 Lambkin, *Opposite Religions Still?*, pp. 40ff. Further page numbers are cited in the text.

14 Steve Bruce, *The Edge of the Union: The Ulster Loyalist Political Vision* (Oxford: Oxford University Press, 1994), p. 142.

15 I deal with endogamy and education in Patrick Grant, *Breaking Enmities: Religion, Literature and Culture in Northern Ireland, 1967–97* (London: Macmillan, 1999), pp. 72ff.

16 Frederick W. Boal, Margaret C. Keane and David N. Livingstone, *Them and Us? Attitudinal Variation among Churchgoers in Belfast* (Belfast: Institute of Irish Studies, Queen's University, 1997). Page numbers are cited in the text.

17 See Lambkin, *Opposite Religions Still?*, p. 20.

18 The following quotations are from Steve Bruce, "Prods and Taigs – The Sectarian Divide", *Fortnight*, 7 July 1986, pp. 5–6.

19 See Boal, Keane and Livingstone, *Them and Us?*, pp. 73, 21.

20 See Bishop and Mallie, *The Provisional IRA*, pp. 126ff; Martin Dillon, *The Dirty War* (London: Arrow, 1991), pp. 1ff; and see also Conor Cruise O'Brien's "Foreword", pp. xiff. On the influence of the Christian Brothers, see Malachi O'Doherty, *The Trouble with Guns: Republican Strategy and the Provisional IRA* (Belfast: Blackstaff, 1998), pp. 14ff.

21 See Bishop and Mallie, *The Provisional IRA*, pp. 57ff, 133; and Sean O'Callaghan, *The Informer* (London: Bantam, 1998), pp. 20–1, who offers a firsthand account.

22 Dillon, *God and the Gun*, p. 131.

23 On the hunger strikes, see David Beresford, *Ten Men Dead* (London: Harper Collins, 1994); Padraig O'Malley, *Biting at the Grave: The Irish Hunger Strikes and the Politics of Despair* (Boston, Mass.: Beacon Press, 1990).

24 Brian Campbell, Laurence McKeown and Felim O'Hagan, *Nor Meekly Serve My Time: The H-Block Struggle, 1976–1981* (Belfast: Beyond the Pale Publications, 1994), pp. 36–7.

25 Bishop and Mallie, *The Provisional IRA*, p. 275.

26 Dillon, *God and the Gun*, p. 174; and Peter Taylor, *Provos: The IRA and Sinn Fein* (London: Bloomsbury, 1998; first published, 1997), p. 195.

27 See Bishop and Mallie, *The Provisional IRA*, p. 181.

28 See Dillon, *God and the Gun*, p. 208.

29 See Padraic Fiacc, *Ruined Pages: Selected Poems*, ed. Gerald Dawe and Aodán MacPóilin (Belfast: Blackstaff, 1994), p. 10.

30 "Glass Grass", in *Ruined Pages*, p. 131.
31 "Glass Grass", in *Ruined Pages*, p. 130.
32 "Credo Credo", in *Ruined Pages*, pp. 141–2.
33 See Boal, Keane and Livingstone, *Them and Us?*, p. 147.
34 See *Sectarianism: A Discussion Document*, pp. 23–4.
35 Toby Harnden, "King Rat Knew the Trap was Closing", *Electronic Telegraph*, issue 947 (Sunday, 28 December 1997).
36 Dillon, *God and the Gun*, pp. 64ff. The chapter entitled "Walking with Christ?" provides an account of Wright's career, ending with his imprisonment for intimidation, at which time "rumours circulated that he was back on the 'salvation trail'" (80). Further page numbers are cited in the text.
37 *Is there Room in Heaven for Billy Wright?*, anonymous, without date or place of publication. The librarian at the Linen Hall Library suggests that the pamphlet was published by Wright's supporters in 1998, at either Portadown or Belfast. There are four printed pages, from which the following quotations are drawn.
38 David Rudkin, *The Saxon Shore* (London: Methuen, 1986). Page numbers are cited in the text.
39 The following account derives from Marilynn J. Richtarik, *Acting Between the Lines: The Field Day Theatre Company and Irish Cultural Politics, 1980–1984* (Oxford: Clarendon Press, 1984). Page numbers are cited in the text.
40 Lynda Henderson offered this opinion in a personal interview with Marilynn Richtarik, cited in *Acting Between the Lines*, pp. 199–200.

Chapter 5   Shoot the Women First

1 "Apostle of Violence", in *Captain Lavender* (Loughcrew, Co. Meath: Gallery Books, 1994), p. 80.
2 Thomas Docherty, "Initiations, Tempers, Seductions: Postmodern McGuckian", in Neil Corcoran (ed.), *The Chosen Ground: Essays on the Contemporary Poetry of Northern Ireland* (Pennsylvania: Dufour, 1992), p. 200.
3 See Edna Longley, *The Living Stream: Literature and Revisionism in Ireland* (Newcastle upon Tyne: Bloodaxe, 1994), pp. 248, 54.
4 Clair Wills, *Improprieties: Politics and Sexuality in Northern Irish Poetry* (Oxford: Clarendon Press, 1993), pp. 158ff.
5 See Molly Bendall, "Flower Logic: The Poems of Medbh McGuckian", *Antioch Review*, vol. 48, no. 3 (Summer 1990), p. 369; and Mary O'Connor, "'Rising Out': Medbh McGuckian's Destabilizing Poetics", *Eire–Ireland*, vol. 30, no. 4 (Winter 1996), p. 164. I summarize this body of criticism in Patrick Grant, *Breaking Enmities: Religion, Literature and Culture in Northern Ireland, 1967–97* (London: Macmillan, 1999), pp. 129ff.
6 See Kathleen McCracken, "An Attitude of Compassions", *Irish Literary Supplement: A Review of Irish Books*, Fall 1990, p. 20.
7 See, for instance, Ann Beer, "Medbh McGuckian's Poetry: Maternal Thinking and a Politics of Peace", *Canadian Journal of Irish Studies*, vol. 18, no. 1 (December 1991), p. 202; Susan Porter, "The 'Imaginative Space' of Medbh

McGuckian'', *Canadian Journal of Irish Studies*, vol. 15, no. 2 (December 1989), pp. 95 and 101; Eileen Cahill '' 'Because I Never Garden': Medbh McGuckian's Solitary Way'', *Irish University Review*, vol. 24, no. 2 (Autumn–Winter 1994), p. 270; Wills, *Improprieties*, p. 52.

8   Linda Nicholson (ed.), *The Second Wave: A Reader in Feminist Theory* (London: Routledge, 1997). Page numbers are cited in the text.

9   Ann Rosalind Jones, ''Writing the Body: Toward an Understanding of *l'Écriture féminine*'', in Elaine Showalter (ed.), *The New Feminist Criticism: Essays on Women, Literature and Theory* (New York: Pantheon, 1985). Page numbers are cited in the text.

10 See *The Living Stream*, pp. 192 and 195.

11 Geraldine Meaney, ''Sex and Nation: Women in Irish Culture and Politics'', in Ailbhe Smyth (ed.), *Irish Women's Studies Reader* (Dublin: Attic Press, 1993), p. 238.

12 Sarah Edge, ''Representing Gender and National Identity'', in David Miller (ed.), *Rethinking Northern Ireland: Culture, Ideology and Colonialism* (London: Longman, 1998). Page numbers are cited in the text.

13 Alix Kirsta, *Deadlier than the Male* (London: Harper Collins, 1994). Page numbers are cited in the text.

14 Eileen MacDonald, *Shoot the Women First* (London: Fourth Estate, 1991). Page numbers are cited in the text.

15 The following examples are taken from the essays collected by Linda Nicholson in *The Second Wave*. Page numbers are cited in the text.

16 See Martin Dillon, *The Dirty War* (London: Arrow, 1991; first published, 1990), pp. 235 and 237.

17 For an account of these incidents, see J. Bower Bell, *The Irish Troubles: A Generation of Violence, 1967–1992* (Dublin: Gill and Macmillan, 1993), pp. 365, 395 and 753.

18 See MacDonald, *Shoot the Women First*, pp. 145ff.

19 Chris Ryder, *The RUC: A Force Under Fire* (London: Mandarin, revised edition, 1997; first published, 1989), p. 173.

20 Martin McGartland, *Fifty Dead Men Walking* (London: Blake, 1998; first published, 1997), p. 195.

21 Patrick Bishop and Eamonn Mallie, *The Provisional IRA* (London: Corgi, 1997; first published, 1987), p. 254.

22 Martin Dillon, *God and the Gun: The Church and Irish Terrorism* (London: Orion, 1997), p. 151.

23 McGartland, *Fifty Dead Men Walking*, p. 228.

24 Sean O'Callaghan, *The Informer* (London: Bantam, 1998), p. 148.

25 Mark Urban, *Big Boys' Rules: The SAS and the Secret Struggle against the IRA* (London: Faber, 1992), pp. 236–7.

26 See McGartland, *Fifty Dead Men Walking*, pp. 172–3.

27 Rosemary Sales, *Women Divided: Gender, Religion and Politics in Northern Ireland* (London: Routledge, 1997), p. 71; Anon., *A Brief History of the UDA/UFF in Contemporary Conflict* (Belfast: Prisoners Aid and Post Conflict Resettlement Group, 1999), p. 52.

28 See David Brazil, ''Inside the UDA'', *Irish Press*, 16 Dec. 1974.

29 See Peter Stallybrass and Allon White, *The Politics and Poetics of Transgression* (London: Methuen, 1986), p. 193.

30 See *Daily Telegraph*, 28 Sept. 1972; *Daily Mail*, 6 Feb. 1973; *News Letter*, 14 April 1973; *Daily Mail*, 27 March 1973; *Sunday Mirror*, 9 Sept. 1973; *Sunday World*, 3 March 1974.

31 *Daily Mirror*, 5 Sept. 1975; *Irish Independent*, 5 Sept. 1975; *Daily Express*, 5 Sept. 1975.

32 Liz Curtis, *Ireland: The Propaganda War* (London: Pluto, 1984), p. 124. Curtis offers a political explanation for the Scotland Yard leak, see, pp. 122–4.

33 *Daily Mail*, 27 March 1973.

34 *News Letter*, 25 Sept. 1973.

35 *Daily Mail*, 26 March 1973.

36 Belinda Loftus, *Mirrors: William III and Mother Ireland* (Dundrum: Picture Press, 1990). Page numbers are cited in the text. Loftus points out that the iconography of Mother Ireland favoured by nationalists is mirrored among loyalists, though in a minor key, by such female figures as Brittania, Faith and Ruth (68ff).

37 *Mother Ireland* (Derry Film and Video, 1988).

38 Maurice Leitch, *Silver's City* (London: Minerva, 1981). Page numbers are cited in the text.

39 Jennifer Johnston, *Shadows on Our Skin* (London: Penguin, 1991; first published, 1977). Page numbers are cited in the text.

40 Nuala O'Faolain, *Are You Somebody? The Life and Times of Nuala O'Faolain* (London: Sceptre, 1997; first published, 1996). Page numbers are cited in the text.

Chapter 6   Breaking the Circle

1 *The Bloody Brae: A Dramatic Poem*, in Frank Ormsby (ed.), *The Collected Poems of John Hewitt* (Belfast: Blackstaff, 1992), pp. 400ff. Further references are cited in the text. For Hewitt's notebook entry, see p. 646.

2 The poem is printed by Frank Ormsby as an epigraph to *The Bloody Brae*. See *Collected Poems*, p. 400.

3 Charles Williams, *The Forgiveness of Sins* (Grand Rapids, Mich.: Eerdmans, 1984; first published, 1942), see pp. 78, 4, 1.

4 Chris Ryder, *The RUC: A Force under Fire* (London: Mandarin, 1997), p. 5.

5 Greg Moriarty, "Grief Still for Families of Poyntzpass Victims", *Irish Times*, 3 March 1999.

6 Denzil McDaniel, *Enniskillen: The Remembrance Sunday Bombing* (Dublin: Wolfhound, 1997). Where the following account draws on McDaniel, page numbers are cited in the text.

7 Alf McCreary, *Gordon Wilson: An Ordinary Hero* (London: Marshall Pickering, 1996), pp. 88 and 76.

8 Gordon Wilson with Alf McCreary, *Marie: A Story from Enniskillen* (London: Marshall Pickering, 1990), pp. 89 and 92.

9 McCreary, *Ordinary Hero*, p. 130.

10 A typed summary of the interview exists, apparently transcribed from a tape recording and from notes. See McCreary, *Ordinary Hero*, pp. 136ff.

11 Charles Williams, *The Forgiveness of Sins*, p. 78.

12 Paddy Monaghan and Eugene Boyle, *Adventures in Reconciliation: Twenty-Nine Catholic Testimonies* (Guilford: Eagle, 1998). Page numbers are cited in the text.
13 George Steiner, *Real Presences: Is there Anything in What We Say?* (London: Faber, 1989). The following quotations are on pp. 138–40.
14 George Steiner, *Real Presences*, p. 140.
15 *Carthaginians* was first performed in 1988. It is published in *Frank McGuinness: Plays 1* (London: Faber, 1996). Page numbers are cited in the text.
16 Robert McLiam Wilson, *Eureka Street* (London: Minerva, 1997; first published, 1996). Page numbers are cited in the text.
17 Comic dismissal of the sectarian factionalism of the Northern Ireland conflict among a younger generation of writers, such as Wilson and Colin Bateman (sometimes referred to as "prodigals" – see Gerry Smyth, *The Novel and the Nation: Studies in the New Irish Fiction* [London: Pluto, 1997], pp. 116–17, 132), might indicate current developments in Northern Ireland which duplicate the achievements of the European Enlightenment. In exposing the religious wars and controversies of the sixteenth and seventeenth centuries to ridicule and contempt, Enlightenment thinkers introduced a secular consciousness before which the old religious quarrels would by and large wither, exhausted and rejected, though unresolved. The striking similarities between Wison and Fielding are thus more than fortuitous.
18 The point is explicit. Matt and Mamie "couldn't understand shabbiness or harm. They had no imagination" (111).
19 Francis Bacon, "Of Revenge", *The Essayes or Counsels 1625*, Sidney Warhaft (ed.), *Francis Bacon: A Selection of his Works* (London: Macmillan, 1965), p. 56.
20 John V. Taylor, *The Go-Between God: The Holy Spirit and the Christian Mission* (London: SCM, 1972), p. 173.
21 The full text of both speeches is printed in *The Irish Times*, 14 March 1999.
22 John Hume, *Personal Views: Politics, Peace and Reconciliation in Ireland*, ed. Jack van Zandt and Tom McEnery (Dublin: Townhouse, 1996), p. 85.
23 See Henry McDonald, *Trimble* (London: Bloomsbury, 2000), p. 277: "In line with his policy of seeking 'catholic' advice from different quarters, part of his address was written with the aid of Eoghan Harris."
24 Bernard MacLaverty, *Grace Notes* (London: Vintage, 1998; first published, 1997). Page numbers are cited in the text.
25 Charles Williams, *The Forgiveness of Sins*, p. 78.
26 Jürgen Moltmann, *The Crucified God*, trans R. A. Wilson and John Bowden (London: SCM Press, 1974), p. 186.

Index

.